# TELEVISION, AUDIENCES AND
# EVERYDAY LIFE

**ISSUES** in CULTURAL and MEDIA STUDIES

Series editor: Stuart Allan

*Modernity and Postmodern Culture, 2nd edition*
Jim McGuigan

*Rethinking Cultural Policy*
Jim McGuigan

*Media Discourses*
Donald Matheson

*Critical Readings: Media and Audiences*
Virginia Nightingale and Karen Ross (eds)

*Media and Audiences*
Karen Ross and Virginia Nightingale

*Critical Readings: Sport, Culture and the Media*
David Rowe (ed.)

*Sport, Culture and the Media, 2nd edition*
David Rowe

*Cities and Urban Cultures*
Deborah Stevenson

*Cultural Citizenship*
Nick Stevenson

*Compassion, Morality and the Media*
Keith Tester

*Critical Readings: Violence and the Media*
C. Kay Weaver and Cynthia Carter (eds)

*Identity and Culture*
Chris Weedon

# TELEVISION, AUDIENCES AND EVERYDAY LIFE

# Matt Briggs

Open University Press

Open University Press
McGraw-Hill Education
McGraw-Hill House
Shoppenhangers Road
Maidenhead
Berkshire
England
SL6 2QL

email: enquiries@openup.co.uk
world wide web: www.openup.co.uk

and Two Penn Plaza, New York, NY 10121-2289, USA

First Published 2010

A catalogue record of this book is available from the British Library

ISBN-13: 978-0-33-522869-0 (pb) 978-0-33-522868-3 (hb)
ISBN-10: 0335228690 (pb) 0335228682 (hb)

Library of Congress Cataloging-in-Publication Data
CIP data applied for

Typeset by RefineCatch Limited, Bungay, Suffolk
Printed in the UK by Bell and Bain Ltd, Glasgow.

**Mixed Sources**
Product group from well-managed forests and other controlled sources
www.fsc.org   Cert no. TT-COC-002769
© 1996 Forest Stewardship Council

*The McGraw·Hill Companies*

For Sara, Isaac and Rosie

# CONTENTS

# FOREWORD

The central technical claim of television, the cultural theorist Raymond Williams observed, is its capacity to represent distant events. The word 'television' itself, he pointed out, 'selects this quality, following *telescope, telegraph, telephone, telepathy*, with *tele* as the combining form, from the Greek for "afar", related to *telos*, "end".' Nevertheless, when considering 'most everyday television', the relationship of distance is diminished. 'We are in one place, usually at home, watching something in another place: at variable distances, which however do not ordinarily matter, since the technology closes the gap to a familiar connection,' he wrote. Williams contended that this familiarity 'can be an illusion, but the qualitative change when we see really distant events is usually obvious.' Researchers, he believed, need to examine afresh this sense of connection, that is, the ways in which the cultural conventions of television viewing shape 'our actual living relationships' as we experience these distant realities on a day-to-day basis.

This agenda informs Matt Briggs' approach in *Television, Audiences and Everyday Life*. Television, he recognizes from the outset, occupies a curious status. It is a ubiquitous part of many people's lives around the globe, nonchalantly valued for its comforting presence, but sometimes scorned for its harmful influence. Indeed, when examining perceptions about television's role in our everyday lives, Briggs explains, one is likely to encounter diverse responses, with debates revolving around how it portrays the world around us, whether it engenders 'dangerous effects' on susceptible audiences, risks debasing 'our common culture', or even why we 'waste too much time' watching it, among a myriad of others. This book assumes a different point of departure, however. Briggs seeks to explore the very ordinariness of television by elucidating the nature of its presence in our everyday lives, and in so doing proceeds to defamiliarize its most familiar qualities. More specifically, he strives to identify and critique the ways in which television contributes to our lived engagement with democratic culture – and thereby to politicized forms of citizenship formation – within societies undergoing rapid change.

Such an approach requires new methods of analysis. Rather than setting up either/or distinctions between audience research, on the one hand, and textual analysis, on the other, *Television, Audiences and Everyday Life* unravels the ways in which these issues can be approached through a semiotic framework. Briggs takes us through a number of case studies which focus on key genres (including news, reality and lifestyle programming, talk shows and soaps), exploring the ways in which their significance is negotiated in everyday contexts – such as through gossip, for example, as viewers relax after work in front of the television. In the course of his enquiry, Briggs fleshes out several of the guiding tenets and concepts of cultural and media studies research, such as debates regarding the 'public sphere', 'decoding', 'media ethics' and 'globalization'. At the same time, he considers the value of emergent terms, such as 'play', 'modalities of response' and 'semiosis'. In discerning the basis for an alternative perspective, Briggs revisits the assumptions that have all too often posited audience activity within a narrow, polarized discourse of media effects. His vital insight in this regard is that television has demonstrable effects, which can be opened up for analysis by attending to the subtly complex, frequently contradictory ways in which meanings are fashioned through audience activities.

The *Issues in Cultural and Media Studies* series aims to facilitate a diverse range of critical investigations into pressing questions considered to be central to current thinking and research. In light of the remarkable speed at which the conceptual agendas of cultural and media studies are changing, the series is committed to contributing to what is an ongoing process of re-evaluation and critique. Each of the books is intended to provide a lively, innovative and comprehensive introduction to a specific topical issue from a fresh perspective. The reader is offered a thorough grounding in the most salient debates indicative of the book's subject, as well as important insights into how new modes of enquiry may be established for future explorations. Taken as a whole, then, the series is designed to cover the core components of cultural and media studies courses in an imaginatively distinctive and engaging manner.

*Stuart Allan*

# INTRODUCTION: DOING THINGS WITH AUDIENCE RESEARCH

Many students and academics avoid audience research. After all, it's a bit messy isn't it, and perhaps a bit frightening: having to go out there and get people to talk to you, to tell you about how they watch television, the meanings that they make, the pleasures that are involved, as well as the intimate routines and rituals, habits, avoidances, affiliations and investments which happen around the set. But for all the study of television's texts and the meanings they offer, its history, economics, technologies and institutions, we still know relatively little about what it is to 'watch television'. It is, after all, utterly ubiquitous in western societies, part of the fabric of our everyday lives, a common resource for storytelling, scandal, scrutiny, gossip, debate and information: always there, taken for granted, deeply comforting and perhaps disappointing in equal measure. Television, both as a communicator of meanings, and as a daily activity, is *ordinary*. We shrug it off: when asked what we did last night, we might say, 'Oh, I just watched TV, nothing really'. It is this casual 'just', this mundane 'nothing really' that this book explores. To do so we need to turn to audience research: to all that is available.

In its turn to the everyday realities of television this book doesn't call for *more* audience research. This has been done elsewhere, exhaustively it seems sometimes. As Jenny Kitzinger has noted, cultural and media studies has generated various 'manifestos' for the future of research on media audiences (Kitzinger 2004: 193). Some of these that call for more studies on audience pleasure, on ideological resistance and audience activity, on the grounding of media consumption in the practices of everyday life. Kitzinger herself notes the usefulness of these agendas calling for a renewed emphasis on *media power* 'on the interaction between the "personal" and the "cultural" ' (Kitzinger 2004: 192).

It is only through this intersection of identities, experiences, texts, institutions, everyday practices, routines, talk and public discourse that the media are made meaningful. If we want to know anything about television, it is this that needs our attention.

There are two ways of attending to the everyday cultures of television. The first, as the manifestos suggest, is to do more audience research. We know very little for example about audiences for televised sport, for quiz shows, for television drama (crime and hospital dramas in particular which occupy so much of our screen time), nor for religious programming, current affairs and sitcom. We also know little about the impacts of new media technologies (Internet television, digital video discs (DVDs), satellite services and the like). The second option is to make better use of the wealth of audience research *which already exists*. It is this option that this book pursues for we are not, thankfully, as Kitzinger notes, starting from a blank slate. Rather, we can use what research has been done to refine our understandings: not only of audiences, but also of texts, of meaning making and media power (Kitzinger 2004: 192–3).

This then is this book's starting point. It is a broadly *semiotic* one: to make better use of audience research, not to celebrate audience resistance, or exaggerate media power, but to understand meaning making in *all* of its complexity. The point is to think about the *relationship* between the 'meaning potentials' which are encoded in texts (in their semiotic, generic and discursive modes of address, in their narrative and ideational structures, in the pleasures and points of identification that they offer) and actual audience responses, in which they are made meaningful, in which they create *significance*. This is to pay attention to the fact that 'research into how people actually view, discuss, recall and understand such representations confirms some parts of textual analysis, but challenges others' (Kitzinger 2004: 191). In order to address this we must now turn to questions of method; of how this book explores these questions and what readers can do with the insights that it offers.

## Questions of method

This is a short book, one no doubt with omissions and shortcomings, of which we will return. But first let me make a frank admission: no textbook can cover every single debate or area of concern. Indeed, library bookshelves are heaving under the collective weight of introductory texts on television (e.g. Bignell 2004; Corner 1999; Miller 2002). In writing this book my intention has been to avoid adding to this collection, useful as many of them are. My own experiences, in reading these overviews, are sometimes ones of frustration: 'Yes, yes, yes,' I say to myself, 'This is all very well. I understand that we need to do this, and we need to do that, and that so and so called for more research into this. . . . But what do audiences actually do! What do we know about them! Let me see for myself!' To avoid further frustration our point of departure, and our focus throughout, is rather different. We begin and stay with the research on the audience for television that exists. Through a systematic review this book draws out recurrent themes, emergent issues, ambiguities and clarifications. In doing so it addresses the prevailing assumptions in media theory: testing, clarifying, employing and extending them. All the research presented here is empirically based, which is to say it is the result of the researchers' engagement with television audiences, rather than a theorizing about them in their absence. In doing so, the book can be thought of as something of a jigsaw puzzle, a task which starts with the scattered fragments of insights found here and there (in this journal article, in that research monograph), and builds up, bit by bit, into a coherent picture based on a body of empirical evidence.

While some of this research presented is descriptive, taking the form of 'borrowed' transcripts from published research, the analytical potential in hearing audiences own voices should become evident. In this we see some of the rich texture of their experiences with television, in at least some of their complexity, ambivalence and contradictions. These will then be allowed to *resonate* with more rigorous and systematic conceptualization by bringing them into dialogue with key concepts and debates in cultural and media studies. It tries to flesh them out, to find ways of confirming what we already knew from a theoretical standpoint, but also to suggest new directions, and new *uses* for the concepts. This, I hope, will allow us to increase our understanding of television genres and texts and their relation to culture. I hope it does so in imaginative, incisive and rigorous ways.

In more practical terms, such an approach means that this book is built around close readings of a number of key audience research projects. A glance at the References section will reveal that while many of these have been published since the late 1990s, a few date further back into the 1980s. In the latter case I shall seek to point out the enduring nature of the issues that these 'classic' pieces of research raise across television genres in general. For example, by taking Ien Ang's (1985) classic study of soap opera, which explores audience's emotional responses to the genre, we will be able to reconsider the importance of audience's emotional investments in news or reality television. Likewise, the book's method will demonstrate how the central insights that are made in James Lull's (1980) study of the 'social uses' of television can be employed to think about the community uses of global satellite broadcasting. In this we see an articulation of very different types of 'home': transnational, national, community and domestic (Morley 2000).

Where the research is more recent I shall seek to draw out the connections between *emergent* and *established* research questions, such as the relationship between play and television viewing (Brown 1994) and audiences' ethical talk and judgements (Hill 2005). In either case the rationale is not just to describe or document audience behaviours. Important as these activities are, this book also highlights and develops a range of key concepts which can be employed in our thinking about audiences. Some of these are quite familiar, such as notions of the public sphere, emotional realism or imagined communities. Others are less well known, such as interpretative repertoires, semiosis or modalities of response. The most important point is that readers should be able to see how the concepts have *emerged* from detailed empirical research as much as from more *theoretical* academic debate. Seen in this way, it is my hope that this book's close reading of audience research will take us beyond persistent notions such as 'decoding' or 'interpretation' which inform too much thinking about the meanings that are on offer in television's genres and texts.

Such a method, Kitzinger (2004) notes, is not a rejection of textual analysis for audience research, but rather a semiotic marriage between the two, one which seeks to explore the continuing controversy into 'how the media might impact on how we think' (Kitzinger 2004: 193). Such a close reading, and the grounded methodology that informs it, I believe, is one important thing that we can do with audience research. If properly referenced both audience's descriptions and the researcher's voices can be *recycled*, taken up, *deployed* in our own work, be it student essays or academic research. In doing so, we can use it, and the concepts we have at our disposal, to make sense of our own research questions, our own texts, puzzles and queries, whatever they may be.

To set the scene, not only to flag the prior knowledge that this book assumes, but also to make clear the lens through which the audience research was viewed, the following sections present an introductory overview of the key concepts employed. These are the ones which informed the literature review: those which I had 'in mind' as I read the audience research and mined it for those insights which seemed most important and salient to the overall picture that was emerging. Perhaps the most important is that of the public sphere, and it is with this that we will start.

## Public sphere

This is arguably one of the most useful, but contested, concepts employed in the study of television and the broader media. Originally derived from the writings of the German philosopher Jürgen Habermas (1989), the term is now widely taken to refer to the space for the exchange of ideas, of common debate and opinion formation which is either sustained or, in some accounts, attenuated by television and other mass media (Dahlgren 1995; Gitlin 1998). This 'space for discourse' is taken to be essential for the healthy functioning of a mature representative democracy, not only in respect to the formal right to vote, made on informed choices, but also to hold accountable those who have access to power, influence and wealth. In Habermas's own words, it is a 'forum in which private people, come together to form a public'. In doing so they ready themselves to 'compel public authority to legitimate itself before public opinion' (Habermas 1989: 25–6).

In this, its most classical formulation, the public sphere is a space for rational, reasoned and informed debate, a space in which people can in principle come together, regardless of status or position, to participate in public life, free from constraint and coercion. Indeed, as John Corner points out, this should be a space which exists as independent from the institutions of the state, as well as from constrains of private or corporate interests (Corner 1999: 21). Habermas argues that this space originally developed around the emergent press and coffee houses of the late seventeenth and early eighteenth centuries, and in principle formed a common discursive arena, or a 'general interest' which reflected the growing complexity of social, political and economic relations. As Luke Goode (2005) puts it, while access to this was restricted to a bourgeoisie and intellectual strata, 'a piece of news was no longer a private affair, something of interest only to those whom it directly implicated, but was part of a larger communicative environment premised on a putative general interest' (Goode 2005: 6).

While Habermas argued that the increasing commercialization of the press led to an attenuation or 're-feudalization' of the public sphere, where commercial interests limited the opportunity for extended discussion and distanced reflection (Goode 2005: 20), other writers such as Paddy Scannell have made an argument for the public service broadcasting to be seen in terms of its contribution to a public sphere. In his terms this is to think about television's contribution to the creation of a shared culture. It places much less emphasis on ideological questions which stress the television's role in the maintenance of hegemony (Hall 1982). Rather Scannell (1989) asks us to revaluate public service broadcasting's contribution as essential to modern democracy, a 'public good' that has 'unobtrusively contributed to the democratization of everyday life' by generating new 'rights to discourse'. As he puts it:

> I believe that broadcasting has enhanced the reasonable character and conduct of twentieth century life by augmenting claims to communicative entitlement. It does this . . . through asserting a right of access to public life; through extending its universe of discourse and entitling previously

excluded voices to be heard: through questioning those in power, on behalf of viewers and listeners, and trying to get them to answer. More generally, I have suggested, the fact that broadcasters do not control the communicative context means that they must take into account the conditions of reception of their utterances. As such they have learned to treat the communicative process not simply as transmission of content, but as relational processes in which how things are said are as important as how they are said. All this has, I think, contributed to new, interactive relationships between public and private life which have helped normalize the former and socialize the latter.

(Scannell 1989: 162)

The concept, as well as its relation to television and other mass media, has been the subject of quite intensive scrutiny in cultural and media studies (see for example Curran 1997; Dahlgren 1995; Dayan 2001). Scannell for example has been rightly criticized for his avoidance of questions of power, the coercive and ideological role of the media, and for ignoring the ways in which television might address a homogenized imagined community which excludes as many as it includes (Morley 2000: 110–13). Likewise there has been widespread criticism of the classed and gendered nature of this space, or indeed assumptions that there was ever, or continues to be, a single public sphere (Fraser 1992). While we shall return to these issues throughout the book the most salient critique is the insistence on the sober and rational nature of its discourses.

The basis of such a requirement to rationality is in part based on Habermas's argument that the public sphere should conform to what he termed the 'ideal speech situation'. This refers to the way in which members of a public sphere conduct themselves, and the opportunities for communication that are afforded by its structures and communicative resources. These should sustain four 'validity claims': to comprehensibility, truth, appropriateness and sincerity (Price 1995: 25). In this it is assumed that reasoned debate should triumph over emotion, passion, laughter, scandal, sociability and the pleasures of communication on one hand, and narrative, rhetoric, performance, ritual and spectacle on the other (Buckingham 2000: 24).

Questioning these validity claims, audience researchers, such as David Buckingham (2000), Greg Philo and Mike Berry (2004) and Elizabeth Bird (2003), have pointed out that the belief in objective truth and impartiality, in scientific rationality, and in formal and abstract knowledge as providing reliable and unmediated access to reality is deeply flawed. Their empirical research into television news audiences has found for example that the 'validity claims' of trust, sincerity, comprehensibility and appropriateness cannot rest on sober reasoning and impartiality alone. Rather audiences want and expect to have emotional responses to the news, they need to be shocked sometimes, and while they desperately want access to all the relevant history and facts, they also want to identify with those who appear in the news, to understand how they felt and why they acted in the way that they did. In this they want to get angry, or saddened, they wish to speculate, laugh and gossip. This builds relationships of trust, sincerity and most importantly, authenticity.

In these less ordered discursive encounters some writers have made a convincing case for an 'emotional public sphere'. In this emotional expression and the revelation of intense personal conflict can placed at centre stage and made the focal point of television's discourses (Lunt and Stenner 2005). Buckingham (2000) reflects upon his work with young news audiences and suggests that we cannot make a strict delineation between *reason, emotion, pleasure* and *performance*, that 'Habermasian distinctions between information and entertainment, between reason and emotion, and between public and private, cannot be sustained in light of the complex ways in which audiences make sense of, and respond to, what they watch' (Buckingham 2000: 29).

Despite such criticisms and refinements the concept does offer a useful starting point for analysis, as long it is approached through empirical research. In these terms the concept reappears throughout this book to explore the diverging ways in which television addresses its audience, how audiences in turn respond, how they negotiate with the 'validity claims' of its discourses, and how it contributes to the meanings, values, ethics and debates of everyday life. This is a rather different endeavour from theorizing about what audiences should be doing, or what they are assumed to do (or indeed what they fail to do, as the case may be!). Rather it is to start *with what they do*, and to use the concept as *a way of thinking about the relationship between television, audiences and ethics* in all their complexity.

## Working through

While debates over the public sphere concept remain as a very useful conceptual mooring point, John Ellis's (1999, 2000) concept of 'working through' is also employed throughout this book. It is used to make sense of the ways in which television and its audience relate to the wider world of individual and cultural experience. In many ways it offers a way of further expanding and understanding what it is that actually happens in the public sphere, what sort of meanings are exchanged, and how audiences do so. Borrowing the term from Freudian psychoanalysis, Ellis (1999) argues that television is best seen as a 'vast mechanism' for processing the world, for worrying over it, in order to make some sense of it, offering explanations, but no resolutions. As he puts it:

> Television attempts to define, tries out explanations, creates narratives, talks over, makes intelligible, tries to marginalize, harnesses speculation, tries to make fit and, very occasionally, anathematizes. . . . Television does not provide any overall explanation; nor does it necessarily ignore or trivialize. Television itself, just like its soap operas, comes to no conclusions. Its process of working-through is more complex and inconclusive than that.
>
> (Ellis 1999: 55)

Television news for example tries to create some sort of stability from the disorder that it presents, but in doing so constantly speculates. The audience wants closure ('what will happen next?'), as much as it enjoys the process of narration, of chatter, discourse and speculation. Not content, as Ellis suggests, to let events unfold at their own pace, television news presents a welter of unstoppable speculation (Ellis 1999: 58). Chat shows and the many formats of reality programming in their turn intensify this verbosity, they proliferate the voices and the divergent perspective that can be heard.

These genres display, worry over, try out, and proffer psychological explanations, fragments of life stories, confessions, moral failings, family breakdowns and cries for help (Ellis 1999: 57). They invite the audience to judge, themselves and others, to introspect and project, to gossip and be scandalized, to compare and enlist the authority of experts (Rose 1999). Soaps, likewise, with their multilinear narratives, their continuous nature, and their roles as a common talking point (Brown 1994), take up and incorporate these issues of social and cultural concern. They preset us with stories which resonate with our own experiences, with the 'texture' of our own lives (Silverstone 1999: 1–12). They 'narrrativize, in the same time of experience as the lived time of the audience, the moral dilemmas in the lives of their characters' (Ellis 1999: 60).

Ellis's concept therefore gives us another richer, and perhaps more generous and inclusive way of thinking about what happens in the public sphere. It is a concept which attunes us to the various *modalities* in which we make sense of ourselves and others: as we think through, ponder and believe, as we reject, judge, argue and debate, as we get angry, impassioned, saddened or repulsed, as we imagine, pretend, fantasize, dream and hope, as we anticipate, wish, identify and empathize with those that we see on our screens (Barker and Brooks 1998: 94).


## The embedded audience

While the notion of working through highlights the way in which meaning making is always 'embedded' (Abercrombie and Longhurst 1998) in a cultural context formed by historical events and processes, discourses, politics as well as moralities and identities, it would also be a mistake to see the television audience as a homogenous mass. Television audiences make sense in relation not only to these 'macro' concerns, but also to the individual circumstances of everyday life. As Ellis (1999) suggests, television's working through coincides with audience's *discontinuous* use of television. No one can possibly watch everything that television has to offer – not even on a single channel. Rather it is taken up and used in a distracted manner, one which nevertheless belies the importance it has in the conduct of their daily lives: in our routines and rhythms (Gauntlett and Hill 1999) and the care of the self (Hill 2005). As Ellis (1999) puts it:

> It is important to emphasize that television nowadays is a highly intimate part of the domestic experience of almost everyone in the developed world. Television's special domestic status means that it is given a low level of attention most of the time; but it is the same low level of attention that is given to much else (and most other people) in the domestic space as well. Television in intimate, and therein lies its power. It underlies television's social status as a mechanism for working thorough and exhausting society's preoccupations.
>
> (Ellis 1999: 68)

Bird (2003) makes this clear when she suggests that we are never *just an audience*; rather we come to television always as something else: as mothers and fathers, soldiers or doctors, as environmentalists or motorists, as shoppers or homeowners, as concerned and attentive citizens, or as those distracted by the need to eat a hurried breakfast before getting the kids ready for school. As such we must differentiate meaning making in terms of social identity and the politics of location (such as ethnicity, race, gender, sexual orientation, class, age, faith, political belief, nation, region and neighbourhood). These are all things which will shape our relation to television as at once, a cultural practice, a technology, and as a mediator of meanings (Silverstone 1994). This embeddedness will also include personal experiences (such as health, family relationships or work patterns) and interpersonal relationships, social networks activities and contacts which govern our 'public connectedness' (Couldry et al. 2007).

The method of this book is therefore not to try to isolate these as so many 'deep structures', an endeavour undertaken by David Morley (1992) in the *Nationwide* studies. Such a task, as Michael Billig (1997) points out, is bound to fail given the sheer complexity of who we are and where we come from. Rather than look for correspondences between 'social structure' and 'audience decoding', this book makes liberal use of the audiences' own voices as they work through their relationship with television. I hope that in these conversations something of the texture of their lives will come through; not as the 'variables' of class, gender, faith, age, region and so on; but rather as *their experience of them* (Askoy and Robins 2003: 94) and the way in which it orients and inflects their meaning making: of how television is drawn into semiosis.

## Semiosis and everyday life

While we will go on to explore many of these aspects and experience of audience embeddedness in the following chapters, from the outset it should be clear that we must reject too easy assumptions that such activity and complexity automatically and unambiguously act as barriers to media influence, producing the so called 'resistant readings' of the encoding/decoding model (Hall 1973; see also Fiske 1987). Rather, as Philo (2008) and Kitzinger (2004) suggest, we should not see the ample empirical evidence of audience activity as contradicting theories of media power. Rather we should see them as 'integral to any efforts to understand how that power operates'. Drawing on the work of Elihu Katz and Sonia Livingstone (see Livingstone 1998), Kitzinger makes the cogent point that it is not that 'the multiplicity of factors which mediate between television and viewers undermine media effects', rather 'it is *only* through such complex mediations that any effects could occur at all' (Kitzinger 2004: 180–1, emphasis in original). In this view, recognizing that television audiences are active does not render the medium ineffectual. Rather it is to examine the ways in which the discourses and meanings of television are drawn into semiosis is a constant and incessant conversation between different and always unequal voices that audiences will encounter in everyday life.

This dialogue can be usefully thought about in Gunter Kress's (2000) terms. Drawing on the work of the Russian literary theorist, M.M. Bakhtin (see for example Bakhtin 1981), he argues that any one text, any one representation, any particular articulation of discourse, must necessarily interact with what has gone before, and with what will follow. Audience engagement with any one text is therefore but one moment where meaning halts for a brief second before entering into an ongoing exchange with what follows: it 'punctuates' the ongoing and incessant production of meaning. In this view the public sphere is a space where different texts, discourses and practices 'weave' together (Kress 2000: 134–5). This notion of semiosis goes well beyond the study of the single text, and single encounter with television alone:

> This view raises the questions of boundaries. In the weaving notion of text (the metaphor connects with texture, textile) the flow and dynamics of meaning in the complex social environments in which I find myself

are the basis of the text: a constantly shifting flow of meanings, in which meanings constantly alter in response to the dynamic of the wider social environment, constantly remade by those that participate in an interaction.

(Kress 2000: 134)

In these terms, meaning (what I am calling *semiosis*) is not the product of an 'interpretative encounter' between a single text with preferred meanings and a single viewer. Rather it is an ongoing exchange which unfolds across different texts at different times, between different people. Indeed, the view of semiosis developed in this book pays particular attention to the everyday contexts in which meanings are made, both when people sit down and watch at home, but also as they take up and exchange meanings through other practices, such as in everyday conversations about soap operas, in text message exchanges about the latest contestants in *Celebrity Big Brother*, or as they argue over and comment about last night's news at work.

This account of semiosis is significant, for 'negotiation' and 'audience activity' are practices *not only* of entering into a dialogue with texts, but also of entering into the realm of everyday life. As Joanne Hollows (2008) argues, this will concern the dynamics and politics of the household, the allocation of time and space, of family relationships, and our interactions with those in communities and other public spaces. Shaun Moores (2000) likewise usefully suggests that we can think of these everyday dynamics as a type of *mediated interaction*. In this conceptualization, we are required to focus on the ways in which television, both as a technology and as a set of texts, is 'knotted into' everyday encounters in which we form and maintain relationships with others. This is how the little dramas of day-to-day living are enacted with television as a stage prop for interpersonal behaviour and the exchange of meanings (Moores 2000: 144–6).

This book's method then, as I argued above, is to *develop a model of semiosis that captures the complexity and specificity of television's meanings*. By entering into a close and sustained reading of the existing audience research this book develops a number of arguments and concepts. Many, as a quick glance at the Glossary will reveal, have been posed before, and this account clearly benefits from them. However, what I hope is distinctive is the wider picture that emerges, the sorts of *ethical questions* that I encourage my readers to ask about television, its audiences and its meanings, and the model of semiosis that emerges. If nothing else, what I want readers to take from this is an understanding of television as a complex set of *everyday practices*, not just of textual meanings, but the ways in which these are taken up and circulate in everyday life. This model of semiosis focuses on the diachronic aspects of language, on meaning making taking place across different times, spaces and practices. It does not assume that these everyday activities will serve to *insulate* audiences from the ideological effects of the media. Indeed, on the contrary, it rejects this and in its place asks the following four questions:

- How are media texts drawn into *semiosis* in *everyday life*?
- What *types of meaning* do these everyday practices generate?
- What *concepts* and models do we need to make sense of these meanings and engagements?
- Given this, how do we now evaluate broader questions about television's *ethics*?

## Rethinking decoding: modalities of response

We can see how some of these four concerns will develop throughout this book for the concepts of 'working through', 'audience embeddedness' and 'semiosis' call into question some of the key terms and assumptions of television studies, such as 'decoding', 'polysemy' and 'resistance'. These ideas, originally developed in Stuart Hall's (1973) 'encoding/decoding' model, have tended to be adopted in ways that downplay the role of television texts in the shaping of meanings, and focus on assumptions that any audience activity will tend to resist television's dominant or 'preferred' meanings. These concepts were invaluable in moving debate away from the textual determinism of psycho-analytic screen theory, which was prevalent in the late 1970s (Morley 1980). However, the audience research reviewed in this book suggests that television audiences make meaning in ways which outrun them, and that they may have reached the limit of their usefulness. This is especially the case, as Kitzinger notes, for applications of the model tend to focus on 'diverse audience responses' rather than considering 'the origins or consequences of such responses'. As she suggests, we still need to pay attention to the fact that television texts have preferred meanings, and that these meanings are themselves 'products of a time and place, embedded in powers structures, shaped by patterns of everyday life, conventions and common sense' (Kitzinger 2004: 188–9).

A central argument of this book is that this must not be lost sight of, and that it is a mistake to automatically associate audience activity with ideological resistance, as was assumed by influential writers such as John Fiske (1987). This fundamentally removes the critical and ethical component of research. As Kitzinger (2004) suggests:

> People's ability to deconstruct, reconstruct or oppose a particular message should not be seen as inherently progressive. There is a need to go further than simply documenting the various ways in which people 'decode' or

'resist' messages to identify the origin of such diverse readings and reflect upon why they matter. Rather than seeing these patterns of evidence of 'consumer sovereignty', we should examine how they are shaped by their socio-political context, including by the conduct of people's social interchange.

(Kitzinger 2004: 189)

While this book will introduce several other essential terms, concepts and debates, one final one is particularly important; that of a 'modality of response'. The concept, developed from Martin Barker and Kate Brooks' (1998) audience research, is intended to catch hold of the different *types of meaning* that are on offer in particular circumstances. These are 'cued' or made available by different texts and genres as audiences are invited to *orient* themselves to their modes of address, their stories, discourses, representations and narratives. It also alerts us to the ways in which these meanings are generated in response to audiences' embeddedness, to their wider cultural experiences and practices, the range of everyday routines which the media are an essential apart of, and the uses to which television is put (Briggs 2006, 2007a, 2007b, 2009).

This view is particularly useful as it suggests a much richer range of responses than are allowed by the concept of 'decoding', which relies on a strictly cognitive or even computational model of meaning. In this the question of television's diverse uses, beyond its ideological resonance, are strikingly absent (Barker and Brooks 1998: 94). The question as such is not to get tied down in a debate about 'polysemy' and to map this to the degree of 'audience resistance' or acceptance of 'preferred meanings', but to see what is *hidden behind* the very general notion of 'decoding': to see what it obscures, and the ways in which different types of meaning relate to the issue of media power. This is a question of exploring the modalities through which semiosis is generated, their relationship to the different genres, and that perfectly ordinary habit that so many of us have, of 'just watching television'.

## What is an audience?

As this discussion makes clear, the question 'What is an audience?' is being addressed in a very specific and *semiotic* way in this book, one which is securely focused on *how* meanings are made and the *nature* of these meanings. As I have suggested, the key concept in this endeavour explore the nature of *semiosis*: the encounter between audiences and texts in everyday life. Of course those who have different research agendas in mind will ask very different questions, and use different methods and concepts to do so. The question of how to think about the audience in the broadcasting industry is becoming increasingly fraught for example, as young people turn to computer games and Internet television, or expect their texts to exist across a number of different interactive media (Ross and Nightingale 2003). New technologies such as satellite television, mobile phones and DVDs expand the manner in which people watch and the attention they give to texts. How broadcasters can capture audiences' attention, and indeed sustain it, are becoming major issues as advertising revenue migrates to the Internet. As such most of this industry research continues to be concerned with *measuring* audiences and is therefore outside the concerns of this book. However, as Henry Jenkins (2006) makes clear, there is an increasing concern in the media industry with the *quality* of the viewing, with audience investment, their patterns of meaning making and with brand allegiance, and this type of research is likely to become more important for them as time goes on.

These issues, as Karen Ross and Virginia Nightingale's (2003) book in this series outlines, are becoming increasingly important. As they rightly point out, it will certainly become increasingly difficult in the very near future to comfortably talk about this thing that we are calling 'television'. There may even be some sort of convergence between different research paradigms as broadcasters become increasingly anxious, and mystified, by the migratory practices of new media audiences (Jenkins 2006). We will return to this issue in the conclusion, but the position of this current book is that it is time to consolidate what we have learnt about television audiences in the past 30 years of media and cultural studies, and to interrogate this research with one foot in the future. The task as I see it is to form a *conceptual basis* for audience research that is adequate to the task of maintaining a concern with a broad project of *media ethics* (Couldry 2006). It is also a question of clarifying the concepts that enable us to understand audience, cultural and technological change. The following overview should provide a roadmap for this critique, a summary of the questions that will be posed, and the genres that will be considered as we do so.

• Chapter 1 starts with an examination of news discourse, exploring the ways in which audiences respond to the issues represented, the ways in which the genre either develops or hinders their understanding of public events, and of course, the manner in which it informs their beliefs and opinions. The key concept of the public sphere is employed as a way of framing these responses. The question in respect of this is to understand the genre's contribution to public knowledge, ethics and understanding (Corner et al. 1990). While the research presented here does not deny that television news has a strong ideological influence, it seeks to understand and demonstrate that audiences responded in terms of their critical thinking, the ways in which they argue over and work through the contrary themes and 'ideological dilemmas' (Billig et al. 1988) which characterize television news, as well as the consequences of the lack of contextualization and history which blights the genre (Philo and Berry 2004).

- Chapter 2 considers the rather less high-minded genres of reality programming and talk shows. Both have been seen as indicators of a wider 'dumbing down' of television, and a weakening of the idea of a public sphere. While there is some truth to this, this chapter explores the ways on which audiences' responses can be thought about in ethical terms. Audiences are seen as they argue over the conduct of those represented, as they debate the rightness and wrongness of their motivations, and as they judge them. In doing so they 'work through' wider cultural discourses, standards and values (Hill 2007: 86–7). Indeed, this chapter explores the ways in which these genres are part of a wider project of reflexivity and identity formation in which the audiences are under an increasing pressure to scrutinize their own behaviour. This, as we shall see, makes a contribution to key debates about the governance of the self, identity formation, and ethical conduct (Hill 2005: 108). It will also allow us to examine the ways in which meanings are exchanged in a wider and more complex range of ways than allowed by ideas about the 'rational' public sphere.

- Chapter 3 is the last to deal specifically with one particular genre, that of the soap opera. Perhaps even more scorned than reality game shows, the concerns of Chapter 2 are extended as we consider the essentially *playful* modalities through which audiences respond. This chapter explores the ludic space that they offer, as an opportunity to play with the boundaries of fiction and reality, to test the limits of and subvert contemporary cultural values and expectations, to gossip and mock, and to reflect upon life's experiences, one's feelings and relationships (Spence 2005). This, extending this book's spatial metaphors, is thought about as a *ludic space*, a space where meanings can be exchanged through the audience's common expectations and understandings of the genre, and the shared cultural reference points that they produce (Scannell 1989). Once again the notion of 'working through' will be a key concern, one which extends our understanding of the public sphere and media ethics through detailed empirical research.

- Chapters 4 and 5 move away from the examination of audience responses to discrete genres to consider the *contexts of reception* in some detail. Television, as readers' own experiences will testify, is being watched in an increasing array of different spaces, in different ways, by different people (on mobile phones, in shops and bars, on home computers, through personal video recorders (PVRs) and DVDs). All of these raise questions about what we mean by both 'television' itself, and what it is to be an 'audience' (Couldry and McCarthy 2004). This noted, Chapter 4 reviews the research on what is still arguably the most important context for television viewing: ordinary homes. By 'ordinary' the research does not assume a standard nuclear family, rather it assumes that television is a habitual part of people's everyday lives: stitched into their daily routines and expectations; the ways in which they spend time with those with whom they live, or avoid them; the way in which they relax after work, or set themselves up for the day; the ways in which they find topics for conversation, for keeping the children entertained, for breaking an awkward silence or for easing feelings of loneliness; for exerting power and authority, for pressing values on one's family (Lull 1980). In examining these domestic spaces this chapter adds texture and contextual detail to the responses explored in the previous three. This is to explore the ways in which television in *not simply* a textual medium, in which meanings are encoded in texts, but also the ways in which meanings are to be found in the *act of watching* itself (Bausinger 1984).

- Chapter 5, while not a conclusion, attempts to draw these debates, concepts and methodological approaches together. It explores the ways that global space is experienced by diasporic audiences: those who have settled in different countries and who have to negotiate their place, their relationships with their 'roots', and their sense of who they are now. This chapter explores the manner in which transnational television can act as a symbolic mooring point. In this audiences cling to a idealized version of the homeland: an 'imagined community'. However, this chapter also presents contrary and more complex arguments. These explore the ways in which transnational television is used as a symbolic resource which enables audiences to work through the different experiences of domestic, community, national and global space. In this we shall explore the habitual nature of these audiences' use of television, and the modalities through which they respond. In doing so, by drawing in what is in some ways an *exceptional audience*, we shall be better placed to understand the more persistent and *utterly normal* logics through which television is used, and its relationship to culture more generally (Askoy and Robins 2003).

- In conclusion the final chapter draws these concerns together and highlights the importance of thinking about television through an *ethical framework*. As we go on to consider a medium that is in transition (through technological and cultural change, economic upheaval, media regulation and policy), it will be essential to ask questions about what it is that audiences actually do, to have the concepts in mind to interrogate this as we go into the future, to make a case for the politics of the medium, of what *it is* now, and what it *should be* in the future.

# TELEVISION, NEWS AND THE PUBLIC SPHERE

News, as Jackie Harrison (2006) argues, is something modern societies have come to rely upon. We trust it to accurately and truthfully update us on current events, events which are significant to our functioning as members of a common culture. We 'keep up' with the news for lots of different reasons, all of which are important (Hill 2007). It may be that the story is interesting or entertaining in itself, that it directly affects us, that it makes us pause and think, or evokes our compassion, anger or concern. News, as such, is taken as essential for a healthy democracy, as a linchpin in guaranteeing freedom of speech, as ensuring a plurality of voices which will monitor the exercise of power and justice, and to challenge abuses of each. It is a space where private individuals can participate in public dialogue (Harrison 2006: 3–4). News is the genre which is often and most readily associated with the 'public sphere', as that space in which ideas, knowledge, beliefs and meanings can be exchanged; in which our world appears before us (Silverstone 2007: 27).

While such views are vital to our understanding of news, this chapter seeks to extend them and explore audiences' *understanding* of that discourse, and the ways in which it is *employed* in the public sphere. This chapter addresses these concerns by dealing with a central paradox between 'media power' and 'active audience response'. We will examine the considerable skills that ordinary people possess for 'working through' (Ellis 2000) matters of public concern, and the potential they hold for an active and engaged understanding of the world. Indeed, insofar as television news may support a public sphere there is a huge potential here for its role in sustaining citizenship (Couldry et al. 2007). Following the work of Mikhail Bakhtin (1981) the public in this sense are seen as possessing the *potential* to engage in 'dialogic' forms of communication:

in the cut and thrust of discourse and debate, argument and discussion, of reply and rebuttal, of questioning and seeking answers.

However, whatever the potential we see for such a critical engagement, this chapter also attends to a rather more pessimistic reality. In this the structure of broadcast news discourse actually undermines people's active engagement in the world. In doing so it diminishes rather than sustains the public sphere. The view taken here however is that this failure is not the fault of audiences alone. Rather it is a consequence of news' institutional structures and generic conventions, a mode of address which systematically decontextualize 'news events' from history (Philo and Berry 2004). This is hardly surprising: if events are *seemingly* too complex to understand, if the history and causes are obscured by a constant focus on the 'new', then it will be difficult for audiences to show an interest: they will struggle to come to an informed opinion on the central issues that a culture faces. In tracking between these two positions this chapter investigates the ways in which television news actually shapes audiences' views and opinions, and indeed, the ways in which they understand the world. In doing so we will see what it is that audiences actually do with the texts, discourses and representations that are provided by television, and how they not only *enable* understanding and engagement, but also *weaken* it.

## Textual power and audience resistance

This dual approach is necessary as it will allow us to use audience research to negotiate the split between theories of television news which emphasize its power to shape culture through ideological process, and those which place much more emphasis on the ways in which audiences subvert and resist such power through their interpretative practices. This has normally been thought about in terms borrowed from Stuart Hall's (1973) encoding/decoding model, as well as its subsequent 'test' in David Morley's (1980) *Nationwide* study. This model poses the question as a battle between textual power and audience resistance. On the first side of the equation, television news is investigated for the ways in which it 'prefers' some meanings over others. This is said to legitimize power, to make it seem to be 'natural, inevitable, taken for granted' and therefore to work ideologically to support a hegemonic viewpoint (Hall 1973: 12). On the other hand, texts are polysemic and audiences are said to have the power to 'resist' or 'negotiate' with news discourse and representations.

The former critical position is characterized by writers such as Greg Philo (2008) and the Glasgow University Media Group (see Philo 1995, 1999). They quite rightly argue that many applications of the encoding/decoding model have seized upon textual 'polysemy' and the audience's capacity for negotiated and oppositional decodings, and that they have done so at the expense of examining the power of television to shape our understandings of the world. This they suggest is a mistake and research should reorient itself to this critical agenda to explore television news 'in relation to the development of social attitudes and beliefs' (Philo 2008: 535). This is not to deny that audience responses are complex, and textual meanings open to interpretation and differently inflected evaluative accents (Vološinov 1973), but to sever the assumed association between audience practices (or activities) and ideological resistance. As Philo (2008) argues:

> We have not in our work underestimated the capacity of audiences to engage actively with texts, but nonetheless, there is a powerful body of evidence which shows the influence of media messages on the construction of public knowledge as well as the manner in which evaluations are made about social action and what is seen as necessary, possible and desirable in our world. For us, media power is still very much on the research agenda.
>
> (Philo 2008: 542)

The later 'optimistic' position, which Philo is arguing against here, was most ardently championed by John Fiske (1987), who has concentrated on the openness of texts, the indeterminacy of meaning and the freedom of audiences to shape meanings. Indeed, he has gone as far as to suggest that audiences should treat television news in much the same way as they treat fictions, that 'it is important that readers treat news texts with the same freedom and irreverence that they do fictional ones' (Fiske 1987: 308). The emphasis here is clearly less on questions of power (although this is never far from Fiske's attention) and more on the potential lack of influence the news media may exert in everyday life.

In these debates there is something of an unhelpful *opposition* between theorizations of an overtly passive audience which is influenced by single news programmes at the point of decoding, and audiences who are somewhat depoliticized, and who celebrate textual openness and pleasures at the expense of *ethical engagement* in the public sphere. More recently however, researchers such as Jenny Kitzinger (2004), Annette Hill (2007) and David Buckingham (2000) have taken a somewhat more grounded approach. Their research takes into account a wider range of audience practices and responses. In doing so it moves beyond the limited terms of the encoding/decoding model by situating the power of television news in relation to a real and much messier public sphere, in which meanings circulate between people in the contexts of everyday life. Rather than seeing this as process in which audiences simply 'decode' television news, their research demonstrates the ways in which audiences think and talk, the ways in which they judge, argue, speculate, gossip, laugh, ignore and contradict themselves, in which they emote, feel, identify, fantasize, get angry and sad, apathetic or engaged.

This is important for, as Morley himself suggests in discussing his own *Nationwide* studies, 'the encoding decoding metaphor is unhappily close to earlier models of communication in the sense that it implies a conveyor belt system of meaning that is far from fulfilling the promise for a cultural, cyclical model of communication' (Morley 1992: 121). The empirical research presented in this chapter is therefore very much centred on issues of media power. But rather than employ the concept of 'decoding' it looks at meaning making as *semiosis*: as a processes of *thinking* and *dialogue* which takes place between texts and audiences in everyday life. This dialogue however is nevertheless uneven and sometimes inadequate. To ask *why* we will first need to outline a theory of semiosis, one which is employed throughout all the chapters in this book.

## A theory of semiosis

All of the audience research in this chapter, and indeed the majority of the research employed through the book, uses interviews and focus group discussion to explore the ways in which audiences *talk* about television. The benefit of this over notions of decoding, or of simply asking 'what did you understand' as one might on a questionnaire for example, is that it sees talk and understanding as unfolding as cognitive, emotional, rhetorical and imaginative process: not only 'within the heads of individuals', as Michael Billig and Jonathan Shotter (1998) put it, but also 'between them'. It doesn't look for definitive decodings (be they resistant, dominant or negotiated), but rather the inherently social nature of understanding in which meanings and understanding are generated through talk, in which they shift and change according to the ebb and flow of the conversation, to who is present, and to what they want to achieve, in relation to the cultural, historical and discursive context (Billig and Shotter 1998). As Buckingham (2000) explains in relation to his own experiences with news audiences:

> Talk is an exceptionally slippery medium. In interviews such as these, individual speakers will often prove to be incoherent, inconsistent or downright contradictory. They will proclaim one thing at one moment, only to deny it at another; they will make statements that are effectively undermined by their own qualifications and uncertainties; they will collectively talk themselves around to a given position despite their disagreements; they will invent evidence, or wilfully misrepresent what others

have said; they will make generalized statements that conflict with their judgements about specific cases or examples, and so on.

(Buckingham 2000: 63)

This, as Buckingham notes, is a long way from meeting the utopian and rational communication imagined in Habermasian accounts of the public sphere. It is nevertheless what audiences appear to do in everyday life: it is therefore this that we need to understand.

Buckingham's position in this is useful for it borrows the fundamental understanding from discourse analysis that talk and text are inherently social (Jaworski and Coupland 2006). In focus groups for example, not only are audiences 'providing interpretations of, and judgements about, what they have seen', but also they were presenting themselves in certain ways, 'defining themselves as certain types of people, or claiming particular social identities' (Buckingham 2000: 63). As he notes:

> The key emphasis in this approach is that all these dimensions are inherently *social*. In talking about television, individuals construct – or at least make claims about – their own identities and their relations with others; but they do so using resources that are not of their own choosing. These resources are partly in the form of texts they discuss, which constrain the potential diversities of meanings and pleasures; they also take the form of wider social definitions and discourses, which texts may invoke, and which individuals bring with them to any particular encounter with the medium.
>
> (Buckingham 2000: 63–4)

In this news texts become resources for thinking and acting, for identity work and self-presentation, for the active search for understanding and relevance. They are far more than simple carriers of meanings which have to be decoded.

Gunter Kress's (2000) work on text and intertextuality can be usefully drawn on here to explain this model of dialogue, as well as the methodology employed in audience research. He argues that while texts are normally understood as 'fixed' material things (an episode of *Newsnight* or *CBS Evening News* for example) everyday speech must also be understood as 'text'. In this sense there is little distinction to be made between the texts that are produced 'for us' and the texts we produce 'between ourselves'. As he explains:

> As speakers we participate in making texts, and we do so as hearers also. Texts are social – whether as 'text in the making' or text as completed, material object – reflecting the purposes of their makers and the social characteristics of the environments in which they are made. Consequently we always encounter language as text, and we encounter text in generic form.
>
> (Kress 2000: 133)

Kress argues this for he sees any one text, including our own chat, discussions and arguments, as a 'weave' of other texts. Any text, be it a news broadcast, or our own conversations, will take up, repeat or borrow from these previous texts and discourses. They will do so in a more or less transformative manner. Each textual moment merely 'punctuates' the incessant circulation of meaning that characterizes our media culture. As he puts it, 'the text and its boundaries do not stop this process of semiosis: they provide the punctuation only. . . . In this approach semiosis is ongoing, ceaseless: it is punctuated as textual forms, produced in the environments of particular social occasions' (Kress 2000: 135).

This view of discourse is important, for as I suggested above, this chapter is built around a contraction which arises in the audience research, and indeed in most theorizations of television and the public sphere. There is a *conserva-tive* and pessimistic position which sees audiences' meaning making as being constrained and firmly moulded: in closing down meanings, in limiting the universe of available discourse, of obscuring facts and key information, and of offering accounts of the world which at best attenuate the public sphere, and at worst are inherently ideological, working for 'meaning in the service of power' (Thompson 1990). However, the more optimistic account focuses on the *trans-formative* and dialogic nature of audience understandings; it places much more emphasis on the complexity of the processes where texts are 'drawn into semiosis'.

Just what the relationship between the conservative and the transformative aspect of semiosis will frame this chapter's interrogation of the audience research literature. There is good evidence to suggest that both positions are right; that as long as we do not look for some utopian ideal of pure, abstract and rational discourse promised by the Habermasian public sphere, then the semi-otic activities of audiences are complex, and impressive. However there is also much evidence of the ways in which the very structures of news discourse limits audience's patterns of understanding, engagement and public connectedness. In this conservative position we will consider the ways in which key knowledge and perspectives on the world are *seldom made available and accessible*. This will be an indictment of television news discourse, rather than of audiences.

## News, recall and everyday life

Without doubt, the most significant body of work on the audience for television news has been conducted by the Glasgow University Media Group. The majority of this has utilized a relatively simple, but powerful methodological device which they term the 'news game'. This is a simple procedure where groups of naturally occurring participants, such as colleagues or pre-existing social groups, are asked to write television news bulletins based on a few selected images. This is usually done a year or so after the news event in question, but it has worked upwards of two or three after the event. Regardless of the time scales involved, the 'bulletins' subsequently become the basis for both group and individual discussions (Kitzinger 2004: 28–31; Philo 1990: 12–26; Philo and Berry 2004: 200–4).

In line with Kress's (2000) view of language outlined above, the news game is very useful for it indicates the salience and recall of news' representations of the world. In doing so it suggests the complex ways in which news discourse provides the audience with a lasting discourse for talking, thinking and arguing. It also allows for discussion of audiences' media and critical literacy. As this has emerged as perhaps the most useful method for assessing the influence of news, as well as its contribution to the public sphere, we turn now several pieces of research which employ the method. In doing so we shall pay attention to four important points:

- The nature and significance of the news game methodology itself
- What the method can tell us about audiences' patterns of meaning making, understanding and engagement
- How we can use such audience analysis to evaluate news discourse and its mode of address
- The conceptual clarification and development that such a process allows, as well as its contribution to our developing model of semiosis.

The news game was first developed by Philo (1990) in his study of the 1984–5 miners' strike.[1] What is notable in this, and other studies that employ the method, is the very high degree of accuracy with which groups can recall and reproduce the language, structures and themes of news discourse. This occurs with very little prompting, and for some years after the initial coverage. Philo's (1990) respondents for example were asked to recall their perceptions of how the strike was reported by television news, as well as their memories and beliefs about this. The dominant perception of the coverage was that it concentrated on moments of extreme violence, with confrontations between the miners and the police appearing in all of the bulletins. Here for example is the bulletin which was produced by a group of electronics workers:

Today large crowds gathered outside Bilston Glen, consisting of miners and police, which led to an escalation of violence between riot police and miners. At the scenes later a shot gun was recovered by the police. A police spokesman later said 'violence of this nature can only lead to somebody being seriously injured or even killed'.

(cited in Philo 1990: 79)

Compare that with this BBC news bulletin:

> A dozen Yorkshire pits were targets for the worst concentrated violence of this dispute so far . . . it was hit-and-run mob destruction. . . . Outside Hickleton colliery a crowd overturned two cars and set them on fire. They belonged to Coal Board officials at the pit and their destruction marked another bitter escalation in the bitter struggle inside Britain's mining industry.
>
> (cited in Philo 1990: 139)

In one respect the similarity between these two accounts suggests the conservative ways in which the discourses of television news become 'stitched' into everyday conversations and audience thinking. As Philo puts it, 'some news themes and specific language from the strike have passed very deeply into cultural memories. The ability for people to reproduce accounts of the news which are so close to the actual news is quite remarkable' (Philo 1990: 136). This granted, and while the similarity in the language and themes in the two accounts is striking, we should approach this with some caution, and not as a direct indication of overwhelming television influence. In more moderate terms we can see this as an indication of news' potential to *inform* audience understanding rather than to *determine* it, or if you like, as an indication of the continued *availability* and *salience* of such discourses. These, as we shall see, form what we might call a 'discursive reservoir' which is ready to be drawn upon at any particular moment.

While this might point to the conservative or 'pessimistic' position, the notion of semiosis would also suggest that the ability to recall and reproduce the language of news discourse doesn't necessary amount to *belief* on the part of audiences. Rather Philo found that there were considerable differences among the groups in the ways in which they talked about the bulletins produced in the news game, and that they were engaged in quite important *transformative* activities. These differences were generated by a range of different sources of knowledge and understanding. These included direct experience of the strike through involvement or observation, knowledge of miners and their families, logical deductions based on the scale of the picketing, direct experience of other industrial action, political affiliations or close experience of the media industry and the ways in which its news values frames its representations (Philo 1990: 46).

Those who had some *experience* of the strike, for example, as police officers, trades unionists, as miners' wives or support group workers, believed that television news coverage of the picketing had 'overwhelmingly shown violence'. This contradicted their own experience, that the picketing 'was mostly peaceful' (Philo 1990: 47). Other respondents, however, especially those with no connections to trade unionism, no direct experience of this strike in particular, nor of industrial action more generally, seemed much less critical in their evaluation of the news. Their discussions in the news games were much more closely aligned with the television news discourse. As Philo puts it:

> There were several examples of people with tightly organized sets of ideas, strongly influenced by the television news and the press . . . one secretary for example, wrote that the gun had belonged to 'a striking miner left behind after riot', and that 'picketing mostly involved trouble – assumed this by what was seen on TV'.
>
> (Philo 1990: 64)

More generally Philo found that while some people accepted the accounts given by television news, others adapted parts of the discourse and 'changed key elements of the meaning' (Philo 1990: 149). Some for example believed that the strike was mostly violent, but blamed the police for provoking the violence. These viewers recognizing that this view of events was quite at odds with the accounts in the television news, which portrayed what was an overwhelmingly peaceful (if bitter) strike from the perspective of the police. In other groups the belief that the strike was mostly violent was maintained, along with a high degree of trust in television news. But in this there was also a high degree of sympathy for the miners, and a belief that 'outsiders, infiltrators and militants' had been the cause of the violence (Philo 1990: 149).

In other cases the activity of the news writing account itself demonstrated the shifting and flexible nature of audiences' understandings, as well as their relationship to other discourses, beliefs and sources of knowledge. A group of electronics workers initially thought that the picketing was mostly violent, only to move away from this as they collectively discussed the nature of television with its 'focus on the sensational'. As Philo notes:

> In these cases, the exercise itself seems to have provided the stimulus for the emergence of this view. But it is important that the belief about picketing had in a sense *rested with them* until they were pressed to explain it. These again seem to be examples of the message being absorbed in spite of other beliefs which were held.
>
> (Philo 1990: 149)

The crucial insight here is the emphasis on the practical and cognitive aspects of semiosis, the fact that audiences use discourse as a *resource for thinking with*, for making judgements informed by our own experience of reality, and by juggling the contrary themes, discourses and representations which we have at our disposal (Billig et al. 1988: 6; Shotter and Billig 1998: 18). In the sense given by Valentin Vološinov (1973), various evaluative accents are placed on news discourse and in this there is a constant 'struggle over meaning' (Hall 1982: 77–8).

## Interpretative repertoires

This view of language, which sees texts as being 'drawn into semiosis' rather than 'decoded', is significant for our use of audience research in general. It points to the ways in which meanings are made in relation to specific contexts, the ways in which meanings flow between texts and audiences, as well as the ways in which they are generated between people in everyday life. While some of this semiosis may be 'silent' and 'internal', as Kress (1997) suggests, taking place inside our heads as an inner dialogue, other aspects take place between people as a particular type of talk and social action. This 'news talk' is a specific type of discourse and can be usefully referred to as employing, and indeed generating, what Jonathan Potter and Margaret Wetherell refer to as 'interpretative repertoires' (Potter and Wetherell 1987: 138–57).

This concept refers to the ways in which diffuse and complex bodies of discourse produced in various institutions, genres and texts become 'stripped down' into socially shared and commonplace ideas and theories. These form the basis of 'practical thought' and 'common sense'. Repertoires are 'bits and pieces of social knowledge' which are socially available, shared and acceptable; they circulate in the media, in our thinking, and in our everyday conversations (Billig 1991: 57–61; Billig et al. 1988: 15). Indeed, Potter and Wetherell (1987) have demonstrated the ways in which interpretative repertoires have a basis in the actual *language* of news discourse as much as the *knowledge* they produce. They are often organized around specific and reoccurring figures of speech, metaphors, phrases and images, a 'recurrently used systems of terms' as they put it (Potter and Wetherell 1987: 149).

Alexia Hepburn (1997) suggests that we also need to be aware of the contexts in which interpretative repertoires are used, the uses to which they are put, and the power relations which are involved in doing so. Rather than thinking that they reflect some essential and fixed belief she suggests that people will employ different interpretative repertoires strategically and flexibly to achieve and warrant different claims at different times (Hepburn 1997: 43–7). Philo (1990) for example found that during the news writing exercises consensus was easily reached, but that this was at times a coercive process:

> It was remarkable how quickly some of the groups established the parameters of their own political culture. With the Glasgow women, for example, the presentation of a 'BBC news' was greeted by calls of 'they tell lies, the BBC' and 'ITN was worse'. By contrast members of the Beckenham residents' group established a very different tone, by making remarks about 'that awful Scargill'. Such comments revealed what was assumed to be 'known' by the group and also what was assumed to be 'acceptable'. It was

not simply cultural competence which was being displayed here but also an element of cultural policing. The assumed political culture could exert considerable pressure on anyone who disagreed.

(Philo 1990: 132)

Indeed, Philo notes that each respondent was also interviewed separately to account for this. One woman, who had moved from a mining town in Lancashire to St Albans, a relatively conservative area in the south east of England, disagreed with the group about the actions and credibility of the police during the miners' strike. However, she had not liked to say so, feeling herself an outsider. Philo suggests that 'she said that she had been brought up "Labour" and sympathized with them, but "didn't like to say so in St Albans" ' (Philo 1990: 132).

The idea of an interpretative repertoire is therefore useful as it alerts us to the inherently social nature of semiosis. Semiosis is social because the frameworks for understanding that audiences employ in thinking and engaging in the world come from wider discourses, such as those which find their way into the news media. However, semiosis is also social for they are employed by social actors, engaged in various different interpersonal contexts, who have particular histories, complex investments and purposes in mind. When we situate meaning making in everyday life, we see that respondents do not necessarily display a fixed 'attitude', as something which is outside of discourse, and then finds its expression in talk. Rather they will draw on a range of different repertoires, or at least acknowledge them and work them through as they struggle with others', or indeed their own, partial understanding of what is an increasingly complex and interconnected world.

## Misunderstanding the news

Philo and Berry's (2004) research demonstrates the relevance of such a theory of semiosis, as they explore audience understandings of the Israeli–Palestine conflict. Their research is based on a comprehensive review of news discourse which consistently places emphasis on Palestinian *action* over Israeli response and *retaliation*. This is a constant pattern in television news in which 'Israeli perspectives tend to be highlighted and sometimes endorsed by journalists' (Philo and Berry 2004: 199). To explore the ways in which this shapes audiences' interpretative repertoires, Philo and Berry conducted in-depth qualitative research with more than 100 people. The research explored their beliefs about the conflict as well as the sources of these beliefs. As we have seen above in the discussion of the news game method, there was a very close match between the representations and discourses which are repeatedly used in the television news and those employed by the audience groups. This shapes the viewers' under-standings on the conflict; it gives them a set of interpretative repertoires which they use to make sense of the conflict through their talk and discussion:

| | |
|---|---|
| Female student: | You always think of the Palestinians as being really aggressive because of the stories you hear on the news. I always put the blame on them in my head. |
| Moderator: | Is it presented as if the Palestinians somehow start it and then the Israelis follow on? |
| Female student: | Exactly, I always think the Israelis are fighting back against the bombings that have been done to them. |

(cited in Philo and Berry 2004: 223)

Others commented that the Israelis are 'vulnerable' while the question of legit-imate state violence over illegitimate terrorist violence was raised by another:

Middle-class male: The Palestinians are always regarded as terrorists, Israel as the ideal state which is being attacked by terrorists . . . if it wasn't for the Palestinians and their suicide-bombs, the thing would run perfectly well.

(cited in Philo and Berry 2004: 223)

This last respondent's comment is useful for it shows the kind of critical response we saw above. Here the viewer is well aware of the way in which the conflict is represented in the news (as illegitimate terrorism versus legitimate state action) but seeks an alterative frame of reference: 'how anybody could think that the images of tanks smashing down buildings, of Israeli soldiers armed against boys throwing stones is sympathetic to the Israelis defies logic' (cited in Philo and Berry 2004: 223).

While this may be a very good example of an oppositional decoding (Hall 1973), the wider point remains that these representations are used both by producers and audiences in making sense of what are often inexplicable and alien events. This is very clear in the following account, which is at odds with the true figures at the time, which reflected a ratio of one Israeli death for every two or three Palestinian fatalities:

Middle-class female: I couldn't remember any figures, but then I thought it was the one, I remember it was a suicide bomber. They are the ones who go in and take maybe a whole busload and I thought it would be more Israelis. I don't remember anything showing me the amount of Palestinians who have been killed – I don't remember that, but when it's something about Israelis being killed that has more effect on me – maybe there is more publicity about that.

(cited in Philo and Berry 2004: 232)

As Philo and Berry (2004: 231) argue, although it does not follow that the respondents always believe what they are told, audience members appear to have absorbed 'both the language and the structure of news accounts'. As they make clear, in the western media, representations of the conflict in television news are dominated by the official Israeli perspective while there is little knowledge of alternative accounts, or of the origins of the conflict (Philo and Berry 2004: 225). While other perspectives could be pieced together through other media, most audiences do not and rely on television news. In short, as we shall see in the next section, audiences *rely* upon television news, even if this *trust* is frequently betrayed by incomplete, incomprehensible and biased reporting.

## Bad news from Angola

What we are beginning to see in this audience research is a complex picture of meaning making. Audiences move between trust and suspicion, bias and balance, activity and passivity, critical reasoning and rhetorical skill. While, as we should expect, this is in part a response to the diverse and *embedded* nature of the audiences, who come to television with all sorts of prior knowledges, experiences, identities and political investments, it is also a consequence of the particular generic and discursive structures of television news. These are patterns which naturalize what are highly structured version of reality, in which a hierarchy of voices, sources and discourses appear as natural, as common-sensical: as 'what is' (Allan 1999: 87–92). These institutional and generic issues are particularly evident in Philo's (2002) study of the ongoing civil war in Angola.

In this study Philo and his team screened a report by the journalist David Shukman. This was originally broadcast over two nights on the BBC television news in May 2000, covering the human effects of the conflict and the tragedies caused by landmines and the reasons for the continuation of the war. The former concentrates on the fate of a family of refugees, three members of which have lost limbs through landmine injuries; the latter on a brief history of the conflict, the arms trade, on how oil wealth is controlled by the government and the diamond wealth by anti-government rebels. Finally the report examined the stark contrasts between the wealth and corruption of the government and the fate of the refugees and those caught up in the conflict (Philo 2002: 178–9).

The focus groups were given still images from the report and were asked to write their own news items, before being shown the full report itself. In doing so the news writing exercise was designed to explore the following:

- The knowledge base used for the story that was written by the group members
- Their level of comprehension of the issues involved in the story

- How much was added to their understanding by viewing the news item
- What additional knowledge would be required to produce a better understanding
- How the structure of news discourse shaped their levels of interest
- What could be done at the level of news discourse to increase their interest.

To their credit, those who participated in the news game did examine several of the themes in the BBC report before seeing it in full. Based on the still images, several respondents mentioned details drawn directly from the story, while others drew on a much wider range of knowledge. This included knowledge of western arms trade, most of which was derived from their previous engagement with other media reports. The striking fact however, as Philo (1990) and Kitzinger (2004) have commonly found, is the high degree of resemblance between the original news story and the news game reports. In both the problem was seen as a specifically African issue. This ignores external influences and structural factors such as the international trade in arms, diamonds and oil.

This resemblance between the news game bulletin and the actual report is significant for television news coverage of Africa is routinely concerned with images of famine, disease, poverty, fleeing refugees and conflict (Beattie et al. 1999). This emphasis, as Philo (2002) argues, hardly takes the explanation beyond popular misconceptions of 'tribal enemies', 'ethnic war', 'chaos', 'anarchy', 'wild men' and 'insanity'. Respondents commonly reproduced images of men dancing in grass skirts brandishing spears in front of mud huts, while one respondent was surprised that the liberal and tolerant capital city of Rwanda, Butare, should have a university: 'Oh you don't think of them having universities,' she said (cited in Philo 2002: 176). This woman from Philo's study sums it up well: 'Well, every time you turn on the television or pick up a paper, there's another war starting or there is more poverty and destruction. It's all too much' (cited in Philo 2002: 177).

In this, audiences' interpretative repertoires also closely resembled the discourses and explanations found in television news. These focus on current events, with what happened today, rather than with historical and structural causes, contextualizing background and processes. It is hardly acknowledged in the textual address of news bulletins that audiences will not always 'keep up' and carefully follow a story from the very beginning, that they will miss reports, and that they will require background information and analysis which needs repeating and developing throughout the story. As this respondent puts it:

Respondent: It is whether or not you catch a story young, like the first time it has been on or whatever, then you will follow it through. If you hear about it and you haven't seen it on the television you tend not to know much about it.

(cited in Philo 2002: 177)

Another explains his lack of understanding: 'I have a constant sense of not being properly informed about background to issues and things like that'. Others commented on the ways in which television news assumes too much knowledge and careful attention of the part of them: 'sometimes with the East Timor thing, it's assumed that you know exactly what is happening . . . but I don't understand what is happening' (cited in Philo 2002: 177).

It is significant to note in these terms that viewing the actual Angolan news item itself did little to change these conceptions of the conflict. This is despite the report's brief attempt to broach the underlying causes of the civil war. These include issues such as US dependency on Angolan oil or BP's significant activities in the country, the international diamond trade and the movement of funds to Europe and Switzerland through the international banking system. For instance while there was support for the banning of landmines, and calls for British military or diplomatic intervention, most respondents felt that the situation had little to do with the UK, or indeed with developed nations more widely. In this the situation was taken to be hopeless and the only reasonable response is to send foreign aid and money (Philo 2002: 180). In this the *cause* of the conflict was attributed to corruption and poor levels of education, rather than being identified as *symptoms* of the conflict itself.

The important point here is the appalling lack of historical, economic and sociopolitical understanding that would allow the respondents to put the conflict into the appropriate context. As Philo notes, 'no one in the groups related the continuing problems of Angola to their own actions and there was little or no sense of the world system of socioeconomic relationships that sustain such conflicts' (Philo 2002: 180). In this sense the news game both suggest the role of television news in shaping audiences' frameworks for understanding, as well as its inability to develop them.

These points become partially clear in the discussions which followed the news writing exercise. In these Philo pursued the audience's misunderstandings in more detail. These discussions were based around the four central themes of the BBC report: the role of education, the arms trade, international finance, and trade links. While lack of access to education is a problem facing many different countries in Africa, the assumption of the focus groups was that this was universally the case. Philo found for example that respondents expressed surprise that the moderator had known a good many well-educated, religious and principled African people who were denied access to the political process. It was only through the discussion that the moderator initiated (rather than through viewing television news bulletins) that the focus groups began to question failures in democracy as a *symptom* rather than a *cause* of chronic underdevelopment. As one exchange goes:

Moderator:   Why can't the population actually resolve it?
Female 1:    They have got no power over it.
Male 1:      They haven't got any say in the matter. Do you know what
             I mean?
Moderator:   So who has got the say then?
Male 1:      Your government again, and the rebels.
Moderator:   Why would the government and the rebels have more say
             than the people?
Male 1:      They are the ones with the arms, the guns.
Male 2:      And the money.

(cited in Philo 2002: 181)

As Philo (2002) suggests, these points *had* been covered in the news item, and the respondents readily understood them when pushed to do so. This suggested at least some short-term recall. However, the respondents were characteristically much less clear about the *external* socioeconomic relationships which fuelled the conflict. While they understood that Angola had no armaments industry and that the weapons were imported from outside Africa, this was attributed to the countries of the former Soviet Union rather than to the United States or to western Europe. Likewise, while they understood from the report that this was financed through the trade in oil and diamonds, and that surplus funds were siphoned off to European banks, this complex of trade and finance was not readily *understood*, nor was it drawn upon in the discussions. However, it is not that such information and analysis is not available in the media, but rather that it appears in decontextualized and disjointed form. As Philo suggests:

> Although such information can be identified in the media, the crucial point is that it is not routinely referenced in television news accounts and when it does appear in the media it is in a diverse and fragmented form. It is as if all the pieces of the jigsaw puzzle which are needed to explain Angola appear one at a time and in different places. It is not therefore surprising that there is little effect on public consciousness.

(Philo 2002: 182)

It is remarkable that once the audience is given access to the information, coherently presented, their *understanding* and *interest* develops. In talking about the news item, and by contextualizing it in the moderator's additional explanation, the respondents readily grasped the socioeconomic causes of the conflict: that as long as two powerful elites had control of Angola's oil and diamond wealth, little could be done to develop a representative democracy. Crucial to this however is the developed world's implication in this, for in continuing to support such trade the country's economy remains dependent on simple extraction processes (oil and diamonds). As long as no integrated indus-trial and commercial economy exists there will be little progress on political representation and civil rights (Philo 2002: 182).

Of course this simple explanation, as Philo reports, had a significant impact on the audience's understanding and engagement. It challenged their concep-tions of the conflict as an essentially African issue caused by tribal factions who are incapable of self-governance. In place of this it developed their under-standing of the issue as one of international finance and trade. As such they came to see that something could be done about it (that such relationships could be changed) and that their own purchasing behaviour and political franchise could have a direct influence (Philo 2002: 182). As Philo suggests:

> for most of the people in the groups the effect of making the link between their own conduct and events in Africa was both a shock and a sense of revelation as if they had been given 'secret knowledge' that 'opened their eyes.
>
> (Philo 2002: 183)

In doing so, these women developed a powerful new interpretative repertoire:

Female 1:    When I looked at all these photographs you could look at them all as separate photographs . . . they could all have a separate story. It is not until you see not even the first film but the second one and then the discussion as well that you can actually put it together and say now I know what it is all about. I have got a better idea of what caused it now and who is involved . . . it certainly makes a lot more sense in my head now . . .

Female 2:    As far back as I remember watching news, there has always been something about Africa or whatever in the news. Now you understand why it has been going on for so long there is so much wealth involved and so many other people involved that you just don't know.

Moderator:    It's not hard to understand, is it?

Female 1:    No it is not.

Female 2:    Once you make the obvious link.

(cited in Philo 2002: 184)

That the respondents had gained so much understanding, so quickly, through a simple discussion in which some key contextualizing facts and clarifications had been introduced led some to be dissatisfied with the news media, and to be suspicious of government censorship. In actual fact, this was raised by each of the focus groups. The following exchanges are typical: 'The government wouldn't allow you to come out with things like that. It would be cut out, wouldn't it?'; 'Politicians wouldn't say it in the first place because they would be worried that they would be kicked out' (cited in Philo 2002: 184). Some felt that the government was complicit in this:

Female 1:  I think people would find it shocking.
Female 2:  Yes.
Female 1:  Why not put the message across? Because the government doesn't want us to feel that way.

(cited in Philo 2002: 184)

Hill (2007) has found a similar lack of understanding which suggests the need to make the news *contextual* and *relevant* if it is to engage audiences' interest and develop their understanding. In Philo's research this was a case of explaining how foreign policy and the activities of companies and financial institutions are a part of the problem, and how we as citizens and consumers play a part in this. In this, Hill found that some of her respondents felt disenfranchised by the news, rather than publicly connected. The scale of the issues covered, and the tendency towards abstraction, made them feel 'hopeless'. As one respondent put it, 'that can lead to, I don't know, despondency or, I don't know, giving up all together of any involvement at all, and increasing alienation' (cited in Hill 2007: 149). In the same way as Philo's research, the respondent feels alienated by the news as she cannot see how she can make a change, or how national or international events are part of her lifestyle. In place of this she goes on to argue that she would like to see how news connects to her community, so that she might do something with the information that is presented.

Taken together this research highlights in quite unambiguous ways the manner in which institutional structures of news discourse works against understanding and diminishes the operation of the public sphere. Indeed, as Philo suggests, coverage of conflict tends to focus on dramatic, tragic and violent images with little of the context and explanation that audiences require to make sense of them. Audience repertoires in this case remain fixed on 'internal issues' rather than connecting African development to the developed world. It also leaves audiences free to fall back on easier neo-colonial discourses which characterize the problems as ones which are innate to faults in Africa and Africans (Philo 2002: 185). In place of this contextualization should be a *routine* aspect of news reporting, which is not alluded to in passing, but which is built into the repeated structures of news discourse. As these two respondents suggest, issues of taste should come second place to *ethical* concerns and *political* action:

Male 1:  That is where Western corruption comes in and I think it would open up a lot of eyes.

Male 3:  I think you have just got to shock people. If you want to do a story it has to start off gory with arms or legs or silence [saying] you're caused this or . . .

Male 1:  Like you say you would get thousands of letters but it wouldn't stop the person watching the news the next evening.

(cited in Philo 2002: 185)

## Discourses of abuse

Kitzinger (2004) has found a very similar range of responses in which the discourses of television news shaped audiences' understandings of childhood sexual abuse. This, as we have seen, involves the generation of powerful interpretative repertoires which are ready to be 'activated' when needed. In this case an opposition is set up between poorly trained, incompetent, over-zealous and perhaps malicious social workers, and innocent and loving families falsely accused of sexually abusing their children. This is a powerful discourse which may actually exonerate abusers and put children at risk. It certainly serves to limit the possibilities of frank and honest discussion of abuse and hinders the measures appropriate to protect children against it (Kitzinger 2004: 180–91). It is then, in these terms, an issue which demonstrates the ways in which television news fails as an agent of the public sphere. It will also serve as a useful case study to demonstrate the ways in which television news functions more generally.

  To explore audience responses to television news about sexual abuse, and to allow us to feed audience research back into our understanding of the ways in which these discourses function, we must spend some time outlining the discursive context for audience beliefs. Kitzinger explains that before the mid 1980s there was very little public knowledge and understanding of sexual abuse. While there was a tacit acknowledgement that it went on, it wasn't considered to be particularly harmful, especially compared with murder, abduction and non-family sexual abuse which is best exemplified by the 'exceptional' and high profile crimes of Myra Hindley and Ian Brady.[2] In addition to this, and more harmfully perhaps, incest and so called intergenerational sex were seen by some in the medical, academic and the legal professions through the discourse of 'father and child seduction'. Indeed, as Kitzinger explains, it was the social taboo that was seen as the cause of harm rather than the act itself. This served to exonerate abuse and left the power to define the situation in the hands of the abusers. It does so for these are the only interpretative repertoires which are available to make sense of abuse (Kitzinger 2004: 34).

  During the 1980s, Kitzinger explains that we see a quite dramatic shift in public discourse, away from the 'stranger danger', 'serial sexual predators' and 'paedophiles' that characterize Hindley and Brady to something that is very much more common, perpetuated by family members, unseen and unsuspected in the community. Gradually the media recognized the harm caused by abuse, 'confronting the idea that father-daughter "seduction" was an act of violence' and that children were often and systematically exploited by trusted adults within their social networks – rather than by dangerous strangers (Kitzinger 2004: 34). A major catalyst for this in the UK was Esther Rantzen's *Childwatch* in 1986. This programme broke the previous taboos articulating a new 'sexual abuse discourse'. The discourse centred on the relevant facts and figures, case studies of survivors, advice, discussion of harm, and its consequences. Following from this ChildLine was launched, a telephone service through which children could confidentially report their abuse and receive help. Horrifyingly ChildLine received some 50,000 calls on the opening day and between 8000 and 10,000 thereafter. This generated a lot of coverage in the news with such a discourse giving audiences new ways to think about, discuss, argue over and make sense of sexual abuse. Between 1985 and 1987 for example *The Times* newspaper saw a three fold increase in mentions of sexual abuse while it was also common in television news and documentaries and current affairs programmes such as *Brass Tacks, Everyman* and *Horizon*.

In 1987, just a short year after the very positive opening up of discourses of sexual abuse, what became known as the Cleveland scandal broke in the news media. Entering into the public sphere as a very high profile case, television news and the press reported on contested allegations of incestuous abuse and accusations of inappropriate intervention by social workers and police in Cleveland, a county in the north east of England. A total of 121 children from 57 families were taken into care as parents faced allegations of sexual abuse in the home. All of the children were examined by one of two paediatricians, either Marietta Higgs or Geoff Wyatt. Their methods and competence were fiercely contested by parents, local community groups and the local MP Stuart Bell. Bell together with the parents launched a high profile campaign with a televised press conference. Subsequently most of the children were sent home. This was widely taken by the media as evidence that 'no abuse had occurred and that no intervention had ever been necessary' (Kitzinger 2004: 57). The news discourse was therefore quite at odds to the more positive discourses seen earlier with *Childwatch* for example. As Kitzinger (2000) summarizes:

Events in Cleveland were accompanied by a national media outcry on the behalf of parents. Although the contemporary media coverage was not uniform the broad thrust was that these were innocent families falsely accused by over zealous and incompetent paediatricians and social workers.

(Kitzinger 2000: 63)

In order to trace the ways in which television and wider media discourse circulates in the public sphere Kitzinger examined the similarities between the reporting of the Cleveland case in 1986, and the case of allocations of sexual violence against children in the Scottish Orkney Islands in 1991. In this last case nine children from four families were placed in care under suspicion of sexual abuse from members of their families (Kitzinger 2004: 79–80). Kitzinger found that there was a striking consistency in the patterns of reporting, where the Cleveland case functioned as a 'template' for the later Orkney story. As such it had a very significant effect both on how this recurrent social, cultural and political issue is framed and the definition of the situation by audiences.

In this way headlines in the television news and the press made reference to Cleveland over 200 times in 1991 with headlines such as 'How the nightmare of Orkney ignored the lessons of Cleveland', 'How could this happen again: Storm as sex abuse kids fly home' or 'For the sake of broken hearted families we must get rid of the social workers and think again' (Kitzinger 2004: 58). In such a way the prior case framed the subsequent news discourse and the definition of the event. As one television news editor put it: 'I mean, at the time there had been several cock-ups by the social workers all over the bloody country and the assumption is that you are going to side with the families' (cited in Kitzinger 2004: 59).

## Talking about abuse

The question then, as originally asked by the encoding/decoding model, and as developed in this chapter, is how do such news discourses find their way into the public sphere, how do they circulate, and what are the consequences of this meaning making? To begin to explore this, Kitzinger employed the news game. Some two years after the Orkney scandal Kitzinger asked focus groups to jot down a headline about sexual abuse. Once again, as with Philo (1990) and Philo and Berry's (2004) research, the groups almost unanimously reproduced the language and structure of the news discourses, with almost exact headlines such as 'Orkney dawn swoop by social workers' and 'Social workers to blame for Orkney farce'.

We will return to this below, but it is worth noting that the later Orkney case made a very big impact on public perception, serving to place emphasis on the effects of *allegations* on the families, and on distrust of social services and the medical profession rather than on the effects of the *abuse* on the children and the danger that they were in:

Male:      I just remember what was in the papers; they were took screaming from their beds.

Female 1:  Kids getting snatched at dawn.

Female 2:  Aye, that's right, children getting taken out of their homes . . . their parents not knowing anything about it.

Female 1:  All I know is that they were lifted in the middle of the night . . . swooping on the island at four in the morning, uplifting all the weans out their beds.

Female 3:  Them getting taken away from their parents.

Female 2:  In the middle of the night out of their beds, that's horrific.

Female 1:  I mean it's tragic for the mums and dads, I mean it must have been dreadful for them. I think it was awful really awful; I really do.

(cited in Kitzinger 2004: 85)

In actual fact the children were taken into care in a joint operation with the police, at seven in the morning when all the family members would be together (some 30 minutes before the school bus arrived). This was lost on the respondents:

Respondent: What was so shocking was that they were removed from their homes by the police, at the crack of dawn and taken by helicopter to another piece of land, away from their parents . . . that had quite an impact. The fact that they lived on this island and they were flown to the mainland and you had this image, that that might be the child's first flight, and they were almost like being abducted. They were being abducted in fact, like a real childhood sort of horror story in a way.

(cited in Kitzinger 2004: 86)

Kitzinger (2004) suggests that the 'dawn raids' news coverage may have made such a strong impression for a number of reasons. These include the dramatic images of police and social workers 'raiding homes' which acted to brand the story. Likewise, as this is a horrific crime, which is difficult to talk about, the discourse offers an easy framework for avoiding the abuse, for placing it in the hands of the authorities, rather than the parents or abusers. It also simplifies what is complex and ambiguous, offering a clearly defined position. This frames the event in terms of conflict, in an opposition of good parents versus bad social workers (this was not helped as social workers were constrained from talking to the media for legal reasons, and were also defensive as they under attack). Indeed, as Kitzinger argues, there is innate drama in the representation of parents demanding a voice, and considerable room for empathy and identification through the emotionally power of the story (of the thought that this could happen to you and your own family).

In many ways this opposition was also strengthened by the news coverage which placed emphasis on the 'idyllic' and 'innocent' islands with their traditional and tight-knit communities, which was in direct opposition to the assumed corruption of Glasgow for instance (Kitzinger 2000: 68). As Kitzinger summarizes:

> It was these fears, empathies, memories and associations around Cleveland which informed reactions to subsequent reporting of events in Orkney. Indeed people not only confused details of the two cases but explicitly used Cleveland to help them recall and reconstruct what happened in Orkney.
>
> (Kitzinger 2000: 68–9)

While the precise details of the case remained unclear, the respondents who participated in the news game were able to recall and employ the same phrases, facts, themes and explanatory structures that were found in the original news discourse. This was a minimum of two years after the event:

Female 1: Orkney is that . . . Oh no, I'm thinking of another one. I'm thinking of Marietta Higgs.

Female 2: No, that was the Cleveland child sex abuse. Yeah I remember the stupid woman, because she had five kids.

Female 1: They put something in the vagina or something and they said if the vagina dilated the child had been abused. Well, it was something incredible like that and it was Marietta Higgs that was at the front of it all.

Female 3: They were testing any child that had been taken for *any* reason.

Female 2: Bet they didn't test Marietta Higgs' children! And there was a big outcry because then they discovered that this method was not a good indication . . . but of course at that point . . .

Female 3: The damage was done.

Female 2: People's lives had been ruined and men were committing suicide.

(cited in Kitzinger 2000: 67)

Once established, these make up their interpretative repertoires. As these respondents put it:

Female 2: There was one case where, it was a big headline, children being removed. One of the children hadn't even been able to say cheerio to its mother and they were taking the child out the

Female 1:  door and it wasn't allowed to take its toys, I found that's the sort of thing that sticks the most.

Female 1:  Everybody was frightened, nobody could relax, it put the fear of Christ up a lot of people.

Male:  You get your little girl, when they're about three or four; you get into bed and give them a cuddle. And now you're afraid that they might go to school and say 'My Dad was in bed cuddling me' you know, next thing, you have got to be careful.

(cited in Kitzinger 2004: 85–6)

Here we see the respondents repeatedly talk about 'innocent families being falsely accused' through an arbitrary test which had, in their words and quite incorrectly, been 'completely discredited'. Indeed, the incorrect assumption was that the tests had been carried out at random:

Female 1:  Here you are taking your weans [children] to the hospital to get a stookie [plaster] put on their leg, and before you know where you are there are these strange people doing all these things. . . . All the kiddies all squealing and screaming and people doing things to them and there's no mammy and daddy.

Female 2:  Takes *us* all our time to go for a smear test, how do the weans feel?

(cited in Kitzinger 2004: 61)

Despite the inaccuracies in the reporting, the incompetence discourse clearly framed these audience perceptions of the case. This formed an interpretative repertoire which was latent and ready to be activated and drawn upon the next time a case was exposed. In this way it entered into personal or public discourse providing a ready made framework for understanding. The respondents were absolutely adamant about the facts of the case, as one said, 'basically we know what happened'. They trusted their memories and did not question what the media reported, suggesting that in this case at least they had access to all the 'important and relevant facts' (Kitzinger 2004: 88). Only a handful of respondents questioned if the raids occurred in the manner suggested, while they could reproduce news discourse very accurately, even some time after the event. In this sense, as we look at the relationship between the discourses of television news and audience interpretative repertoires, we are not dealing so much with discrete 'decodings' of a particular television news broadcast. Rather we must consider the ways in which news discourse enters into collective memory (Volkmer 2006), both those of journalists who use it to shape news reports of subsequent cases, and audiences' understandings and responses to them.

We have also seen a common baseline of *trust* in television news. Throughout this chapter we have seen examples of how the genre is oriented to with an expectation that it will be a reliable and authoritative source of information, debate and analysis (Harrison 2006). This is nevertheless sometimes tested and undermined as audiences' expectations fail to be met, as they draw on their own experiences, on other sources of knowledge, and as they manipulate news discourse to form the basis of their own position. In this, audiences are not above producing biased arguments themselves, and indeed, of accusing television news of bias. Both of these disrupt epistemological claims to 'truth' and suggest its constructed or discursive nature, and it is to this that we must now turn.

## Truth, trust and bias

Hill's (2007) research suggests a tension in regard to audiences and the trust they place in television news. They want to see it as a useful and authoritative source of information which can be relied upon to provide constructive knowledge and debate. As this respondent puts it, 'I think there is a trust in the news. I think there is a cultural thing you know. This is the news!' (cited in Hill 2007: 135). Part of this is to do with the presence of familiar newscasters, and the institutional status of news in the schedules: 'We have to trust the newscaster and feel confident because that way, when you watch the news and you know that you feel confident that it's true, and that it is correct' (cited in Hill 2007: 135).

However, while this trust may be comforting to journalists, many of Hill's respondents also reported less positive experiences in which they felt let down by television news. In this regard the very high expectations of objectivity and balance which are expected of news are not always achieved. As this respondent suggests, 'It's an acceptance of truth, it may not be, but it's this kind of social acceptance. And this, in particular, is kind of constructed in a way that it must be the truth' (cited in Hill 2007: 137). Likewise, this respondent *wants* to trust the news, but is often forced to step back and interrogate his trust in quite a critical manner:

> 30-year-old male: I kind of believe what I see when I watch the news. But I sometimes think it's also being picked. You know, like, what's important and what's not important. And you never know, you know, it can be subjective in that way. . . . But you don't know whether you get all of it, like a full range.
>
> (cited in Hill 2007: 135)

As Hill suggests, this oscillation between 'trust and distrust' is quite typical. As this respondent puts it:

> 29-year-old male: It's a picture of reality. . . . Well if you trust the person, or the people making the programme, then you can perhaps relate to it and think you get some kind of overall picture of some major events in society. But I think you are fairly aware that it is a picture. I don't think you think you'd get some genuine knowledge of reality.
>
> (cited in Hill 2007: 135)

Respondents were thus quite aware of news conventions, and drew attention to editing and news values. They were also aware of editorial policy and pressures to present official accounts (Hill 2007: 136). This viewer for example questions the epistemological value of 'truth' and hunts for a range of different perspectives: 'I read a lot of news, I watch news programmes and things, to see how it covers it. 'Cos I mean – there is no such thing as "truth" ' (cited in Hill 2007: 136). Indeed, while some singular notion of 'truth' may be an ideal which is held up for television news, audiences are much more flexible in the ways in which they come to their collective understandings. This suggests that notions of truth and bias may be based on relational and interpersonal agreements, struggles and negotiations, as much as they are qualities which can be objectively defined.

Buckingham (2000) has explored the ways in which such agreements about truth and biases are generated in and through talk. In doing so he pays particular attention to the rhetorical functions that such claims serve. Respondents often felt no need to be balanced in their *response* to television news. While there was much talk of bias throughout his focus groups these accusations were often made *less* on epistemological grounds, and more as a rhetorical means of supporting their own positions and of presenting the self in favourable terms.

Buckingham's 14-year-old respondents for example were vocal and dexterous in their critical skills. In arguing they were committed to developing an ethical and political position through which a shared understanding of the truth of the situation would emerge. In doing so Buckingham demonstrates the ways in which definitions were generated through discussion, agreement and debate, as they developed and supported their own positions, challenged those of others, questioned their own arguments, looked for and tested contradictions and weaknesses, and balanced opposing positions (Buckingham 2000: 141).

More rhetorically however his respondents were not above exaggerating, inventing 'facts' and hypothesizing outcomes to support their own position. In this, opposing views were parodied and exaggerated, often with the explicit intent of undermining them (Buckingham 2000: 142). Indeed, this has some surprising outcomes in terms of perceptions of bias. Some respondents for example wilfully ignored the presentation of views which opposed their own, and simply took what she wanted from the text. This in turn then led them on to accuse the items of bias (Buckingham 2000: 144).

As I argued above, this has consequences for the ways that we think about audiences' relationships to news discourse and the interpretative repertoires that they form. It points to the importance of considering the contexts in which it is drawn into semiosis, the prior investments or commitments of the audience, as well as the functions that the talk is serving. As Buckingham (2000) suggests,

> Judgements of bias need to be understood in terms of the social contexts in which they are made, and the social functions they serve. 'Exposing bias' – or at least alleging that it exists – is a powerful discursive move. It seems to place the speaker in a position that is distanced from the text, and by implication, less vulnerable to its influence that others who fail to perceive it . . . it can appear to place the speaker in a position which is beyond the domain of mere personal opinion. At least it represents a *claim* so such a position – even if it cannot guarantee that this claim will be accepted by others. While we need to account for the power of the text, we also need to account for the power of the viewer – not merely in relation to the text itself, but also to other viewers – both real and imagined.
>
> (Buckingham 2000: 149)

## Conclusion

Despite the lively thinking that Buckingham outlines here and the reality of everyday talk which is somewhat removed from the purely rational and 'ideal' conditions of the Habermasian public sphere, there are still some rather negative consequences of the research reported in this chapter. These, as other writers have suggested, deplete the effective operation of the public sphere (Dahlgren 1995). Audiences are certainly capable of critical thought, and are capable of arguing *with* and *against* news discourse. However, in many cases incomplete and inaccurate reporting, marked in particular by a lack of context, leaves audiences *ill informed* and *unengaged*. Indeed, this is exacerbated, as Kitzinger suggests, for avoiding media coverage, forgetting it, or not really paying attention will not necessarily serve to protect people from the influence of television news. Rather inattentive and disengaged viewing may actually *increase influence*, precisely because it precludes the questioning and critical dialogue that we saw in the first part of this chapter (Kitzinger 2004: 187).

In this respect it is worth considering these examples from Philo and Berry's (2004) research. In them audiences feel that television news journalists take too much prior knowledge, information and understanding for granted:

Female student: Every time it comes on [the Israeli–Palestinian conflict] it never actually explains it so I don't see the point in watching it – I just turn it off and go and make a cup of tea or something. I don't like watching it when I don't understand what's going on.

(cited in Philo and Berry 2004: 240)

Male student: I've not heard any historical context from the news at all. They don't tell us that – they don't say – they leave in on the short scale. 'This fighting was due to yesterday's fighting, which was due to the day before'. But they don't go back to all that, I don't know anything about that [history]. The reporter will say 'The Israelis fired into a Palestinian refugee camp today in response to a Palestinian suicide bomb yesterday', but they won't say why the Palestinians are fighting or why the Israelis are fighting – it doesn't go back any length of time.

(cited in Philo and Berry 2004: 216)

This type of response is directly related to a sense of confusion and misunderstanding on the one hand, and to a lack of interest and engagement on the other. Simply put, it is difficult to imagine how audiences can be engaged in issues which are inadequately contextualized and explained. As Philo and Berry put it, 'in principle, to see events as having causes can be a first step towards understanding the possibilities for change, and to engaging with what is shown and to having opinions about it' (Philo and Berry 2004: 239).

Contextualization and clearer explanation do indeed seem to provide the basis for more sustained and critical audience engagement. In some cases, as we saw with Kitzinger's research, respondents drew on first hand experience, a wider range of sources, or expert knowledge to refute the incompetence discourse. In doing so they would take the position that 'there is no smoke without fire'. Moreover, in other discussions some respondents took the opinion that because social workers were assumed to have made such a huge mistake in the Cleveland case, the Orkney case was much more likely to be correct, as they wouldn't risk making such a mistake again. As these respondents put it:

Female 1:  I don't think that the social workers would have acted like that [in Orkney] if there had not been. . . . They're not going to put their careers on the line.

Female 2:  Especially after Cleveland.

(cited in Kitzinger 2000: 71)

Indeed, more emphatically, new interpretative repertoires can quite easily be generated once new information is made available. This respondent for example had the opportunity to watch the documentary *Cleveland: Unspeakable Truths* during Kitzinger's research. Her new understanding of the background to the case, and the detailed knowledge that it provided, generated a very different framework for understanding:

> Female: From what I remember at the time, it was completely hidden that some of the parents already had convictions. Of course that makes a difference to what you'd think. Also I thought Marietta Higgs had wrongly diagnosed, and the programme suggested that she was right. . . . I bought it [the original reporting] hook, line and sinker, Marietta Higgs was damned. I hadn't realized that Marietta Higgs and that man (I still can't remember his name, even after watching the programme) hadn't been struck off – so they were clearly vindicated by their profession. I'm sorry if I had said Marietta Higgs was a sleaze ball. I take it all back.
>
> (cited in Kitzinger 2000: 73)

In this, then we see a clear indication of television news's ability to shape *thinking*, to set the parameters for public debate, action and reaction.

The research methodologies which I have reviewed in this chapter continue to be of central importance to the concerns of cultural and media studies, and for this they have warranted our close and sustained attention. Philo and Berry's and Kitzinger's use of the news game for example has clearly demonstrated the ways in which audiences are not 'duped' by television news, but rather poorly served by it. We have also seen the importance of triangulating studies of news coverage, production process and audience understandings. News in this is found to be systematically biased in terms of elite sources: hard pressed journalists rely on easy assumptions and ready-to-hand discourses while their focus on the new systematically decontextualizes what they report from complex histories, structural issues and political-economic processes. As a consequence we see audiences as they *struggle to make meaning*: they draw the texts and discourses of television news into semiosis, sometimes creatively, argumentatively, and defiantly, sometimes less so.

To add to this complexity we have seen some of the ways in which these meanings are generated in everyday life. While we will return to this in Chapters 4 and 5, we have seen the benefits in asking audiences to talk about news texts, about their beliefs, feelings, investments and understandings. By doing so the research in this chapter has demonstrated the ways in which semiosis is shaped by our audiences' experiences, by prior beliefs, politics, knowledge, values and assumptions, and by their identities and feelings. It has also shown some of the ways in which it is shaped by the everyday contexts in which we talk and live out our lives. However, in this news, discourses are also distilled into stock responses, easy assumptions and half truths. In many cases they provide the interpretative frameworks for *poor thinking*, as they enter into our memories, our associations and our conversations (Kitzinger 2004: 180). The prospects for an effective public sphere based on television news, in this case, seems slight.

## Notes

1 The strike started in 1984 when the National Coal Board announced that it intended to close 20 coal mines with a loss of some 20,000 jobs. As a result many communities in the north of England and in Wales would lose their primary source of employment. The strike must be seen in the context of a wider class struggle where the Conservative government under Margaret Thatcher was systematically reducing the power of the trade unions. Thatcher famously referred to the striking miners as 'the enemy within' and that recognizing the miners' cause would be tantamount to surrendering the rule of parliamentary democracy to the rule of the mob. The strike received widespread coverage, not least regarding the role of the police, who made over 11,000 arrests during pickets outside coal pits.

2 Myra Hindley and her lover, Ian Brady, were convicted of murdering three children in Britain between 1963 and 1965 in the so called 'Moors murders'. Both subsequently confessed to two additional murders. Hindley died in custody in 2002 while Brady is unlikely ever to be released from prison, which adds to the continued controversy over the cases. Both remain well-known and significant figures of hate in Britain.

# 2 | REALITY TELEVISION, AUDIENCES AND ETHICS

Television makes a spectacle of everyday life. Its concerns are increasingly focused on 'backstage behaviours', on those things which go on behind closed doors, or more precisely perhaps, behind how we normally present ourselves: as good, as just, as decent, as moral (Goffman 1969). Jade Goody, an early star of *Big Brother UK*, was a case in point. At once celebrated and vilified she entered television's public sphere, scorned for being an 'air-head', but affectionately championed for her naive authenticity, for being an ordinary girl who had 'made good'. Later however, appearing on *Celebrity Big Brother*, she revealed herself to be a racist and a bully. Questions were raised in the UK Parliament, on news channels and chat shows: what is the nature of ordinary, everyday and taken-for-granted racism, what are the responsibilities of broadcasters, how should individuals conduct themselves in the midst of this? Tragically, as she lay dying from cancer, the ethical debate continued: had she redeemed herself, was she right to exploit her death for financial gain (to provide for her children in the future)? Were her publicists exploiting her, or simply revealing the pain and tragedy of everyday life?

This revelation of backstage behaviours, as Nikolas Rose (1999) points out, is pervasive: a television talk show discusses a woman's feelings when she discovers that her husband is a transsexual; the sex lives and personal conduct of footballers and a host of celebrities are pored over; talk shows, documentaries, lifestyle programmes and docusoaps 'abound with stories of the hidden horrors of family life: physical and sexual abuse, emotional humiliation, drunkenness, spousal abuse' (Rose 1999: 263). Television's address in this, however, is as much ethical as it is salacious, as much moral as scandalous. It is, in John Ellis's terms, a vast mechanism for working through: it worries over such questions, holds them up as examples, as much for our scrutiny as for our pleasure (Ellis 1999). Television, as such, is something akin to a modern confessional (Shattuc 1997: 111–13). But what, in this, is the relationship between thought and emotion, the self and the other? Through what modalities do audiences respond, and how might this relate to the public sphere?

To address these questions this chapter takes the question of television's ethics and uses it to expand arguments about the public sphere. It does so by considering audiences' relationships to what is commonly seen as 'trash television'. We will look at the various formats which make up what has come to be known as reality programming. Our main case study here will be on the hugely popular and global game show *Big Brother*. This has generated by far the most interest in the area by audience researchers and it serves to highlight a very different type of public sphere, one based on the forms and pleasures of *game play* and *ritual* (Couldry 2002). However, while this may sound frivolous and far removed from the high-minded intentions of television news, this chapter argues that reality game shows may actually engage audiences in various forms of ethical judgement, reflection and thought. It is a case, as Annette Hill puts it, of exploring what reality and lifestyle programming can teach us about the 'application of ethics in our everyday lives' (Hill 2005: 121).

This ethicalization, however, is not the dry and sober debate of the classical public sphere. Rather it is one which is based on the rather more bawdy forms of scandal, speculation and gossip. These types of language can be traced back in popular traditions such as fairs, carnivals, popular theatre, music hall, vaudeville, ballads and burlesque, as well as the street literature, the tabloid and the 'yellow' press (Manga 2003: 6). Indeed, as Elizabeth Bird argues, the emphasis on 'the personal, the sensational, and the dramatic' has always been a part of public culture: not only in the news, but also in the ways in which television discourse circulates in everyday life, as audiences gossip, speculate and spread rumour (Bird 2003: 22).

A range of researchers are increasingly making this point. Peter Lunt and Paul Stenner (2005) for example suggest that talk shows, such as *Jerry Springer*, can be thought of as a part of an 'emotional public sphere'. Likewise, Peter Dahlgren (2005) argues that while reality television can hardly aspire to an objective rendering of the world, its emphasis on 'the personal, the sensational, the subjective, the confessional, the intimate' does allow significant forms of public engagement. While we may think and develop frameworks for understanding through our cognitive abilities, they will nevertheless come tinged with emotion or affect (we feel *passionate* about a political party, or *enraged* or *moved to tears* by an injustice) (Dahlgren 2005: 416). These different ways of knowing must be recognized, for as Hill comments, reality television formats and talk shows enable complicated movements between rational and affective responses, and these disrupt the notion of a singular and normative public sphere (Hill 2007: 14).

Following this concern this chapter will go on to look at two further 'ethical spaces'. The first is that of lifestyle programming, with examples such as *Honey We're Killing the Kids* or *How to Look Good Naked*. As Hill (2005) argues, these are primarily concerned with questions of identity, with 'what sort of person should I be'. They view the self as an ongoing project in which 'our identities, or life biographies, are constructed on a daily basis' (Hill 2005: 89). Our framework here will shift from the ritual and playful to the 'ethics of care' and the discourses through which we are governed. As the Foucauldian scholar Rose (1999) puts it, what we are concerned with here is the ways in which these programmes address us through a plethora of expert discourses – those of the law, of religion, medicine, nutrition, childcare and psychology, of fashion, gardening and interior design. Each of these demands that we take responsibility for our own conduct; that we govern ourselves in the name of our own self-realization. This, he suggests, results in an 'ethicalization of existence' (Rose 1999: 264).

The stage set, we will go on to consider audience responses to television talk shows. Drawing on audience research by William Gamson (1998), Livingstone and Lunt (1994), Julie Manga (2003) and Jane Shattuc (1997), we will see how the self is put into discourse in the form of confessional narratives, and how audiences respond, both emotionally and ethically. This constitutes an ethical public sphere, in which the 'battle lines' are drawn between that which is acceptable, and that which is transgressive (Gamson 1998).

## Modalities of response: game play and authenticity

If television news presents itself as a serious, truthful, objective and authoritative representation of the world, reality programming is characterized by much more uncertainty. Indeed, as various writers have suggested, its mode of address is playful and ritualistic, a sort of game in which audiences are expected to participate. Nick Couldry (2002) for example sees *Big Brother* as a type of modern ritual or a media event which does not reflect a pre-existing reality. Rather it quite explicitly foregrounds its format and play-like structure, through emphasizing the house rules or by inviting audience participation and interactivity. Drawing on anthropological definitions of play as a 'liminal' or 'indeterminate space' between reality and fantasy, Couldry suggests that reality television functions as a ritual where audiences can reflect upon their shared culture. This can be seen as a process of 'working through', a space 'where society's members address the central values and meanings that they share' and 'takes cognizance of itself' (Couldry 2002: 284).

Hill (2005, 2007) has also found such an indeterminate or liminal relationship between the reality programming and everyday life. She suggests that audiences oscillate in their attitudes towards the programmes, making judgements between *truth and sincerity* on the one hand and *performance and artifice* on the other. Her detailed quantitative data suggest that viewers place little value on people *not* performing in reality formats. Indeed, they enjoy the game-like structures and judge people on the manner in which they 'play' the game rather than in how 'true to life' it really is. In this way audiences don't question whether reality programming is 'fake'; it is taken for granted that they are, although subtle judgements will be made between different formats (Hill 2007: 125–6). Nevertheless by orienting to the text playfully they look for authenticity *within* the 'rules of the game'. This means taking on multiple roles, roles which resist any easy judgements about the relationship between fact and fiction, truth and artifice, and authenticity and inauthenticity. Sometimes we will connect with who and what is shown, forming quite intense or loyal relationships; at other times we will question our motivations for watching, and be troubled by what we see (Hill 2007: 89).

It is helpful to think about this in terms of the modalities of response which are generated, ones which engage a double way of looking (Barker and Brooks 1998). Audiences describe a type of response which involves *closeness* and iden-tification with the characters. They are seen as real people who are engaged in various dramas, tests of character and ethical dilemmas. But their relationship to the text is also governed by a critical and scrutinizing *distance* over the same participants, who are simultaneously seen as actors or performers in a staged format. This double way of looking that characterizes this modality of response is seen clearly in the following respondent's remarks. On the one hand, this recognition of the gaming aspects of the genre acknowledges that reality parti-cipants are acting, or in Erving Goffman's (1969) terms, involved in various 'presentations of self'. On the other, they still look for the truth *behind* what is represented as a playful negotiation of the 'authentic' and the 'staged'. As this respondent put it:

> Jamie: You can still see people's characters, even though they do it in a way that is quite extreme, but you know if somebody is crying, they are crying, if somebody is laughing, they are laughing and if somebody's acting selfish or kind they are still people. They are *real*. It's just that the situation is set up.
>
> (cited in Hill 2007: 116)

Likewise for the following respondent there is a pleasure in forming character relationships (Hill 1997) with the participants. She 'feels like she really gets to know them':

Angela: *Big Brother*. I felt like I knew the people in there, 'cos after a while, although there's cameras there, in the beginning they all did act up but you can't do it all the time. You know when you're upset and crying you can't act happy, you know what I mean. And you really get close to the people, 'cos you, like, get to know them. It's really weird, 'cos, like, we're talking about them now as if we know them and it's people we've never ever met in our lives who are on TV.

(cited in Hill 2005: 71)

The ways in which such a character relationship governs an oscillation between *closeness* and *distance* can be seen in the following discussion, as Angela and Sharon continue to explain their pleasures. In this the participants are constantly scrutinized and judged. This depends upon the ways in which they relate to the character and your 'attitude towards them':

Angela: Yeah, but if you genuinely like them. Say, I liked Anna and if someone said, 'Oh, Anna's this, oh, Anna's that', I wouldn't think she's acting up, do you know what I mean? I think it depends on your attitude towards the person. Do you know what I mean? 'Cos people genuinely didn't like Nick 'cos they'd seen that he was doing these kinds of things . . . yeah and I hated Mel so whatever anybody said that was good about her, I was like, 'Oh I don't like her, whatever she does, she's a bitch'.

Sharon: I think the only people that could tell if these people are acting up are the people that knew them. We don't know them so we *couldn't really judge*.

Interviewer: Do you end up judging anyway?

Sharon: Yeah, well I do!

(cited in Hill 2005: 72)

This response suggests that reality programming tends to invite a critical viewing mode. The very nature of the genre, in its playful address to the audience explicitly invites audiences to engage in debate, to question what is authentic and what is staged, to judge the actions of participants (be they in game shows or lifestyle programmes) when they are faced with challenging situations. The genre in short invites viewers to judge its 'truth claims'. This is in part because the genre deals with human interest. Audiences will therefore have first hand experience of the issues that come up in the programme, such as social and personal behaviour, relationships and emotions.

Developing these points, Hill's research suggests that audiences are a good deal more critical with reality programming than they are with the news. The genre in this regard is based on a 'chain of distrust' where audiences naturally question the relationships between authenticity and performance. In these terms performance becomes a necessary part of the genre, something that is essential to its forms and address, rather than something which renders it as inauthentic or fake. For some this led to a more scrutinizing orientation to the text, more so than with news for example, which is assumed to be objective and true (Hill 2007: 142). This however is not always unproblematic. For the following respondent the question of emotional responses and authenticity becomes foregrounded in docusoaps, which are generally seen to be much more authentic than reality game shows. The powerful nature of the story and his emotional involvement blurs the lines not only between fact and fiction, but also between entertainment and uncomfortable voyeurism. This becomes a question of media ethics:

> 44-year-old male: I was particularly moved by last night's episode of *Children's Hospital* in which a little girl has her plaster casts removed. I'm ashamed to say that I felt that it was entertaining. It's become a sort of soap opera along the lines of *Casualty*. It's increasingly difficult to distinguish fact from fiction. People's distress is being repackaged as entertainment, and that disturbs me.
>
> (cited in Hill 2000: 202)

Audiences enjoy the combination of information and melodrama which characterizes the genre. In this, Hill sees the 'vicarious experience of witnessing near tragedy and death' which make such stories exciting, and for many, pleasurable to watch (Hill 2000: 203). For instance she reports on a respondent who was deeply involved in a story on the reality programme 999. In this a lorry driver had been impaled on a fence. The respondent was 'riveted, a bit ill, horribly fascinated, glued to the seat with suspense as the emergency services tried to free him, totally sympathetic to the victim's feelings and reactions' (cited in Hill 2000: 203).

## Working through: dramatizing morality

While the patterns of closeness and identification that are seen in these responses are a source of pleasure and involvement for audiences, they also relate to much broader cultural issues. In this the appeal of human interest stories is nothing new. Bird (2003) for example argues that there is a clear relationship between folklore traditions such as ballads, nursery rhymes and oral storytelling on the one hand and generic forms and themes which characterize reality programming on the other. All are centred on the fears and desires of the audience, as well as points of cultural tension and moral standards. Indeed, by drawing on folklore research, Bird suggests that tabloid culture serves to validate cultural norms and educate audiences in the values of a culture, while also offering an outlet for fantasy, desire and longing (Bird 2003: 32–5).

Hill (2007) likewise draws on Ellis's notion of 'working through' to make a similar point. She argues that we are living in an age of uncertainty, one which is characterized by profound changes in our lifestyles, in our expectations, identities and roles. In this our cultural values are constantly shifting. The role of television in the midst of this uncertainty is to provide a means of coming to terms with and understanding the confusion of modern life. As Ellis (2000) puts it, television provides 'multiple stories and frameworks of explanation which enable understanding, and in the very multiplicity of those frameworks, it enables viewers to work through the major public and private concerns of their society' (Ellis 2000: 174).

This working through does not seek to once and for all settle cultural tensions and values. Rather it is a constant and interminable process where it poses questions, narrates, speculates and gossips about the life of a culture. Most of this is open-ended and indeterminate, for television rarely offers definitive answers. Indeed, as Hill suggests, the very repetitive nature of television, with its genres, series and serial forms, its open-ended narratives and cyclical schedules offers a constant deferment. News follows the same daily structure, with ongoing stories, allowing audiences to 'witness on a daily basis'. Soap operas and docusoaps have ongoing narratives with 'no clear endings'. Television in this sense is inherently open: 'a relatively safe area in which uncertainty can be entertained, and can even be entertaining' (Ellis 2000: 82; Hill 2007: 87).

Central to this working through, as Sue Holmes suggests, is the way in which reality programming is 'structurally and deliberately *primed* to make this discursive "struggle" and talk a central element in its experience' (Holmes 2004: 222). *Big Brother* for example becomes a media event and a common talking point. Its working through spreads across newspapers, spin-off shows, Internet chat rooms and everyday conversations (Scannell 2002). Participants enter the diary room and confess their own feelings and the motives for their actions. They pass judgement and nominate. As they scrutinize the behaviour of others, we ourselves are invited to judge, to gossip and speculate: to be scandalized, prurient and salacious. Such talk is the engine of semiosis: it drives our meaning making. As this respondent puts it, 'I mean coffee break talk is to a fairly large part caused by what's happening on TV' (cited in Hill 2007: 162).

While we shall see in Chapter 3 that some of this gossip can generate a challenging and transgressive discursive space, Bird (2003) finds it to be morally conservative, a form of talk which at once delights in the transgressive behaviour while simultaneously condemning it. She argues that gossip tends to police the boundaries of law and order, justice and wrong doing, civility and manners, sexual propriety, gender roles, decency, identity and behaviour (Bird 2003: 32–4). Here for example we see a respondent talking about his identifications with those on *Wife Swap*, and what he can learn from them:

> 60-year-old male: *Celebrity Love Island, Big Brother, I'm a Celebrity.* They're kind of salacious. . . . I think the interesting thing about *Wife Swap* is that there is often something to learn from it, about the way relationships are and how people have them. And you have to look at your own behaviour in some ways. Although, it's meant to be entertainment. I mean, it's entertainment. . . . They're both *salacious*, they're both *suspicious*. But they both contain things about the ordinary drive of life. Ambition, envy, relationships. What actually does go on in the reality of some people's lives . . . there is something you get from them.
>
> (cited in Hill 2007: 105–6)

As Hill (2007) comments, the notion of 'the ordinary drive of life' is significant and seems to offer a range of different pleasures and modalities of meaning for this viewer. These oscillate between carnivalesque pleasure and celebratory involvement in the 'salacious' on the one hand, and a 'suspicious' and scrutinizing impulse to pass judgement on the other. For Hill this includes being 'immersed in the experience of watching' and also a more reflexive process, whereby audiences think about 'how this relates to them'. This reflection occurs not only as the text unfolds, but also later, as the semiosis continues through gossip. Part of this is about being 'grossed out': of *at once* celebrating *and* worrying about the ways in which the boundaries of taste fairness and decency are being exploited (Hill 2007: 107). Sharon captures this well:

> Sharon: That's almost a pleasure in being grossed out by something. It's a weird way of putting it, but there is always a sense of enjoyment, you know, why do we go on fairground rides when they freak us out, but there's enjoyment at it and I think certain people get a pleasure from watching those programmes, and they go 'Oh, oh, oh, that's horrible!' And they are kind of being pushed to the edge a little bit.
>
> (cited in Hill 2007: 106–7)

The oscillation between the salacious enjoyment and the suspicious and uncomfortable ethical dilemmas is central to Rachel's reaction to reality television in the following extract where she reflects on the moral dimensions of *Big Brother*, feeling bad about the choices she makes as viewer, not only worrying about the rightness of producing the programme, but also thinking about how the contestants' behaviour relates to her and her own life:

Rachel: I think there's something a little bit worrying about reality TV itself. I mean if you take *Big Brother*, for example, it does cross the boundaries every year, you can see steady continual things getting a bit more . . . on-edge, it make you feel, 'Oh, maybe we shouldn't be watching this' or 'Maybe we shouldn't be broadcasting it'. It's about identity isn't it, *Big Brother* as well, we watch it, we can remember these characters who we can identify with . . . or maybe they're characters we don't want to, we hate them because we can see a bit of ourselves in them . . . and I think. . . . Where is TV going to take us?

(cited in Hill 2007: 109)

Janet Jones's (2003) study of *Big Brother* makes a similar point, for she highlights the ways in which such curiosity, scandal and gossip is 'part of the game' precisely because the structure of the show encourages audiences to seek out backstage behaviours (Goffman 1969) which are normally hidden. It, she suggests, 'encourages viewers to lift back the curtains of their neighbours' living rooms' (Jones 2003: 407). This focus on the backstage is for some viewers more compelling than soap operas. As one respondent in her study puts it, 'They seem so two-dimensional now I have *Big Brother* to watch'. The programme as such has much in common with the thematic concerns of soaps, with their emphasis on human interest, psychological motivation, moral conduct, judgements and suspense (Jones 2003: 408).

It is interesting to note that the respondents in Jones's study relied heavily on continuous footage, either on the official website or on the digital channel, E4. By doing so they could circumvent the more salacious and dramatic edited highlights in the daily show, and seek the truth out for themselves. In this case the constant scrutiny ensured that the participants were 'exposed', that they were 'laid bare' and had 'nowhere to hide'. In the former case there is distrust of the production team: 'We only see what Channel Four wants us to see. We only see the extraordinary event rather than what people are usually like' (cited in Jones 2003: 411). In this we can see that the values of authenticity and sincerity are what audiences were seeking, and what they voted for. This respondent in her study for example voted for a particular contestant 'because she hasn't got a conniving bone in her body, she is not putting on an act, she is genuine and her naivety makes her more appealing'. In contrast, those that played the game too well, who appeared to be two-faced and scheming, and who tried to manipulate the situation, were ultimately judged for it and voted out of the house:

Female: I dislike Elisabeth: I think she is managing to hide what she is really like. That slip when she shouted at Paul showed her real side. So far she has managed to get people on her side by being understated and nice but then she has given them a good slagging off behind their backs. Like when the girls were wearing bikinis and she made a sly comment about them to Stewart.

(cited in Jones 2003: 413)

While these ethical questions are clearly articulated through the pleasures of story, they also generate responses characterized by process of self-reflection. One respondent suggests that going onto a reality show is the only way of really seeing the truth of who you really are: 'I would love to see how I actually am as a person. I have opinions about myself but have never seen the real me. It [being in the house] brings out the real personality of the person that's there' (cited in Jones 2003: 409). Such responses are seen most clearly when audiences talk about lifestyle programming and talk shows, and it is to these genres that we turn now.

## Lifestyle programming: identity and an 'ethics of care'

Television in this genre therefore becomes an ethical space. A space where moral values are worked through and judgements are made about 'the right and wrong ways to live our lives' (Hill 2005: 109). Drawing on Guy Hawkins' (2001) work, Hill argues that reality game shows and lifestyle television 'make a spec-tacle of ethical crises'. As we saw above, this is not a clear-cut distinction between good and bad conduct. Rather there is a constant worrying over ethical issues and cultural standards of conduct, in which the programmes 'invite us to enter into a zone of ethical uncertainty'. In this liminal zone 'clear positions and sides are not necessarily evident' (Hill 2005: 120). The relationship between reality programming, identity and ethics in this way can be seen in Foucauldian terms as a project which places emphasis on the way we live our lives. It provides information about the care and management of the self (Foucault 1977b). In these terms audiences and contestants both participate in the 'quest for truth about the self'. As Hawkins puts it, 'in infotainment we can see how ethics operate as a form of self-shaping, as a shifting terrain of practical rules, judge-ments and techniques for managing the self and its relations with others' (Hawkins 2001: 413).

In these terms we can see two of Hill's respondents as they discuss how programmes like *Wife Swap* and *Faking It* are useful resources for identity work:

Emma:  You have these families that are really dysfunctional and have no idea why. I mean, it's hard to see yourself from the outside. And so you can sit down and see this family and see all the mistakes they're making and it's just so crystal clear. And it's interesting, how a little bit of work really helps. It's almost like therapy, you know.

Anja:    I think it's interesting because, yeah, you can kind of recognize
         these people. . . . And it's interesting to see how they change.

(cited in Hill 2007: 161)

In these lifestyle programmes semiosis is generated by audiences as they
work through standards of personal conduct and responsibility. These include
the ways that we manage our relationships: in sexuality and infidelity, in criminality and deceit, honesty and dishonesty, in selfishness and selflessness, malice
and self-gain, in dependability, forgiveness, loyalty, shame, in guilt, innocence
and remorse. Identity in this sense is less a fixed property, but rather a
'problem':

> Problematization is the necessary first step in the calculation of an ethical
> telos. It refers to the conditions in which we query what we are, what we
> should be, how we should be in the world. This process of reflexivity, or
> turning the self into an object of moral inquiry reveals, not simply how
> problems become moral concerns, but also the operations of 'conscience'
> as a self-shaping and regulating practice.
>
> (Hawkins 2001: 416–17)

As Rose (1999: 263) argues, this ethical problematization is not simply related
to reality game shows. It is much more pervasive across television's talk shows,
documentaries, lifestyle programmes and docusoaps. In *Cheaters* those who are
unfaithful to their partners are filmed in the act. Evidence is presented to them:
their motivations, their shame, their guilt and dishonour are interrogated. They
are shamed in front of a global audience, they are judged. In *How Clean is Your
House?* standards of hygiene, the quality of domestic space and the care of the
self are interrogated. Those who infringe are scorned, held up in their disgust:
how, we ask ourselves (as we watch, or gossip later) can these people live like
animals, like filthy pigs? As this young man puts it:

> You're going to be judging them when you're watching a programme obvi-
> ously. But at the end of the day . . . they are, like, basic standards that
> people should live to. That's what I am saying, everybody should be clean,
> more or less.
>
> (cited in Hill 2007: 198)

In *Supernanny, How Clean is Your House?* and *Wife Swap* parenting and
family life come under scrutiny. The discourses, the vocabulary and the techniques of developmental psychology, of nutritional science, of pedagogy and
childcare are enlisted. As in the Catholic confessional, external appearances
and conduct are used to make judgements about the real person and their 'soul'.
This is a focus on backstage realms and the truths about the self. It focuses on

judgements about the people that exist *beyond* their presentation on our screens. It is characterized, as Rose (1999) puts it, by a fascination in the

> relations between inner reality and external appearances, in which the outer, the public, the visible, the surface is to be interrogated to see how it expresses, is shaped by or disguises an inner personal truth, where the essence of the individual is to be found.
>
> (Rose 1999: 263)

However, while we judge others, and see what a mess they are making of their lives, we also interrogate our own: we 'pick up tips'. As this respondent puts it:

> I think after watching a few *Supernanny* techniques, I will kind of use those with some of the kids I work with, actually. I think 'No, Supernanny wouldn't do that!', so yeah, I think there is a certain element of taking stuff on board.
>
> (cited in Hill 2007: 161)

This ethicalization is not solely about our thoughts, however, nor the talk and gossip that they may provoke. It is also about the forms of feeling that accompany them, and audiences' emotional responses to the programming (Briggs 2007b). Ethical thought is therefore attuned to the occasional visceral moments with television. Of the moments that move us: the disgust of the houses in *How Clean is Your House?* or the quite disarming feeling of discomfort when watching *Honey, We're Killing the Kids*. Here we see an ethically motivated respondent who talks about his emotional responses as a child goes in for her 12th operation in *Children's Hospital*:

> Respondent: Yeah, I feel it's a very good programme and it does upset me quite a lot to watch it but it's a programme I do like watching because it makes you realize that maybe yourself or other people around you, you haven't really got a problem at all . . . until you look at someone like that. And then it makes you start thinking, why am I worried about my car when, er, the person you have just watched the night before, their 6-year-old son is dying of cancer. . . . I think the majority of people on the outside world haven't really got a clue of what a problem is until they see something like that, um, er, I think it must be really hard to deal with something like that if it ever happens to you, which I hope it doesn't. So I think the programme is good 'cos you really do actually see what other people, out there, are going through. And I think you do need reminding that it does go on.
>
> (cited in Hill 2005: 132)

In these emotional and ethical modalities of response audiences move between rage ('I cannot watch this for another second!') and emotion (tears filling eyes, unexpectedly and unwilled). This has some significance for debates about the nature of the public sphere. As Hill (2005) suggests, with such lifestyle programming 'we see the ways in which ethical and moral judgements can never be about abstract reason or rational thinking alone'. They are also about feelings and emotions, for emphasis on the rational and cognitive aspects of the public sphere, knowledge and communication 'completely deny the visceral and affective intensities that inform, underpin and circulate about thinking and reason' (Hill 2005: 121).

## Talk shows and everyday life

In the final section of this chapter we now turn to consider this same movement between emotional and rational and ethical responses in audiences' engagements with television talk shows. This is interesting as they have been considered not only as the lowest form of television, as 'Trash TV' by some, but also as a fairly transgressive and democratic ethical space by others. Shattuc (1997) for example takes a relatively optimistic position, arguing that television talk shows do in fact live up to some of the ideals of a public sphere. Indeed, she goes as far as to suggest that they subvert them towards a feminist political position. In her view 'television has become the central communicator of information' in our culture, and 'no other public forum replicates the town-meeting democratic sensibility better than the first generation of daytime talk shows'. It is not simply that the shows open up a space where 'average' or 'ordinary' members of the public debate important (and albeit sensationalized) issues which are central to their lives, such as racism, sexuality, social welfare and religious freedom. It is also that they continue to be drawn into semiosis long after the programmes have finished (Shattuc 1997: 85–6). As she suggests:

> Not only does viewer give-and-take take place as part of the show but discussions continue on the news, in the workplace, and at home: the popularization of current political, social and theoretical topics. These shows raise questions of fact versus fiction as the audience test the credibility of the stories presented. (In the common vernacular: 'are those people for real?') They test the demarcation between entertainment and news as they mix political issues with personal drama. Further, they use ordinary people to stage social issues that are infrequently disused elsewhere on television: homosexuality, family conflict, sexual relations, and racial divisions.
>
> (Shattuc 1997: 87)

Indeed Livingstone and Lunt (1994) found that their respondents frequently deviated from talking about the actual content of the programmes that were screened in their focus groups, and went on to talk about their own related experiences. These focus group discussions simulated the kind of talk that happens between family, friends and colleagues. As they suggest, 'these stories may be vaguely supportive or critical of the studio audience's accounts, but essentially they represent a separate discourse in which the media provide the opportunity for viewers to manage their identities in relation to others' (Livingstone and Lunt 1994: 85). This, as we saw above, can be thought of as an ethicalization of existence. As this respondent puts it:

> Respondent: It does make you think of your own views on these things. You can't listen for 40 minutes with people talking on the subject like that without thinking in your own mind how you would react or feel about it. In that sense it is educational but not to give a point of view. It makes you sort out your own thoughts a bit more.
>
> (cited in Livingstone and Lunt 1994: 85)

Likewise, here is a respondent from Manga's (2003) research who is talking about the *Jerry Springer* show:

> Janice: So there are issues that, you know, I can look at and I think, 'Gee, we talked about that this morning', or my own persona; – I mean I was in a relationship where I thought my boyfriend was cheating on me. And I found that when I listened to Jerry, I got different pointers. You know, different people saying, 'well, look for this. You do this'. You know. Or – one part that was really good was when – that made me think, 'Oh, gee. Do I want out of this relationship?' . . . But basically with him I know there's something that I'll get from this show that really relates to my life or a person at school or co-worker or whatever.
>
> (cited in Manga 2003: 123–4)

This represents a continuation of some of the key ethical themes that we have identified with the formats of reality television: the emphasis on the personal as a source of truth and authority and the ethicalization of existence. These involve not only standing in judgement over others, but also of returning the gaze to monitor the self. In doing so Shattuc (1997) argues that talk shows are also involved in the problematization of 'objective' epistemologies, where 'truth' is no longer clear and uncontested. Rather, here we see audiences constantly moving back and forth, puzzling over and scrutinizing their 'truth claims'. Indeed, as Shattuc points out, they have been positively evaluated by feminist scholars precisely for these reasons. They disturb official and sanctioned 'rationality' of the Habermasian public sphere, with its tacit opposition between the (masculine) public world and the (feminine) private realm of the body, experience and the emotions (Shattuc 1997: 90).

In order to develop this argument Shattuc draws on the work of Gloria-Jean Masciarotte (1991) and suggests that the sight of women on these talk shows taking pleasure in talking about painful experiences offers a 'subversive yet gratifying venue for the rare public portrayal of women's struggles (Shattuc 1997: 93). This she suggests amounts to a 'counter public sphere' in which controversy, repetition, fragmentation and uncertainty refuse to name a singular and totalizing 'truth'. In doing they reject the separation of experience, the body, emotions and affect from expertise and authority:

> As a result, the talk show participates in a debate arena comparable to Habermas' public sphere. However, the evidence of social injustice has shifted from rational and distant forms to an intersection that collapses personal experience, physical evidence and emotion.
>
> (Shattuc 1997: 94–5)

This 'distrust of both the learned knowledge of expertise and the simulated truths of fiction' (Shattuc 1997: 98) has been well documented by Livingstone and Lunt (1994). Here for example is one of their respondents who places value on the direct experience of ordinary people over the authoritative discourse of experts:

> George: Experts? I think you have to wait until the end of the programme before you draw any conclusion about who the experts are. I think that people who Kilroy thinks are going to act as experts don't always turn out that way. You often get much more useful information from the ordinary person in the studio who happens to be very good at communicating and has something significant to say. What you tend to get from experts is you're reminded of the same things, you often don't get new perspectives from experts. But what you get from Kilroy's programmes is new perspectives, from for example the young offender himself. When he says absolutely I will go out and re-offend unless I'm locked up, you can't really argue with that. No matter what an expert's opinion is, this is the kind of thing that really matters.
>
> (cited in Livingstone and Lunt 1994: 100)

Indeed, Lunt and Livingstone found that two-thirds of their respondent held very negative views about expert discourses, insofar as they were abstract and failed to connect to their own lived experiences. We will recall that this is often a reason given for people's lack of understanding and engagement in television news, while reality programming is generally valued precisely for the focus on the personal. As these respondents put it:

> Respondent:   I hardly noticed them, I must admit, they didn't impress me

at all, because I thought that whatever they said would be so predictable I switched off, mentally.

Respondent: Looking back, I can't remember anything that he said. If you have an expert, you should at least come away with something.

(cited in Livingstone and Lunt 1994: 118)

We do need to address questions about the nature of television's ethical discourse in respect to this. As Shattuc (1997) suggests, there are clear continuities with reality game shows and lifestyle programmes as expert discourses are used to evaluate and monitor the self, to place a 'grid of visibility over existence' (Rose 1999: 270). These talk shows after all are about the 'care of the self' and in line with the Foucauldian critique, they can be seen to address the audience with the discourses of psychology and counselling, as well as those of the church, law, social work and educational establishments. Shattuc quotes Foucault on this, suggesting that talk shows function as a form of modern 'confessional'. The host, the experts, the guests and the studio audience become 'the authority who require the confession, prescribes and appreciates it and intervenes in order to judge, punish, forgive, console and reconcile; a ritual in which truth is collaborated by the obstacles it has surmounted in order to be formulated (Foucault 1977a quoted in Shattuc 1997: 112). However, as she argues, the complex relationship between participants undermines the authority of science and rationality to produce a 'set of power relations which are much more complex and vertiginous than Foucault's':

Who is the therapist? The expert? The host? The studio audience? Who are the patients? Those on stage with reductive name tags such as 'female gang member', 'incest survivor' and 'husband locked her to bed'? Or 'we' the viewers? Or Oprah, who routinely confesses her abusive childhood and displeasure with her body? And to what degree are the confessions, emotions and interactions understood as truth?

(Shattuc 1997: 113)

This is indeed a serious question: what do audiences understand as 'truth'? One thing is certain: audiences demand more ways of knowing than are warranted by the Habermasian public sphere, with its emphasis on rational discourse and emotional distance. Rather, talk shows offer a public sphere which values the subjective, the emotional, the particular, the concrete, the motivated and the suppositional over the objective, the rational and the abstract. Here 'the ordinary person also lays claim to a particular epistemology which should be revalidated' (Livingstone and Lunt 1994: 102). For the following respondent, for example, the 'openness' of the genre and its regimes of truth are valued as a place where ordinary people can be heard. As he puts it, 'why should only professionals have their chance to air their views on television? It's our television; it's our country, why shouldn't we, as ordinary people, have a chance to air our views?' (cited in Livingstone and Lunt 1994: 58).

For many then, there is a degree of trustworthiness about ordinary experience, where respondents are engaged in the now familiar hunt for the 'truth'. As this respondent puts it: 'one of the things about this is that it's real, and it's real people and is different to the normal reality of television' (cited in Livingstone and Lunt 1994: 59). Truthfulness was also defined by a lack of closure, so they can (as this respondent puts it) 'think of both sides and decide myself':

> Maria: I think it's better if they don't [draw conclusions] because I think people are smart enough to come to their own conclusion and think things through for themselves and I don't think we should all think what Oprah or Donahue say.
>
> (cited in Livingstone and Lunt 1994: 59)

This is a process of closeness and distance, or empathy and reflection:

> Respondent: I could identify with some of the problems that those people were putting forward. Personally, it's as though I am having an argument with some people, that's the effect it has on me. It's astonishing really. You say, good gracious, does it do that? Do they live like that? Different people's lives.
>
> (cited in Livingstone and Lunt 1994: 84)

There is a movement here between the distant and judgemental responses on one hand that we saw with reality programming, and a closeness, identification, empathy and self-reflexivity on the other. One respondent in Shattuc's research would use the *Jerry Springer* show as a resource for gossip with her friend, or with her work colleagues. She liked *Ricki Lake* as it was both 'sensational' and 'sincere' at the same time. As she puts it, 'when it comes down to it, a [talk show] is just about human interest stories which are about human behavior . . . about people. It's not a high intellectual level, but it is just about everyday lives'. She 'connects' and 'identifies' with the guests and the issues, likening them to either 'group therapy sessions' or 'anthropological study'. People she argues are 'too fast to trash them because that's the cool way to deal with them'. Another respondent, Pat, valued the shows as she liked their outrageous and scandalous nature, likening them to the tabloid *National Enquirer*. While she did not feel the need to ironize her pleasure, she talked of her playful and gossipy relationship to shows such as *Ricki Lake* where she would 'get into it . . . laughing . . . and talking' on the telephone (cited in Shattuc 1997: 185). One of Livingstone and Lunt's respondents captures this oscillation between trust and mistrust, empathy and gossip, perfectly:

> Respondent: I must admit that I find it disturbing. I think it rouses very different feelings in me. On one side, one wants to be compassionate with these people, but on the other side, I am a reasonable practical person. I think, why the hell are you doing that? I found it very difficult to come to conclusions about that.
>
> (cited in Lunt and Livingstone 1994: 84)

As this quotation suggests, talk shows, much like the various formats of reality programming can be seen as a contested ethical space: a space which is ridden through with contradictions and ambiguities, between closeness and distance on one hand, and between celebrating transgression, and judging those who transgress on the other (Bird 2003). Indeed, while Shattuc (1997) is quite optimistic about this space, researchers such as Gamson (1998) and Manga (2003) are much less confident. While Gamson (1998) for instance duly recognizes that they provide a space for those who are otherwise marginalized in the media to speak, he also sees much more tension in this, as audiences pass what are ultimately conservative judgements on others. For example, what he terms 'liberal heterosexual sympathizers' tend to view the shows as harmful, not because they transgress the bounds of conventional sexuality, but because they focus on the *extreme* at the expense of the *pedestrian*. This at once reinflects homophobia into class distinctions and demarcates 'nice middle class professionals' and their 'nasty, extreme, flamboyant outsiders'. As this respondent argues:

> Jill: It's a shame, because some people are afraid of that, and then they see a show like that and it just confirms their own prejudices. They're all like flamboyant and extremist. They're using these people to make people's hatred go up, you know what I mean, by showing extreme examples. And it's a shame where you see everybody believes that it's this extreme part of the population. They don't seem like normal people, just like individual people. The talk shows, it's not like anyone I know. Everyone I know is pretty much like a professional. That's like the work I think of when I think of like gay people who I know, I think the word 'professional'.
>
> (cited in Gamson 1998: 194)

As Joshua Meyrowitz (1987) and David Morley (2000) both argue, television profoundly destabilizes the distinction between 'public' and 'private', blurring the two spaces as the outside world enters domestic space, shaping its temporal, spatial and interpersonal dynamics (see Chapter 4). This is one major concern for some of Gamson's respondents, who judge guests poorly for discussing what is private in public, for revealing what should remain 'backstage' (Goffman

1969). For example, 56-year-old Barbara complains that 'I can't believe they would air all of this stuff on the air, I mean in front of the general public, so to speak' (cited in Gamson 1998: 202). In part, as we saw above with Shattuc's respondent, there is a common distinction between respectable shows such as *Oprah* and 'sleazy' programmes such as *Jerry Springer*. This is clearly articulated by this 55-year-old white teacher who employs the 'iconography of dirt' (Douglas 1991):

> Judith: I wouldn't watch this garbage. Who's sleeping with who, what's going on between this couple because they were two women living together, or whatever. I can't better myself, I can't get more class to me, and I think class is very important. I think a lot of people have lost it. And this is all just – people are entitled to their private lives. It should be private. And anything that's put on display is just garbage. There's nothing wrong with having sexual topics on television. To put it on display is what's wrong. When it's private, you work with it, but when you put it on television live, it becomes dirt. If you're going to open it up, have a psychologist there, make it a very proper thing.
>
> (cited in Gamson 1998: 202–3)

The metaphors of dirt and pollution are very interesting here, and point to some reoccurring ethical themes which organize Manga's (2003) research, *Talking Trash*. In her work she finds a tension between a carnivalesque delight in the 'transgressions' aired on the show, but also an uneasy and worried relation to it. Indeed, as we saw above with Bird's (2003) discussion of gossip and speculation, such transgression seem to be rather conservative in the last analysis, as the guests are ultimately judged for their 'deviant' behaviour. Many of Manga's respondents for example talked about the 'ritualistic' nature of their viewing, which fostered interpretative communities who would delight in gossip and discussion around the shows. Here is Karen:

> Karen: We'll comment through the whole thing . . . like if it's me, Pam and Francine, it's always, I make jokes through the entire thing, because I'm a very sarcastic person. And I feel I have to make fun of everyone on the show. And then like, if the husband comes back, I'm the one that's like, I'm very loud, or whatever. And I'll be like 'Oh get him out of here!' Or whatever.
>
> Interviewer: So, you're actually commenting about the show.
>
> Karen: Yes. Like I feel like I can talk to the people.
>
> (cited in Manga 2003: 85–6)

This nature of this talk, and the jokes made about the guests, are often judgemental however, and many failed to see these talk shows as legitimate discourse. Here is Michelle who uses the strategies of distancing, as well as delighting in the pleasures of story, to negotiate her relationship with them (Bird 2003: 44–6). She values more serious talk shows like *Montel* as they deal with issues in a serious manner (such as reuniting families that have been long since separated). These are 'serious' shows, which have 'a purpose'. However, *Jerry Springer* and *Ricki Lake* are watched 'because it's funny, and I like to see stuff like that'. As she explains, she can 'learn stuff' from them:

> Michelle: But most of them, they fight. But then, sometimes the show – I mean I watch them to just learn how people are out there and just – it helps me to realize that there are ignorant people out there.
>
> (cited in Manga 2003: 99)

This ethical distancing, however, is not a blanket condemnation. She is understandably angered by the Ku Klux Klan who appeared on the show, 'so stuff like that, I like to watch stuff like that because, although it makes me angry when I watch it, I still know there are people out there like that. I may not have encountered them, but they're still out there'. However, at other times the basis of her judgement is less unambiguous:

> Michelle: And Ricki Lake, sometimes her show – Ricki Lake, her show, I love her show. I don't know why because all – I think it's just garbage. Like people come on the show – 'you slept with my man!' and she wants to tell her baby's father that she was having sex with someone else and stuff like that. And I don't know if I just need a laugh, but I watch those things. But it's not meaningful. It doesn't teach me anything.
>
> (cited in Manga 2003: 99)

It is quite clear that she is in fact 'learning' from the shows, learning about what she considers to be acceptable standards of conduct. It is an ethical stance in which she considers the care of the self. The criterion of 'truth' and 'authenticity' we say above is also evident here, as Sandi adopts the ethical modality of response. Like the reality viewers examined previously, she can see through the production format and looks for the sincerity of characters. This is guaranteed if it allows her to 'identify' and reflect upon her own life, experiences and beliefs:

> Sandi: Yeah, I can relate to a lot of the issues on the talk shows. I mean from child abuse to, you know, having a boyfriend cheat on you. So a lot I can relate to. People on drugs. So, I can relate to a lot of issues that are being brought up. So I can sit down, and I can watch that. And I can be, you know, I can believe that. You know, this isn't a set up. You know what I

mean? 'Cause a lot of times talk shows, I used to think that, you know, they rehearsed it for the night before and they tell you what to say. But because I can relate to it, you know, it's more real for me.

(cited in Manga 2003: 110)

In this we see the now familiar oscillation between two seemingly contradictory modalities of response. Manga (2003) found that the women she researched moved between judging and identifying: from 'taking pity *on* them' to having 'empathy *with* them'. The former involves an act of scrutinizing judgement, the latter an act of close identification and self-reflection (Manga 2003: 120). With identification Sandi speaks of 'everyone's struggle being sort of similar', while Janice takes a more distanced and judgemental stance:

Janice: Sometimes the guests are a little – sometimes I look at the shows and I'm like 'She really should not even have them on there'. And they're like a total disgrace, or 'Where does she get these people?', 'How could they come on TV and embarrass themselves like that?' You know?

(cited in Manga 2003: 125)

However, Janice also reflects on her own relationship to the talk shows:

Janice: I think for the most part it's to – I mean Jerry pretty much likes to let the world know that there are things out there. I guess we shouldn't be so judgemental because people go through all kinds of changes and have all sorts of problems in life. And who are we to sit back and say this person is wrong for doing this? . . . Society as a whole shouldn't be so quick to judge and condemn.

(cited in Manga 2003: 130)

To complicate this picture just a little bit further, Manga (2003) also suggests that the pleasure of story can have a transgressive effect, insofar as audiences clearly enjoy the process of speculating and gossip. This centres on the melodramatic themes of infidelity, avarice, deceit, mistaken desire and identity, on bodily display, sexual appetite, lust, greed, envy and betrayal. In this she suggests that the more extreme talk shows are 'intentionally constructed as transgressing mainstream cultural standards'. This has a distinct 'carnivalesque' character: 'as *excessive* and *performative* – intentionally, flagrantly, unabashedly, and actively privileging that which is genuinely devalued in mainstream culture' (Manga 2003: 161). Here for example is Janice, who clearly delights in the transgression of gender, politeness and bodily decorum:

Janice: If I'm home, I have two or three people call me watching the same show, wanting to know if I'm watching. We really get on the phone and it's, like, 'That's crazy! Did you see the show, so and so was on?' and 'Did you see the one where the drag queens were on and they started fighting and he snatched the wig off?' You know, we really get into detail about it. You know, it's an everyday thing . . . I love it.

(cited in Manga 2003: 169)

Drawing on Bakhtin's (1965) ideas, Manga makes a case for this as a progressive cultural process through which 'an act of expressive behavior inverts, contradicts, abrogates, or in some fashion presents an alternative to commonly held cultural codes, values and norms' (Stallybrass and White 1986, cited in Manga 2003: 162). While this is an attractive position which stresses ideological resistance and an ethical refusal of normative morality it may be more idealistic that empirically grounded. Like Bird (2003), Gamson suggests the carnivalesque elements of talk shows might in effect might stigmatize same sex desire further, sliding 'quickly into the category of things that are not the business of polite, civilized, clean nice people to hear about' (Gamson 1998: 203). This symbolic inversion is clearly rejected by Judi, for example:

> Judi: My girlfriend's sister is gay, and they're living lives the way they want to. On TV they're doing it for a gimmick, they want the attention whereas my friends aren't like that at all. They don't flaunt it around. If they love each other, that's their problem. They don't sit there and advertise it all the time.

(cited in Gamson 1998: 204)

Likewise, with Manga's own data we see a discursive recuperation, where the transgressive is judged, and normal ethical standards applied, through the processes of gossip. Here for example is Joy, whose delight in transgression reveals a rather less progressive mocking stance:

> Joy: I watch it with my friends and we make fun of the people that are in the audience or the guests. I watch with my friends and we just laugh at what people say or what they are wearing or something. I'll watch with a group of people and just make fun of them. That's basically how I watch the talk show. I always watch it with a friend sitting on the other line saying 'Do you believe she said that?'

(cited in Manga 2003: 168)

## Conclusion

This chapter has suggested some of the ways in which the concept of the public sphere can be extended to the formats of reality television and talk shows. In several ways there are oscillations between the close and distanced modalities of response. This does not seem to be an 'either/or' position. Rather it seems to be a pervasive way in which texts are drawn into semiosis, not only the moment of 'decoding', but also later as their discourses, characters and representations circulate widely in everyday life. This ultimately points to the *indeterminate* nature of this public sphere. As such, rather than look for responses which are either 'oppositional' or 'dominant', 'negotiated' or 'preferred', as the encoding/ decoding model proposes, the research points to the rather more contradictory nature of semiosis, as well as the various modalities through which it is generated. The essential point for Manga (2003), for example, in line with Rose's Foucauldian position, is that talk shows and reality programming promote an ethicalization of existence in which self policing and self-monitoring subjects are produced (Manga 2003: 153–4). Unlike the purely rational space of the Habermasian public sphere, where sovereign subjects exercise an independence of thought and discursive will, audiences are seen to introspect and scrutinize the self in the quest for identity. They do so not only through talking, judging and thinking, but also through identifying, emoting and experiencing. As Magna puts it, in this public sphere 'the subject is now not *just* the rational, sovereign subject, but also an *appropriately* emotive and self-disclosing subject' (Manga 2003: 155, emphasis in original).

Hill's research has certainly informed this chapter's argument, and the close reading of it points to the relevance, quality and worth of this research methodology. There are two methodological points that can be made in this regard. The first is that we need more research of this nature, for it is primarily through such detailed empirical investigation that the conceptual basis of our thinking can be tested, problems clarified and new agendas posited. That a book such as this is forced to rely so heavily on one researcher's output speaks volumes in respect of this. Nevertheless, the centrality of *ethics* emerges here for example, as it does in Chapter 1, with the issue of news. While questions of representation, discourse, ideology and power will continue to be important, these issues can be critically approached in very useful ways by interrogating audiences' rights and responsibilities, the ways in which the media enable or attenuate civic engagement, and the ways in which audiences position themselves ethically (see Couldry et al. 2007 for an extended discussion of this). That discussion of the public sphere has largely taken place in reified, abstract and normative terms suggests the further interventions that Hill's work, for example, can be pressed into service for.

The second methodological point therefore is that there is real worth, for students and researchers alike, to make better use of audience research. Through close and sustained reading the knowledge, conceptualization and understanding produced can be imported into our own work with texts and institutions, perhaps in place of primary research where this is not possible, but at the very least to give a grounded conception of what it is that audiences do with texts, the *sort of meanings* that they make, and *the ways* in which they make them. Using this methodology this chapter (like the first) has been able to move beyond the concepts of encoding and decoding and suggest the relevance of a more nuanced conceptual framework.

Hill's research for example demonstrates the complexity of semiosis and the contrary modalities of response through which it is generated. We have seen audiences as they at once scrutinize themselves and others; as they gossip and joke, and also as they identify and emote. We have seen them as they not only introspect and learn, but also pass judgement and pour scorn on those who transgress. This working through both disrupts and reinforces existing cultural boundaries, and it allows us to repose the questions in terms of discourse, ideology and *ethics*. This research demonstrates that there are, in Bakhtin's terms, *centrifugal* delights in transgression which open up a radicalized discursive space, but also *centripetal* forces which pull radical elements back in again, towards unity, consensus and stability (Bakhtin 1981: 271). If we can learn anything from audience research, it is this, for it characterizes the life of language in society: 'a tension filled unity of two embattled tendencies' (Bakhtin 1981: 272, cited in Shotter and Billig 1998: 16). As with television news, we should therefore be wary of either celebrating audience resistance or decrying television's hold upon those who watch. Rather we should attend to the everyday contexts in which meanings are made and the modalities through which audiences respond.

# 3 SOAP OPERA AND PLAY

A quick glance at the television guide reveals much about the soap opera and its importance to television schedules.[1] Once the domain of femininity, a distinctly women's genre, soaps now have a mass appeal; they address men and women, the young and the old, people of all ethnicities, from here, there and everywhere (Gauntlet and Hill 1999). They are flagship programmes; their viewing figures indicate not only the popularity of the soap itself, but also the health of the channel. Economically significant, they bring the highest viewing figures; executives hope that viewers will continue watching, whatever is available elsewhere, on satellite channels and Internet television (Hobson 2002). Culturally significant, they become common points of reference: stories and characters which stay with us throughout our lives, characters that grow with us, and in some cases, die with us (Scannell 1996). What other form of storytelling lasts, as in the case of the British soap *Coronation Street*, for nearly 50 years? What is it to follow stories, to be involved with such a cast of characters: how are soap operas drawn into semiosis?

No other genre, as Dorothy Hobson (2002) notes, generates so much talk and discussion: from the sizeable market for magazines and tabloid press which constantly speculate on, reveal and discuss ongoing storylines, to Internet bulletin boards and the more general talk between friends, neighbours, colleagues and strangers. Talk is at the heart of this genre. The textual form of the genre itself is dialogic and decentred, centrifugal rather than centripetal: the ensemble of characters mulling over, responding and gossiping about storylines and each other's lives, intersecting in myriad ways. The genre contributes to a public sphere: its storylines will resonate with the lives of their audience. Viewers will recognize themselves in the characters, not only in what they do, the lives that they live out and the dilemmas that they face, but also in how they feel. Its realisms in this are as much 'emotional' as they are 'empirical' (Ang 1985). Through these modes of realism soap operas come to 'work through' public debates and cultural events. Soap operas know *who* we are, they know *how* we feel: they address us in our daily experiences, in our daily concerns, in our hopes, our fears, our joys (Askoy and Robins 2003: 97; Elsaesser 2003). This, as John Ellis (2000) suggests, is 'working through' at its most prolific:

> In this sense the soap opera works through news issues – not slavishly, item by item, issue by issue, but by providing narratives with resonance to the everyday experiences of the prevalent thinking of their viewing publics. . . . Soaps narrativize, in the same time of experience as the lived time of the audience, the moral dilemmas in the lives of their characters.
>
> (Ellis 2000: 110)

Taking soap opera as a common cultural reference point and one of our must significant forms of storytelling, this chapter will be concerned with the talk which surrounds the genre. As the title of this chapter suggests, a lot of this talk is playful, or *ludic*. As this is emerging as a key concept media and cultural studies this chapter will bring together important observations in the audience research and consider play's consequences for the public sphere, or the ways, in Mary Ellen Brown's that it provides an 'outlet for a kind of politics in which subordinated groups can be validated and heard' (Brown 1994: 2). While more recent work is used where appropriate, the bulk of this chapter revisits now 'classic' international audience studies conducted by Ien Ang (1985), Brown (1994), David Buckingham (1987) and Tamar Liebes and Elihu Katz (1993). In doing so it draws out the central insights that they have made and demonstrates their continued significance for the field. In particular this chapter suggests that the concept of play provides a new way of looking at old insights, and poses this as an important new direction for audience research and the public sphere.

## Play and ethics

In this, what is particularly interesting, as Brown's (1994) quotation might alert us to, is the specifically *ethical* notion of play that emerges from these 'classic' studies. We see that it is not, as is often assumed, something which is relegated to a distinct period of childhood. Rather it is seen as an essential part of human culture and a pervasive activity that audiences engage in through their everyday lives. Such play, as Roger Silverstone (1994) argues, is an essential means through which audiences *frame* and *experience* their realities. It is not irrational, and it need not be childish; indeed, it is entirely rational. This rationality however is of a different order than that of 'the mundane, and the quotidian'. In play, Silverstone argues that we move into a *subjunctive* space of the 'as if', we blend everyday life and fantasy, the pretend and the real. In this play enables us to look askance at reality: to see things in new ways. It is both of the everyday and somehow removed from it:

> To step into a space and time of play is to move across a threshold, to leave something behind – one kind of order – and to grasp a different reality and a rationality defined by its own rules and terms of trade and action. . . . Play is a space in which meanings are constructed through participation within a shared and structured place, a place ritually demarcated as being distinct from, and other than the ordinariness of everyday life, a place of modest security and trust.
>
> (Silverstone 1999: 60)

To play in these terms is to enter into an agreement into what can be said, and what can be done, into what *sort of meanings* can be exchanged. Play, as such, is a ludic space in which distinct types of meanings are generated and exchanged. It is a space where we can explore our private selves, our relations to others, and that which normally remains ineffable (beyond words, indefinable, overwhelming perhaps). The ludic is safe and retractable ('I was only playing after all'). It is both serious and frivolous. In play we are not accountable for our actions *in the same way* as we are in other realms. As such, we can venture, test and further our involvements with others; it gives rise to 'a deepening level of relatedness' (Kelly-Byrne 1989: 242).

This play is perhaps a matter of boundary crossing, and indeed, of boundary blurring, for in play we move between various different thresholds, some of which are policed more firmly than others. We move between the 'public and the private', between 'front and back stages' (Goffman 1969), between the realms of the 'real and the fantastic' (Ang 1985). We move between 'inner and outer realities' on the one hand, between 'the individual and the social' on the other (Silverstone 1999: 59).

Play is self-conscious. It is, as Denise Kelly-Byrne (1989: 10–11) argues, marked by 'meta-communication': by communication about communication. Play in this sense is governed by rules, rules which are encoded in genres and narrative forms and modes of address, in our expectations of them, and in our joint and coordination and involvement. But adherence to the rules of play is negotiable. Children will step outside of the play frame to bargain over the progression of the game. In our play with television we reflect upon, subvert and manipulate narratives, discourses, characters and conventions. These play-ful moments may be small, they may be ephemeral and passing, but they bring moments of pleasure and release. They punctuate the seriousness of everyday life (of work, domestic chores, responsibilities and childcare). Play subverts their rules, turning them on their head. They 'suspend the regularities of the daily, take pleasure and in some transcendent way, play with the categories and concepts of the world over which they otherwise have no control' (Silverstone 1999: 62). In some small way we see this playful subversion here, this suspension of rules, of norms; a transient moment of *useless* pleasure and of knowing laughter:

Doris:  Liz still think she's married to Don?
Vicki:  Yeah, that's for sure. Something will happen such as a fight or else she'll have a fall or a brain tumour (laughter . . .).

(cited in Brown 1994: 137)

In this we see the knowing relationship that soap viewers have with their genre, a relationship that vacillates between closeness and distance, precisely that which is playful. In doing so they can laugh at their own pleasure, but this laughter, as Bakhtin (1965) argues, seems to subvert the standards of high culture, of 'serious drama'. It turns the scorn that is placed upon soap opera back on those whom mock them. It is not just a refusal of that discourse, it also derides it. Here for example are Ada and Mary. They take delight in blurring the boundaries of the text and everyday life, talking about the events playfully, *as if* they were real:

Ada:    I don't know who that guy is.
Mary:   Oh, he's a new guy.
Ada:    But I've watched it.
Mary:   He was at the wedding.
Ada:    Whose wedding?
Mary:   At Liz and Neal's.
Ada:    I didn't go to Liz and Neal's wedding (laughter . . .).
Ada:    I couldn't make it (laughter . . .).
Ada:    I didn't watch it.

(cited in Brown 1994: 142)

In this we are dealing with what Victor Turner (1980) terms the 'liminal', an area of experiment and play with words, representations and ideas, a space which is full of 'potency and potentiality'. It is, as Brown (1994) puts it:

such a liminal state between fantasy and reality that can be created by the boundaries of soap opera gossip networks. There is a sense, in this unruly world, in which pleasure can transgress boundaries, and that transgression is brought about by laughter.

(Brown 1994: 134)

While for many soap operas are valued for their *authenticity*, for the ways in which they speak eloquently to express our experiences, our feelings and our lives (Ang 1985: 79), for others it is at once also their *in-authenticity* which is valued, their melodramatic excess and the grand scope of their emotions. This, as Bakhtin (1965) has argued, characterizes the 'carnivalesque', a space of laughter, gossip, parody and inversion to which we must now turn.

## Soap opera and the carnivalesque

Brown (1994: 134–7) suggests the concept of the carnivalesque helps us to explore the subversive powers of laughter and pleasure, powers which can function in the service of resistance. The carnivalesque in this context can be thought of as those spaces which license the inversion of cultural norms. This can involve parody, nonsense, exaggeration and excess, all those things which are normally deemed useless and non-productive (which have no 'use-value' in Marxian terms). It can also, as we have seen, work through blurring boundaries and through the uncertainty that this provokes. Here for example Brown (1994) discusses the carnivalesque pleasures of the strong women in the British soap, *Coronation Street*. The ability to speak and be seen is a source of power which subverts definitions of the feminine as passive and demure. Note the laughter that it provokes between the two women:

| | |
|---|---|
| Ellen: | *Coronation Street* is famous also because it has great bawling-out, stand-up fights between women. |
| Interviewer: | The first time I saw that was on *Coronation Street*. |
| Ellen: | Between Ena Sharples . . . |
| Interviewer: | But she's so old. |
| Ellen: | Between Ena Sharples and . . . |
| Interviewer: | Annie would be too sophisticated. |
| Ellen: | Well no. Annie has got a good bag for that. |
| Interviewer: | She's got a good mouth on her! (laughter . . .) |

(cited in Brown 1994: 153)

While this may be a somewhat muted form of carnival, its regular insertion into everyday life can generate small moments of resistance, a tactic against the strategies of the powerful (de Certeau 1984). Simply entering into playful talk, speculation, laughter and banter at work for instance is non-instrumental, it may be a way of commenting on the constraints placed on women, and their experiences. This subverts the prevailing expectations, it insinuates itself into institutional spaces (Hobson 1982). As Bakhtin (1965) suggests, such talk and laughter is 'first of all, a festive laughter':

It is not an individual reaction to some isolated 'comic' event. Carnival laughter is the laughter of all the people. Second, it is universal in its scope; it is directed at all and everyone including the carnival's participants. The entire world is seen in its droll aspect, in its gay relativity. Third this laughter is ambivalent: it is gay, triumphant and at the same time mocking, dividing. It asserts and it denies, it buries and revives. Such is the laughter of carnival.

(Bakhtin 1965, cited in Brown 1994: 135–6)

In the following Brown (1994) sees this 'control' over one's investments, a control and knowledge which is manifested in parody and laughter. This can be seen as a form of empowerment which again mocks the serious, the tasteful, the productive and the sober:

Ada:    I'm naming my kids Bo and Hope (laughter . . .).
Ada:    I'm not being stupid. I'm dead serious (laughter . . .).
Ada:    I don't carry around pictures in my wallet for nothing. I love them. Unreal.
Mary:   Have you got pictures in there. Can I see it? (Ada shows picture).
Mary:   I think that's great.

(cited in Brown 1994: 142)

Here Ada playfully parodies her fandom, and Brown sees in this a form of personal empowerment: the ability to step back and reflect while manipulating standards of 'good taste', as well as the boundaries between fantasy and reality, between real life and the world of the soap opera (Brown 1994: 143). This is full of ambiguity; it serves to pass judgement, to articulate a powerful discourse of resistance and solidarity.

In the following exchange Ada not only displays the same level of subversive laughter, but also raises questions about ethics, identity and power. The solidarity generated by the laughter allows her to articulate a discourse, a discourse which is centred on the contradictions between what is expected of men and women in our culture, and what they actually do. This can be a powerful space for resistance and critique, in which these contradictions and assumptions can be broached in a safe manner. Here it concerns male hypocrisy about female sexuality, that men may have multiple sexual partners, but that women should remain chaste until they are married:

Ada:          She [her mother] won't let me watch it.
Interviewer:  Oh, right, she takes the television set away from you? (laughter . . .)
Mary:         My Mum hates it too. She can't stand it. She says it's a waste of time.

| Ada: | My Mum's addicted to *Neighbours* and she got really emotional during that time when Scott and Charlene . . . she was really angry at it that he was so narrow minded, and for days she would go on about it – 'men are so narrow minded!' |

(cited in Brown 1994: 146)

As Brown (1994) suggests, while there is laughter here about the low valuation of soap operas by some, there is also a powerful recognition of mutual interests across generations, an admiration for the older woman's strong political views. In their laughter they recognize the problems that they face, even if it doesn't make them go away. The laughter is as such a powerful acknowledgement of their subordination. This is pleasurable as the women can speak freely, at once avoiding a male defined version of femininity, rejecting or parodying them (Brown 1994: 146–7). This carnivalesque movement between everyday life and the world of the soap opera (a liminal movement), its parody, its pleasure, and its subversive ethical discourse are seen vividly in the following account where Ellen revoices one of the character's famous one-liners. It is worth repeating at length:

| Ellen: | I mean there's great lines from Bet Lynch that you – things like put-downs mainly, mainly probably put-downs to men, which is why she is popular in her role as a barmaid, how she puts people down, because I don't know whether you've seen it, but there really was this barman Fred Gee, a great big fat obnoxious bloke, who really fancies himself – you know what 'fancies himself' means? I didn't know whether it means the same thing in America. |
| Interviewer: | He was full of himself. |
| Ellen: | Really fancies himself, thinks he's a real hit with the women, but isn't actually and is extremely unpleasant – and obnoxious generally. Most women would find him that, and he would always get into situations where he would dress up and put on after-shave and perhaps a cravat and look absolutely ridiculous, and then he would try and get off with someone. |
| Interviewer: | And then Bet would come in. |
| Ellen: | And he'd be preening in front of the mirror very pleased with himself and he'd say 'How do I look, then Lynch?' and she'd say 'Oh, you look like a well-scrubbed pig.' So you'd use that line – you'd just really appreciate that line. |

(cited in Brown 1994: 147–8)

In this we see a form of working through, a form which rejects the sobriety of the classical public sphere, and instead celebrates the rowdy, that which is in bad taste, that which subverts rules, which mocks, laughs and jeers, which 'works through' playful gossip and the pleasures and the connectedness that it promotes.

## Working through: soap opera and gossip

As this notion of a 'resistive space' might suggest, Brown (1994) sees a some-what different relationship between gossip, ethics and cultural power than we saw in Chapter 2. There we saw the ways in which gossip about reality programming and talk shows seemed to be fairly judgemental: that while it celebrated the transgression of cultural norms it also served to validate and support them. In this audiences were seen to judge the behaviour of those that appear on television. They drew 'moral boundaries between what is acceptable and what is not' (Bird 2003: 33). However, when seen from the perspective of 'working through' gossip can be thought about in a different way, as one which challenges the ideological basis of women's lives. As a properly Foucauldian perspective on power would suggest, hegemony is won only through a constant process of struggle where competing discourse vie for acceptance (Foucault 1977a: 92–102).

The ways in which soap operas are drawn into semiosis, through gossip networks, are, in Brown's view, counter-hegemonic. That is to say that they create a second oral text. This second text brings different perspectives, mean-ings and viewpoints to bare on those areas of cultural life that are represented. The meanings that are generated in this soap talk may resist the power of dominant discourse, its attempt to define the world, our ways of knowing, and ways of being. As Brown (1994) puts it:

> The struggle can be seen as a struggle to resist a confluence of powerful discourses in favour of a resistive discourse. The resistive discourse comes out of the terms of contrast with dominant discourse, much of it situated around women's everyday lives as social subjects. Sometimes the struggle is centred on countering the discourses put forth by the educational estab-lishment. At other times it is more centred on family issues. All of these, of course, are ultimately economic and ideological issues. Ideology, while giving us a way to interpret our lives, also attempts to legitimate structures of feeling beneficial to dominant classes, sexes and races.
>
> (Brown 1994: 17)

Part of this powerful resistive space is generated not only by the interaction between the structures of soap opera itself, but also through the nature of gossip as a form of talk and social interaction. Both, as Brown (1994) suggests, are open ended and resist closure. What is important here however is that while gossip can pour censure on moral and ethical transgressions, it can also serve to interrogate them and validate women's experiences, 'a cultural medium which reflects female reality, a connection between the lives of women who have otherwise been isolated from each other' (Jones 1980, cited in Brown 1994: 31). Such gossip allows a ludic licence in which talk about fictional characters can express things which normally remain unsaid, while also building intimacy between women. As one of Lee Harrington and Denise Bielby's respondents puts it, it provides 'the satisfaction of gossip without the guilt because the people aren't real and can't be hurt or betrayed by what one says about them' (Harrington and Bielby 1995: 119; see also Baym 2000: 72).

## A ludic orientation

To understand this modality of response we need to explore the ways in which it is generated as audiences adopt a *ludic orientation* to the text: as they approach it and draw it into semiosis playfully. As Nancy Baym (2000) puts it, this type of talk can be seen as a game, a game which is played whenever audience sit down and watch, or whenever soap operas and their secondary texts enter into our conversations:

> If one understands soap viewing as a game of making meanings from clues, then the collaborative provision of multiple readings has obvious benefits. No longer limited by one's own time constraints and limited knowledge, the game becomes bigger and more fun to play. The more players the better.
>
> (Baym 2000: 93)

Soap opera narration depends on the considerable knowledge that viewers bring to the text. Indeed, in Wolfgang Iser's (1978) terms, they can be seen as relatively 'open' and decentred texts, rather than linear and closed forms. Rather than engaging in them in a linear reading pattern (as one event following the next) audiences have to 'transverse a textual terrain'. They have to engage in considerable work to *retain* a sense of the story's histories. Audiences have to recall what has happened both in the near and distant past. This is based not only on 'action', but also on what we know about character motivation, on psychological realism and consistency. However, this is complicated by another narrative device. The text not only demands that audiences retain its own past, but also demands that they playfully predict its future. This act of *protension* is based on audiences' anticipation of what might happen. This is open, complex, one story impacting on all the others. This is what Iser (1978) refers to as *lateral reference*. These narrative devices of course generate and draw upon playful speculation, gossip and discussion. Some of it is based on the information gleaned from the tabloid press and soap magazines, which aim to make realistic predictions, while other gossip is wilfully outrageous, playful and perhaps scurrilous, based on precisely what is *not likely* to happen.

In this textual openness audiences are primarily concerned with the pleasures of story; with what is told, as well as with the processes of narrative – with how it is told. That this meaning making involve the pleasures of being manipulated, and that it functions through the processes of speculation, prediction and suspense is seen clearly in the case of these 9 year olds. Drawn from Buckingham's research, we hear them as they talk about a major storyline in the BBC soap opera, *EastEnders*:

| Maxine: | I remember that bit when you see Michelle walking on the bridge and that . . . |
|---|---|
| Samantha: | Near the canal. And Den came . . . |
| Maxine: | You see, everybody came out and they went in their car. And me and my Mum, we didn't know who it was! |
| Samantha: | Yeah, nor did I. And they always stop it when it's so exciting! |
| Interviewer: | Why do you think they do that? |
| Brian: | They've got to save the next bit for the next episode. |

(cited in Buckingham 1987: 167)

As Harrington and Biebly (1995: 129) and Baym (2000: 81) note, such playful speculation is perhaps the most common form of talk about soap opera, and is certainly among the most pleasurable. Indeed, it is a form of orality in which people can engage in the pleasures of storytelling: not only in recounting and explaining past story events, but also in imagining future ones. Some of this speculation is based on a detailed knowledge of the conventions of the genre, and is playful and knowing in this respect.

Here for example a group of 9-year-old children display considerable imaginative and powers. Not only do they display a good knowledge of generic conventions, but also they demonstrate a grasp of adult themes and personal issues:

| Natalie: | Lofty's going to find out. He don't know. And he's going to be Michelle's husband. |
|---|---|
| Preston: | Guess what? He got a ring of Den. And when she finds out, she might get divorced. |

| Vicky: | I reckon that Michelle's not going to turn up, or something like that. Give him the elbow. |
| Maxine: | I think Lofty marries Michelle, I don't know what would happen with Den. His jealousy would creep in, boy. You'll see him get really jealous. |
| Samantha: | He'll try and mess up their marriage. |
| Maxine: | Try and divorce them. Boy. |

(cited in Buckingham 1987: 168)

Some of this speculation is of course fuelled by the sizeable market for soap magazines and articles in the tabloid press. These add a further level of complexity to the actual processes of narration, acting as a spur to playfully interrogate the text in new ways. Audiences might look for 'hidden meanings' and the real truth behind what is shown. Here for example is a fan of the US soap, *All My Children*, who speculates about a storyline, drawing parallels between the actors' lives and the characters that they play:

> Fay: I gotta know this: what is the story between James Kiberd and Kate Collins? Don't they get along? (I need some juicy gossip here!) ☺ . . . Someone who saw Kiberd last year said he hinted that Collins was a lesbian, but again, I heard LeClerc say that he once had a 'relationship' with Collins (now they are just friends), and she is certainly 'involved' with someone. Either way, it's her business and really has nothing to do with her ability to act. However it *does* seem that the chemistry that used to be there between Kiberd and Collins (when they play Nat and Trevor) just isn't there anymore. . . . They used to have a LOT more spark!

(cited in Baym 2000: 92)

## Personalization, character interpretation and speculation

Baym's (2000) research is valuable in this respect as she draws on her long-term membership of a soap opera bulletin board. This has the very significant benefit that unlike focus groups (on which the majority of the research reported in this book is based) the talk and interactions unfolding on the bulletin boards were naturally occurring. This is what this audience actually does in everyday life, as they draw the text into semiosis: they have, if you like, been caught in the act. In this regard it gives us a very reliable form of research materials, albeit of a kind which is based on particularly 'high investors' in the genre (Jenkins 1992). Baym found that this audience's interpretative practices are organized around three different types of talk: 'personalization', 'character interpretation' and 'speculation'.

The first of these types of talk, *personalization*, involves the process whereby audiences make the shows personally meaningful. This involves a movement between the characters, storylines and personal experiences. As Baym (2000) puts it:

> they do this by putting themselves into the drama and identifying with its situations and characters. They also bring the drama into their own lives, making sense of the story in term of the norms by which they make sense of their own experiences.
>
> (Baym 2000: 71)

This is a dialectical movement between the text and everyday life, where the understandings of each feed back into each other. In this, 'collaborative interpretation facilitates a sharing of personal experience, providing the opportunity to explore the story from different vantage points' (Baym 2000: 71). This personalization however cannot really be separated from other types of talk, in particular that of *character interpretation*. In this Baym sees a process whereby viewers discuss the characters in terms of their motivations, their consistency and the consequences for the ongoing story. They do so however by drawing on their own life experiences as well as their expectations of the genre. This is both cultural verisimilitude (what is realistic in terms of real life) and generic verisimilitude (what is probable and believable in terms of the generic conventions).

Here for example these viewers discuss the character of 'Nat' from *All My Children* in terms of the production of the soap, the consistency of her characterization and their own feelings and experiences:

Respondent 1: Nat is also having a grudge towards Trevor, something the 'old' Nat wouldn't do . . . I do not like the attitude they are putting on Nat! Very unreal!

Respondent 2: I also thought that this wasn't right. If my husband accidentally burned down the house and I got hurt I really don't think I would hate him for it. If anything I would try and not make him feel guilty.

Respondent 3: I wholeheartedly agree. I know my husband would feel terrible. For goodness sake the man carried her out of a burning home. I would have thought he would have left her there if he did it on purpose. The new Nat is just not right.

(cited in Baym 2000: 74–5)

In the following posts audience talk about character portrayal and motivation quickly becomes *personalized* as private experiences are brought to bare on the interpretation and on the understanding of the character. This narrative understanding is then used to disclose, explore and discuss personal feelings and experiences. This is a movement, as Baym puts it, between 'immersion in the drama' on the one hand, and 'bringing the drama into real life' on the other (Baym 2000: 76). Here the talk concerns a storyline about domestic abuse:

Lexine:  I was on the receiving end just ONCE – but it was enough to make me get an immediate annulment from a mistake-of-a-marriage. *All My Children* portrayed my ex to a 'T' (professional, likeable) – but completely lost me when they started this ridiculous story with Nat.

Diane:  Boy did this ever bring back nightmare memories . . . I'm not after sympathy, but wanted to tell you from experience, this is *so* typical. My ex-husband did the same thing (he wasn't as psycho a character, thank God). He only hurt me when I asked for it! Then, just to keep the peace, I'd end up apologizing to *him*! He was always remorseful, cried and said it would never happen again, etc. etc. etc. . . . just like they do on TV.

Pam:  Diane, I applauded you for getting out of such a destructive relationship! That took a lot of courage. Waytogo, woman!

(cited in Baym 2000: 76)

As we see in Brown's (1994) discussion of gossip above, as well as in Silverstone's (1999) arguments about play, this type of talk can serve as a way of disclosing different aspects of the self and of exploring these in a supportive environment. As Baym (2000) suggests, a lot of the talk therefore actually discusses feelings and relationships as well as the cultural and ethical norms and standards from which they arise: an important form of 'working through' in Ellis's terms.

Such a contribution to the public sphere, which includes the processes of personalization and character interpretation, can clearly be seen in the responses that Kitzinger (2004) found with the development of a particular storyline in the Channel 4 soap opera, *Brookside*.[2] The teenage character Beth Jordache, played by Anna Friel, suffered years of sexual abuse from her father. She also witnessed him systematically beat her mother. While, true to the melodramatic address of soap opera, she eventually kills him in self-defence, and buries him under the patio, this dealt with the realities of sexual violence and incest in a powerful manner. As Kitzinger (2004) notes, for perhaps the first time a soap opera created a frank portrayal of abuse and its effects. In this people could recognize themselves. It also provided a strong and confident role model which powerfully articulated the new interpretative repertoire. As one woman recalls:

Victims on TV, they're like a big shadow, all blacked out. That makes me feel terrible, they're hiding away. . . . I thought 'I'm going to grow up and I'm going to be scared of everything'. But Beth [in *Brookside*] she was so strong, she's got a grip on everything. Before that everything I saw seemed to say that if you were abused you'd be strange, different, keep yourself in a wee corner. Watching Beth has really helped me.

(cited in Kitzinger 2004: 43).

This was a major story, and represented a pervasive stock of 'common knowledge' (Gripsrud 1999) and a powerful and collective way of working through for the contemporary culture (Ellis 1999). Outrage was provoked in 1995 when news leaked that Beth would end her own life. This resulted in demonstrations by incest survivors' groups outside the production studios, with banners reading 'save our survivor'. Eventually she was written out of the series through death by natural causes (Kitzinger 2004: 44).

## Working through: identity

Soap operas, just like reality programming and talk shows, can therefore be seen to function in some respects as what Nikolas Rose (1999) calls an 'ethical technology'. These, as we saw in Chapter 2, can be defined as 'technical repertoires for the conduct of conduct for particular purposes, of images, norms, evaluations and techniques of selfhood' (Rose 1999: 269–70). In these terms the discourses articulated by soap operas have an ethical component. Through them everyday conduct is brought under a self-disciplining scrutiny. They also feed into the ways in which audiences imagine their futures and think about their pasts (see Briggs 2009). Buckingham for example has found that the young children used soap operas to gossip about adult subjects which are just entering into their horizons of experience: as they consider their futures and what they will become (Buckingham 1987: 164; see also Buckingham 1993b). This is a significant aspect of identity work, and in this, watching soap for younger viewers may hold pleasures akin to voyeurism. As Buckingham (1987) explains:

Television may provide them with representations of aspects of adult behaviour which are usually hidden from them, although they may know of their existence. Discussing television may provide them with a relatively safe way of acknowledging things which they are normally forbidden to talk about; as well as allowing us to look without being seen, television also allows us to pass comment without reprisals.

(Buckingham 1987: 164)

Here, for example, 11-year-old Lisa raises issues of adult sexuality, gender, fidelity and married life in the British soap *EastEnders*:

| | |
|---|---|
| Lisa: | Pete's a bit of a chauvinist. Know what I mean, a sexist pig. |
| Alison: | Pete's been cheating . . . |
| Lisa: | They don't spend too much time together. They just don't talk to each other. When it comes time when Pete wants her, and she's trying to explain to him, he doesn't want to listen. He just wants her for himself, really. |
| Alison: | As his body lover, know what I mean? |

(cited in Buckingham 1987: 165)

The power of this working through is generated as they move in and out of the play frame. They do this in order to engage in moral debate. In the following exchange, for example, the speakers constantly shift between the 'inside' and the 'outside' of the text: sometimes talking about the lives of the characters *as if* they were real, but at others broadening the talk to consider wider ethical, political and ultimately ideological concerns (Thompson 1990). In this playful movement between the world of the soap opera and the everyday world we see the same kind of personalization that Baym identified, and also in the second example with 17-year-old Magdlin and Heba, a sophisticated critique of gender roles and representational issues. First consider four 12 year olds, Natasha, John, Fiona and Lee:

| | |
|---|---|
| Natasha: | Angie's too soft, though, she always says [whining voice] 'I'm sorry Den'. |
| John: | If he was doing that, you wouldn't go out with him. He goes out with Jan right, and you wouldn't stick up with it. I would either leave him, or . . . |
| Fiona: | I wouldn't give him a second chance. |
| Natasha: | She should smack him in the face, or boot him one. |
| Lee: | I know what my mum would do. She'd get a frying pan and knock him over the head with it. |
| Fiona: | And if I was Angie, I would have got Jan and booted her one. |

(cited in Buckingham 1987: 175–6)

In the following exchange, as Buckingham (1987) suggests, we see a disagreement about whether the characterization and discourse should aspire to an ethical position on what life *should* be like, or whether its realism should portray what they take life to *actually* be like:

| | |
|---|---|
| Magdlin: | I think she's dull and boring. She goes on about the same point all the time. About Den going out with that woman. That's the only thing she cares about. |

| Heba: | I don't think so. I think she makes it more interesting. |
| Magdlin: | All she talks about and cares about is men. She said it: her life is useless because of men. |
| Interviewer: | So you think that's the problem? |
| Magdlin: | I think it degrades women a bit actually. |
| Heba: | I don't think so. Most women are like that really, if you come to think about it. |

(cited in Buckingham 1987: 175–6)

This ethical debate, as we would expect, is not restricted to children. In the following example a Korean soap viewer raises ethical questions through the process of personalization. In this the respondent enjoys comparing the portrayal of a strong woman who fights against her husband's infidelity with that of her sister who forgave her husband after he had an affair:

Korean woman: When my friend recommended it to me, she was trying to tell me the plot. At first, I thought it was just another typical story about a husband's affair. But as it was revealed, I was stunned. It was about my sister! So, I told her to stop telling me the story. I wanted to know exactly how it would end and how it would be different from my sister's real life story . . . I loved the way that she treated her husband at the end.

(cited in Lee and Cho 1990: 36)

Likewise in the following example, the playful talk between husband and wife about the US soap opera *Dallas* blurs the boundary between the text and everyday life. In doing so it generates a discussion which works through issues of cultural values, aspirations and ethical conduct.

| Beverley: | J.R. and Bobby, their mother is just heartbroken with the things that J.R. does, and she is sick for Bobby because he doesn't get the things he wants, and this kind of thing, well, this is every mother's reaction, but in our case, I hope that I never have a son like J.R. I would have to be, you know, that sick about it (ha ha). |
| Don: | I would love having a son like J.R. |
| Beverley: | Ah, phoo. |
| Interviewer: | You would love to have a son like J.R.? |
| Don: | You betcha. You betcha. |
| Interviewer: | Why is that? |
| Don: | I would like to have one that is as smart as J.R. (his wife laughs hard) a conniver, a doer. |
| Beverley: | And you would sit back, just like Jock. |

Don:         I made the mistake once, just after we had watched *Dallas* for a year or a year and a half or something, I told my oldest daughter that I thought J.R. was my idol, the kind of guy that you admire and respect; even though he is a fink and a crook, you admire and respect him. She went out and bought me a picture of J.R., and hung it on the wall in my den. (ha ha)

Interviewer: Do you still feel that way about him, that you have some admiration for him and that you respect him?

Don:         Well, you sure have to have admiration for the guy; he accomplishes most things he sets out, no matter how, no matter who he has to step on to do it, and if you are a successful businessman and handling that much money, I think you have to do that in the world today. I don't think you can be Mr. Nice Guy and make 20 million dollars. I think you've got to step on somebody.

                                            (cited in Liebes and Katz 1993: 93)

This is an interesting example, which is worth analysing in some detail, for it demonstrates the ways in which text is drawn into semiosis through several different modalities. In the first instance the text acts as a 'bridge' (Vološinov 1973) between the mother, daughter and husband, a resource for the organization of their family life. In this, however, we also see the second modality, for it is playful. The family blur the boundaries of the text and the everyday, both with the giving of the gift, but also as they imagine what it would be like to have a son who was as ruthless as J.R.[3] The exchange starts off as banter, as something which is playful, and which generates laughter, and perhaps an affectionate recognition of different personalities and beliefs within the family. The third modality however takes on a political inflection. Don seems to become less playful and more trenchant in his validation of J.R.'s values and the free market discourse of big business more generally. In this he seems to be generating an interpretative repertoire which supports the sovereignty of the free market over individual rights and ethical behaviour. This is working ideologically to legitimize the current mode of capitalist production, and he tries to impress this on his family, and his aspirations for his son.

We can think about this in terms of the identity work which is being conducted as Don and Beverley speak in different ways. Goffman (1981) for example alerts us to the *social identities* that are established and enacted as audiences adopt different voices or repertoires, and therefore to the role of language in the maintenance of identity and the 'presentation of self'. He suggests that any strip of naturally occurring discourse, such as that which we see here between Don and Beverley, will be 'laminated' by a constant change of voices. The interactive participants change 'footings' throughout. This change in footing moves us 'towards' and 'away from' the primary business at hand. Here this is a movement between a playful discussion of the soap opera, broader talk of family life and their relationships, and finally a discussion of political ideology and ethics (Goffman 1981: 154). Crucially for my argument this changes the ways that audiences present themselves, and indeed the roles that they assume in the ongoing play. We can therefore expect any example of soap talk to involve the use of different voices, different discourses, and different aspects of the self.

Such a complex and situated play of voice, discourse and identity suggests that it will be fruitless to look for consistent decodings, whether they be dominant, negotiated or resistant (Hall 1973). It is rather more useful to look for the functions that any such talk serves, in specific contexts, as it unfolds between social actors (cf. Buckingham 1993a). As Erving Goffman (1981) puts it:

> A change in footing implies a change in the alignment we take up to ourselves and to others present as expressed in the way we manage the production or reception of an utterance. A change in footing is another way of talking about a change in our frame of events [the voice we use – the business we are attending to]. . . . Participants over the course of their speaking constantly change their footing, these changes being a persistent feature of natural talk.
>
> (Goffman 1981: 128)

Liebes and Katz (1993) have found this play of different repertoires in several of their focus groups. In these we see the ways in which the discourses articulated by the character of 'J.R.' are taken up and drawn into discussions of economics, corruption and political struggle. In some discussions Israeli Arabs, to take one example, label Saudi Arabian sheiks as 'J.R.s', while Ariel Sharon (who at the time of the study was the Israeli Defence Minister, and had just been implicated in a massacre) was called a 'J.R.' by some kibbutz members. In this there is a struggle over different repertoires, between playful soap talk and a politically driven voice which raises an ethical point about political conduct and free market economics:

| | |
|---|---|
| Shaul: | He [J.R.] is Sharon. |
| Aharonchik: | Sharon is a miniature version. |
| Sara: | He steps over the bodies of his best friends. There are a lot of people like that. Take people in politics. It's almost the same thing; the only thing is that they are not shown on television as *Dallas*. |

Shaul:        Don't smear. Why are you smearing?
Sara:         It's exactly that. It's so; it's so. Politicians are dirty people.
Aharonchik:   Sharon is not politics.

(cited in Liebes and Katz 1993: 94)

These activities are quite complex. In them audiences move between different modalities of response; the voices that they generated are dialogic, they anticipate the responses of others, as well as respond to, take up and revoice prior discourses and meanings that circulate in our culture (Bakhtin 1981). On the one hand, these can be ideological: they can legitimize wider cultural practices and the distribution of power and wealth in society (Thompson 1990). They can serve as ethical technologies, through which selfhood and everyday conduct are brought under a self-disciplining scrutiny (Rose 1999). On the other hand, they can also challenge and subvert such discourses and interpretative repertoires, through bad taste, parody, exaggeration and laughter (Brown 1994). Indeed, the playful narrative pleasures of speculation, prediction, gossip and mimicry serve to nourish interpersonal relationships, as a 'knowing' and affectionate relationship with the soap opera is maintained (Baym 2000).

In this, we see the complexity of meaning making, its contingency, the fact that it is always embedded: a product of the social environments in which it unfolds. What is particularly important to note here is the sheer inadequacy of the notion of decoding, the ways it obscures such modalities, and in particular, the playful, knowing and emotionally charged nature of fantasy, of imagination and play. It is to the last of these terms that we turn now.

## Play, fantasy and emotional realism

This playful relationship between soap operas and their viewers has been well documented by Ang (1985) as she explores her respondents' emotional responses to the once hugely popular series *Dallas*. What interests her in particular are the ways in which they found a kind of authenticity in the stories, even as they were aware of its melodramatic and unrealistic qualities. In this she makes an important distinction between 'empirical realism' and 'emotional realism'. In the latter there is a particularly playful aspect to semiosis: a game which they play; a conscious and knowing relationship with text which they enter into in order to seek out moments of authenticity and emotional intensity. In the former the respondents wanted to see their own worlds depicted realistically. This was an expectation that they would recognize the sort of people and events which they come across in everyday life, rather than the unrealistic accumulation of improbable and sensational events which characterized this soap opera (Ang 1985: 37). One female viewer, for example, complains that *Dallas* is 'rather unreal':

> It is a programme situated pretty far outside reality. The mere fact that a whole family is living in one house comes over as rather unreal. What happens in this serial you would never run into in the street or in your circle of acquaintance: very unreal events. The family relationships are so weirdly involved: this one's married to the sister of the enemy of his brother, etc., etc.
>
> (cited in Ang 1985: 41–2)

Other viewers were much less demanding in these terms of cultural verisimilitude. That the soap was set in an alien and fantastic environment, far beyond the bounds of normal credibility, was recognized as a generic convention: these were simply the sorts of glamorous locations and people that populate these fantasy worlds. Indeed, this shapes their responses, and their playful relationship with the text, as it clearly sets up that this shouldn't be taken too seriously: precisely that it is 'pretend'.

Despite this rather more playful orientation, for these viewers' expectations of cultural verisimilitude were also very important. In this we are not dealing so much with the fallacy of the text as a mirror of the world, which can somehow be depicted in some naturalistic manner. Rather the viewers looked for psychological and emotional forms of authenticity. They wanted to see their own *subjective experiences*, their own inner lives, feelings and emotions depicted on the screen. Take, for example, this Dutch viewer who finds a deep resonance between the quarrels and fights she sees played out across the series, and her own experiences:

> Female: I find *Dallas* super and for this reason: the characters reflect the daily life of a family (I find). You sometimes see serials where everything runs smoothly. Never any rows or anything. Not a damn thing wrong. Every family has rows sometimes. It's not smooth sailing. In *Dallas* there are rows, desperate situations.
>
> (cited in Ang 1985: 43)

This woman from the United States similarly describes her involvement with *EastEnders*:

> Female: Women can see they're not alone with misbehaving kids, unfulfilled love lives, legal troubles, drunken relatives. They may receive the inspiration to carry on when everything around them is turning to crap.
>
> (cited in Madill and Goldmeier 2003: 480)

Likewise, this is powerfully seen in Lee and Cho's (1990) research, where this viewer fantasizes about her former boyfriend, while she compares her husband with the one depicted in the soap:

> Female: The man [the husband in the drama] reminds me of my husband. He does alright by his wife materially, but is torturing her mentally. I'd rather be poor, well not really poor, you know what I mean, I'd rather have a husband who cares about me just like the young fella in the drama . . . I wonder what could have happened if I had married him [her ex-boyfriend]. He was always nice to me. I think he would have been a better choice. Well, maybe not.
>
> (cited in Lee and Cho 1990: 40)

What we are seeing here, Ang (1985) suggests, in this emotional realism, is a 'tragic structure of feeling'. In this there is a profound and melodramatic recognition of life's emotions, 'that life is characterized by an endless fluctuation between happiness and unhappiness, that life is a question of falling down and getting up again' (Ang 1985: 46). Indeed, this reflects the phenomenological experience of life: of what it is, sometimes, to be alive, to experience subjectivity, 'an expression of a refusal, or inability, to accept insignificant everyday life as banal and meaningless; it is born of a vague, inarticulate dissatisfaction with existence here and now' (Ang 1985: 79). As she explains, this is not the great suffering of humankind, marked by the tragedies of war, starvation and ecological disaster. Rather, it is the suffering which accompanies everyday life. There are, she suggests, 'no words for the ordinary pain of living' and soap operas may articulate such experiences in quite powerful ways:

> By making that ordinariness something special and meaningful in the imagination, that sense of loss can – at least for a time – be removed. It is in this world of the imagination that watching melodramatic soap operas like *Dallas* can be pleasurable. *Dallas* offers a starting point for the melodramatic imagination nourishes it, makes it concrete.
>
> (Ang 1985: 79–80)

Profoundly moving and immersive as this experience can be, there is no question however the viewers have 'lost a grip on reality', which is to say that they believe in the reality of the show. Rather this modality of response is generated by a movement between closeness and distance, between the 'game' and the 'play'. As Ang suggests, 'these remarks suggest a distance between the "real" and the fictional world. And precisely because these letter writers are aware of this, it appears they can indulge in the excessive emotions aroused in *Dallas*' (Ang 1985: 48). Consider for example the movement between knowing distance and playful involvement with this viewer:

Female: The good thing about it, I think, is that lots of things happen in it taken from life, so to speak. Such as Sue Ellen with her marital problems, though I do find that in the longer run that is a bit overdone, she makes a game out of it. I think the serial writers do that deliberately, because lots of men find it terrific to watch her. And would even like to help her. Oh well. These gallant Don Juans. . . . After a serial like that of poverty and misery, where spiritual character is concerned, because financially nothing is lacking, I often think what a relief, now I can come back to my own world and I'm very happy in it. To have seen all those worries gives me a nice feeling – you're looking for it, you're bringing it on yourself.

(cited in Ang 1985: 48)

Ang goes on to suggest that this 'flight' into a fictional fantasy is not so much an escape from reality, but a playing with it, 'a game that enables one to place the limits of the fictional and the real under discussion, to make them fluid' (Ang 1985: 49). This play is both affirming and pleasurable, an inalienable part of everyday life, experience and identity:

The pleasure of *Dallas* consists in the recognition of ideas that fit in with the viewers' imaginative world. They can 'lose' themselves in *Dallas* because the programme symbolizes a structure of feeling which connects up with one of the ways in which we encounter life. And in so far as the imagination is an essential component of our psychological world, the pleasure of *Dallas* – as a historically specific symbolizing of that imagination – is not a *compensation* for the presumed drabness of daily life, nor a *flight* from it, but a *dimension* of it. For only through the imagination, which is always subjective, is the 'objective reality' assimilated: a life without imagination does not exist.

(Ang 1985: 83, emphasis in original)

## Conclusion

The 'classic' studies that the bulk of this chapter has drawn upon suggest another way in which we can make better use of audience research. The concept of play has emerged as an important issue in recent years, and by employing our methodology we can now go back to the existing research and look at it in different ways. In doing so this chapter has taken what remained marginal and undeveloped in the original work, and placed it at the conceptual and critical heart of the enquiry. In *revisiting* this work this chapter has begun to explore the various playful modalities thorough which soap operas are made meaningful. We have seen, for example, the ways in which audiences respond to the invitation of the text to pass judgement on its characters. But we have also seen the ways in which they relate them to their own lives. While this may not always be sober and rational, it does seem to 'work through' the moral, ethical and ideological values of our culture.

The subversive pleasures of play, laughter and gossip are central to this semiosis. In their small infractions they turn politeness, sobriety, rationalism and realism on their heads. They throw them back in the faces of those who would seek to criticize, contain and control. In this audiences find considerable pleasures in the touching excess of soaps. They are an emotionally resonant space in which they could find recognition of the banality of the everyday life and its tragic structure of feeling. Despite this we should be wary of celebrating the necessarily *resistive* nature of such audience activity, as the encoding/decoding model would posit. Much of what we looked at in Chapters 1 and 2 would confirm this. We have seen the ways in which gossip about television, its stories, and those who appear on it is just as likely to be conservative: to reinforce rather than challenge existing discourses and practices. Audiences' playful responses are less progressive in this regard; they can support the existing lines of power in our culture as well as challenge them.

What emerges from this ludic agenda in particular is the futility in trying to decide once and for all on the 'progressive' or 'conservative' nature of soap opera, or reality programming. In place of this we should rather take a lesson from Bakhtin and see texts as a battleground where a range of different competing voices, discourses and ideological accents converge. We see then that this is the nature of the public sphere, a space where multiple voices, discourses, genres and pleasures interact. The public sphere, in this, cannot be reduced to the singularity of the rational, the balanced and the objective. This is not what audiences do: audiences *work through*. They discuss and introspect. They gossip, laugh and cry. They fantasize, imagine and emote. They develop opinions and beliefs about the world. They mull these over. They are just as likely to assert the discourses presented to them as they are to reject them. They may not always be consistent in this. They may be swayed by mood, politeness, embarrassment or indifference. In these modalities there is a constant struggle over meaning, a constant struggle to define the world and to find authentic experiences. This it would seem is the nature of play. This is the nature of soap opera and its role in this thing we call the public sphere.

## Notes

1 Following Dorothy Hobson (2002: 12–14) the term soap opera is used throughout this chapter to refer to both long-running continuous serials, such as *All My Children* in

the United States, *Neighbours* in Australia or *Coronation Street* in the UK, and also to the high profile and expensively produced series popular in the 1980s, such as *Dallas*, *Dynasty* and *Falcon Crest*. While these share the emphasis on the emotional lives of the characters, they were produced in series of 13 episodes, and broadcast in different seasons over a number of years. Hobson (2002) argues that despite the differences, however, the huge success of these serials broadened out the appeal of soap operas to a male audience, and influenced production and script writing accordingly. In the UK, for example, soap operas such as *EastEnders* (1984) and *Brookside* (1982) introduced stronger action plots based on male characters. Likewise, despite the lack of precision in the definition they were broadly perceived to be a part of the soap genre, an assumption which was shared by audiences, critics and academics alike. Ien Ang's (1985) influential book for example is entitled *Watching Dallas: Soap Opera and the Melodramatic Imagination*.

2  Channel 4 was established as a public service broadcaster in the UK in 1982. Its remit was to cater to minority tastes and interests that were not sufficiently addressed elsewhere and to provide innovative and challenging programming. *Brookside* ran from the initial launch of the channel until 2003, when it was finally dropped due to declining viewing figures and the increase of commercial activity at the channel. During its run it dealt with controversial issues, such as industrial action, incest, domestic and sexual abuse, drug addiction, cult religion and homosexuality.

3  J.R. Ewing was the central character in *Dallas*, a scheming oil baron played by Larry Hagman. He was very well known and became a common reference point in countries where *Dallas* was broadcast, even for those who had not seen the show. The character came to be synonomous with greed, underhand dealing and the excesses of free market capitalism. *Dallas* originally ran in the United States between 1978 and 1991. It was shown on the BBC in the UK when 24 million viewers tuned in to watch the shooting of J.R. (Hobson 2002: 12).

# TELEVISION AND DOMESTIC SPACE

What is it to watch television? To come home from work, exhausted: looking forward to the next episode in this drama, of that soap? To find comfort in this; to know that it will be there, familiar, routine. That it addresses us, our concerns: that it seems to speak to me, that it knows who I am (Scannell 1996). To habitually turn to the news, to switch it on, not only to find out what had been happening today (on this day, and no other day), but also to withdraw from immediate reality (of doing the washing up, reading that report, mending that leaky tap). This turn to television may involve a withdrawal from others, a way of making oneself unavailable; it might just as well forge a way of being together, a point of shared social contact. Television, for better or worse, is a part of who we are; we use it to tell stories of ourselves, and others. We use television to organize the everyday, the here and now, the there and then.

Reflecting on this Ron Lembo (2000) has written about how he remembers his childhood. This, we read, has as much to do with what happened *around* the set, as it has to do with what it screened. There was a 'warmth and safety' in watching *Kojak* and *Baretta* with his father, one of the only points of social contact they shared. These were not moments for his mother to watch, however; she chose to 'busy herself in the kitchen', returning to watch only as they tuned into *The Ed Sullivan Show*. Such moments were not just ones of exclusion (of the gendered politic of domestic space). They were also ones of inclusion: they became encounters for her to tell stories of her own childhood, of

her parents coming from Italy and settling into life in America; about her early years in school; about basketball and football games she went to with her friends; about the various jobs that she and her brothers and sisters had when they were growing up; about her ballroom dancing days, or about how she learned to cook and be a beautician.

(Lembo 2000: 4)

While always on, however, the TV was just as likely to be ignored; it was a constant presence in the background accompanying other daily activities such as the housework, hobbies, reading, dozing (Lull 1980).

Television in all this, however complex it may seem, is something which we sit down and 'watch'. In this lies its difficulty, for how do we make sense of such a seemingly mundane activity? How do we think about its relationship to wider patterns of meaning making: to the 'working through' that we have been so concerned with? It is a question, it seems, as Herman Bausinger once argued, that the 'activities' of watching may be meaningful in themselves; a set of meanings which are distinct, or at least only loosely articulated to, the meanings of the programmes that are screened (Bausinger 1984; Morley and Silverstone 1990). In this can be seen a nexus of meanings which sit on the cusp of social and textual practices. It is this nexus that this chapter explores. It explores the ways that concepts such as decoding or of the public sphere tend to remain, in a curious way, abstract: 'one step removed' from the practical realities of television viewing (Lembo 2000: 10). In this we will see the multiple modalities in which audiences respond; not only the types of meaning, but also their relationship to our everyday lives, our routines and our experiences.

In this, this chapter argues that an account of semiosis, of interpretative repertoires, of ethical thought, gossip and debate, of identification and emotionality, need to be grounded in the practical arrangements of television viewing, the social uses that they are put to, and the social spaces in which it occurs (Lull 1980). The first, as set out by James Lull, builds a typology of television's uses, an empirically grounded account of what happens around the set, the ways in which it fits into, and is structured by domestic space, as much as it structures them and the social relations of the households to which it belongs. The second, one which Scannell (1996) and Lembo (2000) are concerned with, seeks to think about our *experiences* of television, the ways in which it addresses us, the ways in which it makes us feel secure, safe and comforted. It seeks to understand its phenomenological characteristics.

## The social uses of television

First then, we must attend to the *how*, the *when* and the *who* of television viewing, questions which have been admirably addressed by Lull (1980). To do this he has built a typology of the *uses* that television serves. To build this typology Lull presents the data from a very large ethnographic study involving over 200 families. Researchers played a full role in the households, eating, performing chores and socializing with the families. Each family was observed at home for between two and seven days, from mid-afternoon to bedtime. Interviews were subsequently conducted to expand upon such observations (Lull 1980: 201). Lull's aim in conducting such a thorough ethnography was to offer a model of the ways in which television is used in everyday life. It is not only a communicator of meanings, but also a prop in social interaction. It acts as a 'vital resource in the construction or maintenance of interpersonal relations'; it plays a central role in the manner in which households 'interact normatively within their special everyday realities' (Lull 1980: 5).

The method of this chapter is therefore to explore the social uses that television is put to, and in line with the other chapters in this book, to piece this together with examples from the available research. This method demonstrates not only the *lasting relevance* of the 'established' audience research which has informed thinking in cultural and media studies, but also the importance and contribution that empirical research can make to *conceptual development* and clarification in the field. It is especially notable in this regard that Lull's research, which dates back to 1980, can throw considerable light and conceptual clarity on more descriptive ethnographic approaches of Hugh Mackay and Darren Ivey (2004) and David Gauntlett and Annette Hill (1999), which are used quite extensively throughout what follows. To demonstrate such a use of audience research our starting point must be Lull's typology, which can be listed as follows:

- environment
- regulation
- communication facilitation
- affiliation and avoidance
- social learning
- competence and dominance.

## Environment

The first of Lull's uses, the environmental, is concerned with television's sheer ubiquity in households: with the fact that it is a constant source of 'noise' which contributes to the overall semiotic environment. In this television provides a backdrop which accompanies other tasks or activities. This, as Lull (1980) puts it, is to explore the ways in which television is used to 'create a constant background noise which moves to the foreground when individuals or groups desire'.

This 'guarantees a nonstop backdrop of verbal communication against which they can construct their interpersonal exchanges' (Lull 1980: 202). In this Mackay and Ivey (2004) explain how television can be used in a rather distracted manner.

Karen, for example, makes a distinction between forging 20 minutes for herself to read the newspaper when her children are busy doing their homework, which is a luxury in her busy schedule, and the television which she doesn't watch 'properly':

> Karen: I suppose I do watch a fair bit, but I don't really watch it properly, if you know what I mean. . . . I'll watch a bit of *Blind Date* and *Stars in their Eyes* in the kitchen on a Saturday night.
>
> (cited in Mackay and Ivey 2004: 112)

It is interesting to note the assumption that 'proper' viewing is similar to what might (or might not) be found with print media. In this she assumes a mode of discrete and sustained attention. Despite such an assumption this is only a small part of what audiences do with television. Having left university and started working in a new city, away from her friends and family, this young graduate relaxes in the evening in front of the television. This is gratefully used for company so that her evenings might be spent 'vegging out'. As she puts it:

> Graduate: TV is more important to me now, in that I need it to relax when I come home from work. As I live in a horrible bedsit on my own, I switch on the TV the minute I get in the door. The voices, music, or whatever warms the room up and helps me relax. I have to have it on as background noise.
>
> (cited in Gauntlett and Hill 1999: 95)

A retired male civil servant also values this use. At once he seems dissatisfied with the actual content of television, but horrified at the thought of not having it there, as a background to his evening routines:

> Retiree: TV's main purpose is distraction and comforter. I rely on a framework of personal favourites (*The Bill*, *University Challenge*, *Neighbours*, repeats such as *Auf Weidersehen Pet*) to keep me going . . . I no longer watch (so much or even at all) the arts or current affairs programmes; they seem trivial or irrelevant. But it would be an empty, anxious house without the evening TV.
>
> (cited in Gauntlett and Hill 1999: 189)

Intermittent viewing likewise seems to provide distractions or a mood which is both stimulating and relaxing. In this audiences can switch between one sphere of activity (reading a book, cooking dinner) to another, that of attending

# TELEVISION AND DOMESTIC SPACE | 99

to the text. Here is Elizabeth, who finds a resonance between what she watches on the kitchen television and the domestic tasks which occupy her time and attention:

> Elizabeth: Yes, this is a new channel that's just started in the last three weeks or so. It's a channel dedicated to food and cookery programmes during the day. I've watched it quite a lot since it began. I'll watch during the day, although it's mostly repeats of things like *Master Chef*, *The Naked Chef* and *Ready Steady Cook*. There are some good live items on there as well . . . I love to cook anyway, I find it a breath of fresh air from the news all the time and most of the rubbish on Sky.
>
> (cited in Mackay and Ivey 2004: 134)

## Regulation

In addition to such environmental uses, television is also used in a regulative capacity, to organize household time and the everyday routines of family life. This contributes to structuring of the day and also to maintenance of family and household relations. In Lull's terms we are concerned with the ways in which television 'punctuates time and family activity such as meal time, bedtime, choretime, homework periods and a host of other related activities' (Lull 1980: 202). Mackay and Ivey (2004), for example, report on the Swain family, who have several televisions throughout their home. The family comprises the two young children (aged 7 and 8), the father who does shift work, and Michelle, the mother. Like so many women, she juggles her parenting with a busy career. While it was rare for them to agree on what to watch, or even to watch together, Michelle would bring the family together around the set between 6 and 7 each evening. Television in this was used to forge an hour of social contact; a strategy to have 'family time' which was not 'dictated by the children'. As they put it:

> [Michelle] said that is difficult for her as a working mother to have no help at home during the evenings. She has to cook and clean, while the demands of the children for attention focus solely on her. They tend to 'play up' more often now, because they know that John will only be there at the weekend. The media devices in the home seem to be used by Michelle as a means by which she can focus the attention of the children, enabling her to look after them in a way commensurate with her limited time.
>
> (Mackay and Ivey 2004: 75)

Michelle would have had little time to perform her domestic tasks if the children did not have their satellite television or the video recorder. This is not to say that she and John neglected their roles as parents, 'but rather that the media in their home have allowed them time to fulfil these roles as well as they can, under the constraints of time and the other pressures of being in full-time work' (Mackay and Ivey 2004: 75). Television as such provided much needed intimacy. It was an 'easy way' of being together. Through it Michelle gets a small respite from the constant attention, demands upon her, and discipline that she otherwise maintains (Mackay and Ivey 2004: 47–8). This differs from the family's solo use of television. In this Michelle would occasionally watch soap operas alone to 'have her own space', while her 8-year-old daughter would view videos in her bedroom. Television in these cases becomes a private activity, a means to relax away from the negotiations of family life (Mackay and Ivey 2004: 47–8).

## Communication facilitation

In this we see some of the ways in which one of the main tasks with understanding the practice of 'watching television' is to see how it is integrated into people's social relationships, the ways in which they spend time together, and the resources that they employ for this (Silverstone and Morley 1990). In Lull's terms we are concerned with the ways in which television's characters, stories and themes are employed by viewers in their everyday interaction. As he suggests, television examples are used by children to explain to each other, and to their parents and teachers, those real-world experiences, emotions and beliefs which were difficult to make personally transparent in attempts at verbal communication (Lull 1980: 202). It also acts, for others, as a way of easing discomfort, or creating an 'immediate agenda for talk where they may otherwise be none (Lull 1980: 203). While for some such as the Swains, as we have just seen, television is a ubiquitous presence, for others it is used much more selectively.

Mackay and Ivey (2004) report that not all families would constantly have the television on. In the Davies household, for example, television was used in a quite selective manner. Never a ubiquitous presence the family would come together to watch the popular British soap operas *Coronation Street* and *EastEnders*. The programmes in this sense would act as a common centre of attention and a communicative resource. They provided topics of conversation, or perhaps opportunities for brief remarks about the unfolding drama ('he's such a shit that bloke . . .', 'why doesn't he leave her to have the baby alone'). This might be organized in a fluctuation between companionable silence and involvement in the narrative on the one hand, and lively gossip and debate on the other. As Mackay and Ivey (2004) suggest:

[The Davies family] were heavily absorbed in the story line of a tug of love involving the paternity of a young baby girl. The half hour of *EastEnders* seemed quite an intense experience for them, both seemed engaged and focused on the programme throughout and I could sense a release of tension afterwards.

(Mackay and Ivey 2004: 76)

Likewise, here is Jackie from Ann Gray's (1992) study. She explains how she watches *EastEnders* and that it is a nice way of being with her daughter:

Jackie: We're hooked in a sort of comic way . . . like 'is he going to the wedding or not?' . . . you know, I couldn't care less [laugh]. I think it's very easy to join in with . . . it's more like a joke than anything else the way we watch it . . . if Jim's been out he'll come in and say to Jane, 'Well what happened in *EastEnders* then?' . . . Then Jane will say '*Well* . . . [laugh].

(cited in Gray 1992: 96)

This talk, as we have seen in Chapters 2 and 3, will often take the form of either gossip or personalization, and ranges across all genders and age groups. Here a 16-year-old school pupil explains that 'if there was no television I would miss being able to gossip with my friends over *ER* or *Neighbours*, it has become a social thing' (cited in Gray 1992: 95). Ethics and the care for the self (Rose 1999) are also in play here, for it 'allows them to talk about their own problems, indirectly, through a particular character or situation' (Gillespie 1999: 147). This is particularly important in the Bengali families that Maria Gillespie (1999) studied in the UK, a context where strict rules about family pride and loyalty forbids children from talking directly about family problems, even with the closest of friends. As Gita explains, this can be quite elliptical:

Gita: In school or at home we often have teenage problems which relate to our soap . . . but you don't talk about your own family except to really close friends maybe. . . . By talking to friends you come to an understanding. . . . You can think back to what a character did and see they did things the right way. . . . We discuss the problems and how they get solved.

(cited in Gillespie 1999: 147)

The act of sharing the same narrative validates the feelings and pleasures provoked by the story, whether this is 'silent and internal' (Kress 1997: 45–7), or spoken through gossip, discussion and casual asides. This joint meaning making helps to maintain relationships and communicate shared cultural experiences. We see this here, as Valerie Walkerdine (1997) renders a scene from her research, in which a family watches the film *Anne* on television. While there was no talk to record, she was sure that quite profound meanings were nevertheless being communicated:

[Television formed] the *relay point* in a complex and ongoing discussion within the family about their plight. Far from their being no discussion there was a great deal of it. The film offers a way of picking up and talking about issues that are very painful and difficult for the family, and also presents a way of understanding and working through these issues.

(Walkerdine 1997: 115, emphasis in original)

### Affiliation and avoidance

In examples such as these we see something of television's absolute ordinariness, the ways in which the seemingly simple act of watching functions to maintain affiliations between household members. It also suggests that several of Lull's (1980) uses can be active simultaneously. These tend to centre around Lull's description of 'affiliation' and 'avoidance'. In these television serves as a 'potential resource for the construction of desired opportunities for interpersonal contact of avoidance'. As he elaborates:

Television viewing is a convenient family behaviour which is accomplished *together*. The medium is used to provide opportunities for family members or friends to communally experience entertainment or informational programming. A feeling of familial solidarity is sometimes achieved through television-induced laughter, sorrow, anger or intellectual stimulation.

(Lull 1980: 203, emphasis in original)

We can see how this taps into wider gendered discourses, assumptions and practices here, with Janet from Gray's research. Not only does television bring people together, but it also can be employed as a 'social distracter', 'rendering less intense the communicative formalities which might otherwise be expected' (Lull 1980: 203). In this Janet watches American soap operas with her daughter, a pleasure which is not shared by the male members of the household:

Janet: Well [the children] stay up later at the weekends, and my little girl loves it, *Dynasty* and *Dallas*, she loves it, and she really gets involved in it, you know, with me . . . like, I'll go to her 'where did it end last week?' and she'll tell me . . . she really. . . . You know, she's really good company . . . it's nice having her against them three. They sit and think [sneer]. They watch, but they have the same attitude as my husband, you see, if you're sat crying, you know . . . you fill up . . . but my daughter's really . . . she loves it, she loves them programmes, she gets right involved in them.

(cited in Gray 1992: 96)

Gauntlett and Hill (1999) give several examples of how television functions to facilitate communication sometime after the initial act of viewing. It does so by fostering affiliations between this 14-year-old girl's peer group. For her this is more important than the programmes themselves, which she doesn't particularly enjoy:

> Pupil: I have to watch a bit more TV nowadays because my friends talk about TV a lot and so I have to understand what they are talking about but apart from that I still don't attach too much importance to TV – I prefer a good book – sometimes I feel guilty about NOT watching TV because I'm seen as a bit weird 'cos I don't watch as much as my friends and sometimes I think my sister would prefer me to watch a bit more TV and therefore be more normal.
>
> (cited in Gauntlett and Hill 1999: 85)

While the functions of 'affiliation' and 'communication facilitation' are quite close, and certainly relate to the sort of discussions going on here in peer groups, the former tends to be more focused on the specific *meanings of the programme*, which are taken up and shared, and the latter with the *act of watching*, as bringing people together around the television set.

Mackay and Ivey (2004) give a nice example of this distinction as they describe the Protheroe family. The home is a busy one, with the retired grandparents regularly entertaining the extended family. Most of this entertaining takes place in their large conservatory. This acts as a family room and does not house any media technologies. While guests are occasionally allowed into the living room, more often than not this media rich space is used when they are alone. The living room houses the television, video and satellite television receiver, as well as the hi-fi system and a collection of compact discs (CDs). It seems to be divided into 'intimate spaces' through both the arrangement of the furniture and through the use of different media: listening to music with headphones on, concentrating on a sought after television programme, watching a hired DVD, quietly reading a book or a magazine. As such television functions in this household as an element in a larger media ensemble; through its selective use members of the household can be co-present, being together in the same room, but occupying different spaces of attention. This provides a very different social feel from the busy and sociable space of the family room (Mackay and Ivey 2004: 39–40).

While I shall explore this 'social feel' in more detail below, as creating what Lembo (2000) refers to as a 'mindful space', we also see the social feel that television generates in the following. Here James uses television as a way of making the household living room his own physical space, regardless of whether he is watching or not. While he reads the papers and listens to Classic FM on the radio, he also likes to doze in front of the television, 'I have one eye open to watch the television and the other one to rest' (cited in Mackay and Ivey 2004: 120–1). This space was regarded as his domain, the rest of the family using it only when he was out, or by specific negotiation. His wife by contrast enjoyed the company of television to mark out the kitchen as her own personal space:

> Mrs Daniels: I usually sit in here on a Friday night. Someone usually calls in for a drink if they're passing, we'll sit here. James won't have people in the living room when he comes home from work, he'd probably throw them out. . . . It's easier to be in here, if he's sleeping or watching the news I prefer to be in here. I can watch what I want then. Usually I have a stool next to the table. To be honest, I like to be in here having a bit of peace . . . I'll have it [the television] on the worktop when I'm cooking, normally just the HTV news at teatime. It's on in the background normally, but things like *Blind Date*, *Don't Try This at Home*.
>
> (cited in Mackay and Ivey 2004: 122)

Gauntlett and Hill (1999) also suggest the importance of this combination of affiliation and avoidance for a domestic relationship which was marked by discord, and which would soon end in divorce. The couple used television to avoid confrontation in their relationship, to give them something to focus their attention and *not* to communicate with each other. This however would lead to other forms of tension, as her husband criticized her for viewing. As she explains:

> Divorcee: He is apt to be rather snobbish about television and claims that he cannot do anything else whilst watching it as I can – because it's too distracting. He often leaves the room to potter elsewhere away from the TV set.
>
> (cited in Gauntlett and Hill 1999: 104)

Another of their respondents reports the same function: 'in the recent past, television was such a ritual and a crutch to a failing relationship. It provided so many ways of evading "real" conversation – especially from me' (cited in Gauntlett and Hill 1999: 106). As Mackay and Ivey (2004) report, this pattern of avoidance was common in most of their households, with a wide array of media devices spread throughout the dwellings. This enables not only affiliation, as a focus for joint interaction, but also avoidance, as marking out private or personal spaces amid the multiple interactions and demands which made up the households (Mackay and Ivey 2004: 124).

## Social learning

A great deal of what we have seen in Chapters 1, 2 and 3 can relate to Lull's (1980) category of social learning. In this he refers to the way in which 'television programmes are used by parents to educate their children about the topics being presented in accord with their own world view' (Lull 1980: 205). While we have seen the many different modalities through which this learning and occurs, in the following examples we see the ways in which it is specifically organized through the households' patterns of viewing.

Stewart Hoover and his colleagues (Hoover et al. 2004) for example highlight the ways in which the Stevens-Van Gelder family enjoys their regular chance to watch Disney DVDs on Sunday evenings. As a brand, 'Disney' signals that it will be family time, but that while it may be safe in these terms, the films may some-times slip into sexism and racism. This is a chance for teaching their 9-year-old son Brett. It becomes a pedagogic tool (Buckingham and Sefton-Green 2003):

> Actually we sort of laugh about that. Brett really picks up on it, because he's been raised, this is a pretty conscious household in terms of sexuality, racism, all that kind of stuff. And those are the things we talk about all of the time. So he's really aware of it, and he'll laugh about it. He'll see it on a TV show and he'll say 'Oh mo God. All of a sudden the guy's here, now the woman acts like she can't do anything!' And we'll laugh about that and how 'isn't that silly' and that kind of thing. So we just talk about it.
>
> (cited in Hoover et al. 2004: 74)

Likewise, another family in the United States, comprising two men and their adopted 11-year-old daughter, were acutely aware of the values being taught by the media. As one of her fathers elaborates:

> Mark: I think probably if I were not gay, I would not spend so much time asking Lisette – and myself – to think about what the person is saying on the news or what the newspaper article says, and consider whether it's the truth or whether it's an opinion that might have a valid opposite.
>
> (cited in Hoover et al. 2004: 142)

Indeed, this dialogic way in which television is drawn into semiosis in this household is seen in a positive light by the daughter:

> Lisette: In the movies that are bloody or news shows that are bloody or gory, I *can* watch it, but if it's getting too bad then I'll just stop myself. My parents don't really care as long as I'm willing to talk to them about it if I have questions. And I can get up and leave. I don't feel I have to stay there. I have that kind of discipline, so they trust me with it.
>
> (cited in Hoover et al. 2004: 143)

This use of the media as a tool for facilitating discussion was also seen in another of Hoover et al.'s families, the Roelofs. They recognized that banning their children from watching 'R' rated films on satellite or DVD would simply not work, as their viewing could not be constantly supervised. Rather they should openly discuss their reasoning. As they put it:

> Sometimes if you say 'No, you can't watch that', they're going to watch it anyway. But if you discuss why you don't like it and you ask them to watch something else, they usually will. So I almost find it's better to discuss things.
>
> (cited in Hoover et al. 2004: 121)

This is also true for the Vogels, for whom television was about thinking ethically; not of enforcing rules but of helping children make good decisions. This related directly to the content of the television that they enjoyed, specifically the supernatural themes found in shows such as *Millennium* and *The X-Files*. The mother, Isabel, argued that these can have a positive outcome, for despite their dark and often violent themes they can teach 'positive images and life lessons'. They allowed 12-year-old Renee to ponder the depths of evil in society, 'the dark underside of human existence' as she puts it (cited in Hoover et al. 2004: 156). For the Vogels, the decision to let Renee watch 'R' rated material, alone in her bedroom, was one based on fostering openness and trust, where restrictive rules are detrimental to children's growth. As Isabel explains: 'rules don't allow a child to make decisions ... you have to learn to make decisions'. Renee was smart enough, in their opinion, and sufficiently balanced in her emotional life, that she had the self-discipline to avoid mindless sex and violence. As her mother suggests:

> Isabel: I'm always astounded when people say 'you know the influence that TV has on my children is more than I do'. I think, 'Gees, then you're not parenting right'. There's something going on with parenting if you have to really compete with the media. I think I'm teaching her to analyze it, and then that way you can't be as influenced by it. If you look at it and read it carefully.
>
> (cited in Hoover et al. 2004: 128)

In this way, like the other families detailed in this chapter, television was something to be openly talked about; it formed an essential part of the ways in which the families related to each other, and shaped how the rhythms and spaces of the home were organized.

## Competence and dominance

Of course, as we have seen in several of the examples above, the issue of social power is never far from the surface of the little everyday dramas that are enacted around the television set (Moores 2000: 144). This could involve conflicts between parents and children over what sort of programme they should be able to watch, timetabling issues, or whether they had earned the right to watch by doing chores or homework (Gauntlett and Hill 1999: 41–2). While doubtless many households with children do have strict regulations on the use of television and other media, such rules are unlikely to be strictly enforced and are open to negotiation according to the broader habitus of each household (Livingstone and Bovill 1999).

Hoover and his colleagues outline the Ahmeds' media rules with regard to this. Ostensibly they seem very strict, limiting television to one hour daily during the week and two at the weekends. There are strict divisions about when these hours may be used up. Furthermore, while two hours are given 'free', the remainder had to be earned through book reading or through completing household chores (Hoover et al. 2004: 84). However, while these rules were explicitly stated and posted on the fridge for all to see, there was much good-humoured recognition in the family that they were there to be transgressed, and that they could never be strictly enforced. Nevertheless, they stood as a constant reminder of the need to monitor the use of time spent with television, as well as the appropriateness of what should be watched, which was informed by their Islamic faith. These issues of regulation relate to the idea of social learning outlined above, as the mother Jamila explains:

> Jamila: Hasan mentioned dating. Again, what is the purpose of dating? Is it just to – just to be with each other, and eventually, eventually? Is this something, really I mean, what are your intentions and goals? What really do you want to do with this? So that's the same with TV. It's just – are we wasting our life here in front of the TV, in front of the Nintendo? Or are we really doing something? And then at the same time, very realistically, it'd be nice it would be nice if we were much more strict, but – we have leisure time too, and we're, I guess, of the lesser perfect humans! [laughter]. You know, we do just go ahead and waste time, but we try to say, let's limit it a bit.
>
> (cited in Hoover et al. 2004: 87)

As they suggest, such a relationship with television is part of their more general dispositions, an ethical relationship to the self and the other which involves the careful monitoring of their conduct (Briggs 2006, 2009). In this case it was not a fundamental prohibition, such as a ban on eating meat, but as an ethical consideration of the balance and proper use of their time, energy and resources (Hoover et al. 2004: 90).

## Gender

Of course, as critics have pointed out (e.g. Gray 1992; Morley 1986; Silverstone 1994), gender is one of the key vectors of struggle around which households are organized, and the division of labour and leisure is a fraught battleground. Television is not only deeply tied up in this, but also an indicator of wider inequities. There is some controversy in the research around this, however, where the assumption remains that men are in command of the remote control and have the right to dominate programming schedules, and perhaps even the right to watch. Morley's (1986) early research certainly suggested this, as he states in his study *Family Television*:

> Many of the women felt that to just watch television without doing anything else at the same time would be an indefensible waste of time, given their sense of domestic obligations. To watch in this way is something they rarely do, except occasionally, when alone, or with other woman friends when they have managed to construct an 'occasion' on which to watch their favourite programme, video or film.
>
> (Morley 1986: 150)

Indeed we saw this pattern quite clearly with the Daniels family above, where Mrs Daniels watched television in the kitchen while her husband retired to 'his' space in the living room. Here is a particularly striking example from a 40-year-old respondent:

> Male office worker: As far as the main TV in the lounge is concerned, I (if I am at home) seize the remote control – for my own protection. My wife and our daughter invariably know if there is a programme they want. I acquiesce in their choice until it begins to annoy me or insult me, and then I begin rapid channel-hopping until I find something less annoying to settle on. When I feel it might be safe, I switch back. If this system fails, I switch the set off. Those who wish can go and watch in another room.
>
> (cited in Gauntlett and Hill 1999: 243)

It gets worse as he goes on to proclaim that he is the 'virtually exclusive' owner of the remote control, and that he does this to assert his position as the 'unchallenged husband and father' (cited in Gauntlett and Hill 1999: 243).

Despite the unabashed chauvinism that this man displays, Gauntlett and Hill (1999) argue that we should also consider the evidence which suggests that people may wish to watch separately and that there is some pleasure in doing so. While the burden of domestic work continues to fall at women's feet, when they do get to sit down they have increasing power over their media choices. The statistics are significant here with 81 per cent of respondents reporting that viewing decisions are jointly made or that they view different sets, and only 11 per cent reporting that the male partner decides. This is not that much more than the 6 per cent of female respondents who reported that they normally get to decide what to watch (Gauntlett and Hill 1999: 240–1). Indeed, with a growing number of households now having multiple television sets, DVD devices and Internet Protocol Television (IPTV), the following accounts would seem to reflect the reality of the negotiations over what to watch, and where 'we normally watch together, but when there is a difference of choice one watches in the lounge and the other in the dining room'. Another couple reports that '[we] generally watch the same programmes so there are rarely any problems; majority decisions win if there is an argument but my brother and I have TVs in our rooms so we can watch anything there' (cited in Gauntlett and Hill 1999: 26–7). Indeed, in the case of a 21-year-old woman, there is a pleasing reversal of the domestic roles seen above:

> Every time I watch *The X-Files* I do feel guilty. Why? Because my boyfriend thinks it's weird and I think it's great and 'cos any other day around this time is usually our quality and relaxing time together. When the current season ended my boyfriend thought yes, Tuesday night will be ours again until the announcer said 'for those *X-Files* addicts who can't wait until the autumn, the first series is being shown again on BBC2 9pm Mondays'. The reason I feel so guilty is 'cos whatever we're doing at the time when my boyfriend sees *X-Files* about to start he'll tell me to bugger off upstairs and watch and he'll finish things off and 9 times out of 10 we've only just started on the sink full of pots and pans. I feel guilty afterwards too 'cos I realize that the initial guilt only lasts as long as the opening titles.
>
> (cited in Gauntlett and Hill 1999: 26–7)

The issue, as Gauntlett and Hill (1999: 244) suggest, becomes one of who gets to view on the 'main' television set. For some, as we have seen, there are benefits to be gained in marking out spaces other than the family living room as 'theirs', and that various different tactics and strategies are in play here (de Certeau 1984).

## Dailiness

In some regards arguments such as this suggest the need to generate fuller accounts of the subjective intentions and meanings behind watching television, in *why* people turn to television, with as much as with objective accounts of *who* watches *where, when* and *how* (Lembo 2000: 1–3). We have seen some of these subjectively driven intentions above. These include watching television to avoid social contact, or indeed of forging it through the pleasures of talk and companionship. This may range from pleasure and relaxation on one hand to the forceful and deliberate assertion of power and identity on the other. Scannell (1996) makes a very similar case for this experiential aspect of television use, albeit one which is focused on an examination of broadcasting's address to the viewer. Scannell's starting point in this is to account for television's *dailiness*. He argues that through this 'ontological characteristic' we will begin to understand how the media *matter* for us. This has as much to do with our experience of time as it does with the organization of domestic space. Scannell argues that we have to consider time in two ways. As everyday 'domestic' time which is experienced and lived out in its *cyclical*, repeated and rhythmic functions, and that sense of time which endures in a *linear* fashion, which stretches out before us (and perhaps behind us, in memory) over weeks, months and years (Scannell 1996: 152–3).

Television, in this dual temporality, matters. It is one of the 'utterly familiar, normal things that anyone does on any normal day'. A commonplace, as Scannell remarks, is to ask 'anything on television?' The reply might be, 'no, nothing'. This does not mean that there is literally *nothing* on, rather that there is nothing special on, 'merely the usual programmes, on the usual channels, at the usual times'. Indeed, as he argues, it does not mean that we do not watch; most of the time people watch 'nothing', or rather 'just television', ordinary, predictable, daily television which is integrated into our daily routines (Scannell 1996: 5–6).

Here is Nicola Davies again, for whom television is simply there, as part of her life-world, as a normal and expected thing she turns to. As a single parent, living alone with her young daughter, night clubs and pubs no longer hold the attraction they once did for her: 'It's too much hassle and it costs too much'. Rather, she'll have a few friends around to watch a video, to have a few beers and stay up late. While Sarah Cox's show in the radio 'wakes her up, and gets her going' on the days that she works, she'll regularly watch the soaps with her daughter. Indeed this is a regular and sought after part of their routine; simply what they do: 'Louise gets to watch Children's BBC at her grandparents, and has some cartoons on a video to watch at their house'. The media give structure to her habitual movements; this is ordinary, everyday, unremarkable, but ontologically significant, *as a way she makes herself at home*. As she puts it, 'I usually get home before *EastEnders*, so I'll watch that and have some tea' (cited in Mackay and Ivey 2004: 25).

In this way television is owned in an important ontological sense; both as a *possession* and as a *habit*. It is something that 'I' and 'we' do: its space marks the 'hub' of household life (Mackay and Ivey 2004: 32–3). This ownership, this sense of having television to hand, as part of our horizon of expectations, is emphasized starkly by the Protheroe family, who take the card for their satellite television service to their holiday home in France (Mackay and Ivey 2004: 39). Likewise, Mackay and Ivey's account of Michelle suggests this, insofar as her involvement in soap appears has become habitual, so much so that she is surprised by how central they seem to be for her 'sense of days':

> I asked Michelle if she tended to watch any programmes regularly. Initially she told me that she does not get much time to watch television. Her daughter however protested, painting a rather different picture: 'You watch *Emmerdale* and *EastEnders* and *Coronation Street* all the time'. She replies: 'Sshhhh Amy I'm talking. I do like the soaps and the kids will watch them with me, I like the news as well'.
>
> (cited in Mackay and Ivey 2004: 110)

On reflection, as she read back her research diary, Michelle was surprised as to how repetitive her lifestyle had become. Television was central to this: 'Is this really my life?' she asked. Gauntlett and Hill (1999) also found this to be an issue. Here we see a young woman who habitually turns to the television when she returns from work:

> The first thing I usually do when I get in from work is switch on the TV; this means I catch some of the *6 O'clock News*. Tonight I was home in time to catch all of it.
>
> (cited in Gauntlett and Hill 1999: 25)

Why she enjoys serendipitous encounters with new programmes as she busies herself getting supper, and watching with her brother, it is the regular, the habitual, the fixed that she really enjoys:

> At 7.30 it's *Coronation Street* time, it always has been and always will be. I've watched this programme since as long as I can remember. My whole family does. If I know I'm going to be out I ring up my mum and dad to tape it.
>
> (cited in Gauntlett and Hill 1999: 25)

Our 'sense of days', this all pervasive dailiness Scannell (1996) argues for, is shaped by the media. We simply have to ask here if time would feel different without television, radio, newspapers, and now the Internet. Would it run to a different rhythm? He thinks so: 'the effect of the temporal arrangements of radio and television is such as to pick out each day as *this* day, this day in particular, this day as its *own*, caught up in its own immediacy, with its own involvements and concerns'. As he elaborates:

> The huge investment of labour (care) that goes to produce output of

broadcasting delivers a service whose most generalizable effect is to re-temporalize time; to mark it out in particular ways, so that the time of the day (at any time) is a particular time, a time differentiated from past time-in-the day or time as yet-to-become.

(Scannell 1996: 149)

There are contentious issues here, as we will see, for the ability of broadcasters to temporalize time in such a way now, with IPTV and repeats, and the plethora of channels now available, is changing, even from when Scannell was writing. However, this doesn't negate this temporalizing effect of the media, as we see in Gauntlett and Hill's (1999) research, as well as Mackay and Ivey's (2004) research, audiences continue use the media, flexibly, in the management of their time.

Scannell (1996) for example describes how he gets up with the *Today* programme.[1] The name itself orients him to the day's tasks, its formatted structure, regular time checks, updates and weather reports, traffic 'all chime in with my concerns, the tasks that face me now, of gearing up for another day. *Today* brings me "news": what's happened since I went to bed, what's happening "now", what's coming up later in the day' (Scannell 1996: 150). Here is Mackay and Ivey's account of the Chandler and Thomas household, which captures this ontological imperative perfectly:

> I arrive to find Stuart and Ann busy rushing around before leaving for work. They always get up exactly half an hour before they had to be in work. Stuart told me that this was because they live so near, that it takes less than ten minutes to get to work, 'You know what it's like, the nearer you live to work, the more time you think you've got in bed'. Both were dressed and eating cereals in a rushed manner in the living room. BBC News 24 was on the television; neither really took much notice and continued to eat, looking up occasionally at the time shown on the screen. Ann ran upstairs to finish dressing and to brush her hair. They told me that they like to watch the early news bulletins and that there were regular summaries every fifteen minutes on the BBC. They like to know what's been going on that night, or morning: it seems to give them some sort of orientation to the day ahead. Stuart 'would normally listen to Radio Four in the kitchen, if I have time to spare and have a decent breakfast' but today he was very late.
>
> (cited in Mackay and Ivey 2004: 112–13)

As Gauntlett and Hill (1999) suggest, news in this sense is seldom taped to be watched later. It is precisely its cyclical sense of living in the immediate presence, of being 'in touch' which is important. For their respondents news was valued for the 'up-to-the-minute' feel, for its immediacy, for connecting them to a shared present: its 'nowness' as Scannell (1996) would have it. News in this sense is rarely recorded to be watched later, for to do so would destroy this sense of 'timeliness'. As this respondent puts it, 'we find it quite unrewarding to record news or current affairs programming for viewing only a few hours later. It's amazing how quickly "topicality" gets outdated' (cited in Gauntlett and Hill 1999: 56). For many, news is a structuring point to the day, a way of 'orienting' to what is ahead. Several respondents stressed how they make the turn to news as soon as they wake up, not only as a habit, but also as a way of feeling more generally 'connected'. In part, there is a sense of being part of a wider public sphere here, of knowing that others are watching at the same time, which forges a civil connection (Gauntlett and Hill 1999: 57). This unemployed man explains what it would be like without the news:

> I would have withdrawal symptoms for a start. I'm a news addict, especially for instantaneous news coverage. I would feel cut off from the world . . . I feel part of humanity by sharing a television experience with people all over the world.
>
> (cited in Gauntlett and Hill 1999: 57)

Part of this has to do with 'trust' and the personification of authority through the regular appearance of newscasters, who are experienced almost as known others, as always there, a reassuring, constant presence. Here is a 63-year-old clergyman:

> 'I would miss nearly all the BBC announcers – nearly – likewise all the ITV announcers/newscasters. I would miss Jon Snow. They seem like good-class, dignified honourable friends'. Likewise, here is a factory worker: 'the news read by Michael Burke, is about as trustworthy as broadcast news gets'.
>
> (cited in Gauntlett and Hill 1999: 60)

While there is a sense of living in a shared present for these respondents, other respondents stress the psychological aspects more strongly. They do this by emphasizing television role in providing reassurance, an ontological factor wherein in its daily ongoing nature adds stability and meaning in times of flux. In this Hill (2007) argues that television news is a relatively stable genre. It is stable not only in its mode of address and its generic conventions, but also in its place in the schedule. It is always there and punctuates the day and other programming with fixed marker points, while it also gives regular updates on what is happening in the world.

The 'stability' of news is important. While as we saw in Chapter 1, audiences vary considerably in their level of engagement and understanding of its content,

Scannell (1996) and Silverstone (1994) both point to the 'ontological' function of the genre. This adds an additional motivation for watching. Silverstone refers to this as 'ontological security', the way in which audiences have confidence 'in the continuity of their self identity and in the constancy of the surrounding social and material environments of action' (Giddens 1990, quoted in Silverstone 1994: 5). This 36-year-old woman, for example, values the assurance that the scheduled news provides as it is integrated into the daily routine: 'there's something quite nice about that ten o'clock slot, you can put your mind to rest and let go of the day' (cited in Hill 2007: 98). For others the constant presence of rolling TV news is valued:

> Female, 38: It just keeps rolling, regardless whether there's news or not. It's always there. And if you walk in the door and you go 'what's the score last night?' did anything blow up in the Middle East? you go to it, you feed off it.
>
> (cited in Hill 2007: 98–9)

This repetition is important for many viewers, and suggests an important communicative function of television news which is quite absent from the encoding/decoding model, which has no way of accounting for this form of semiotic and psychological 'investment'. Here for example a 21-year-old male artist talks about the rolling news on the 7 July London bombings as a way of, as Hill puts it, providing reassurance and anxiety in equal measure:

> 21-year-old male: The repetition of it is strange, in a way. When it happened I turned the news on and they were reporting what had happened and they were just reporting it again and again, every two minutes until there is something else. It does give you a sense of 'it's still happening', it's still happening', but it just happened once. They just keep reporting the seem news until more happens.
>
> (cited in Hill 2007: 99)

### Dailiness and the elderly

Karen Riggs (1998) offers a very interesting case study in this respect, when she considers the role that television plays in the phenomenological experience of time for elderly audiences. In this the popular detective series *Murder, She Wrote* was used in a ritualized manner. Along with other activities, such as church going, coffee mornings and meetings with friends, watching *Murder, She Wrote* allowed her respondents to recover a 'deep structure of feeling'. She describes this as a structure which is needed to maintain a sense of order to their lives, an investment in the expected, the routine, the safe and the knowable. This involves the preservation of self identity when other things, such as work, or caring for a family have disappeared. As Riggs (1998) puts it:

> For elderly people, the reassuring mystery presents a means to validate the self at a stage of life when one's identity is threatened in many ways by society as a whole. This preference for the genre is akin to the tendency for some elders to repeat their own stories, tales that measure out their lives and reward the teller with reminders of individual stability through time.
>
> (Riggs 1998: 16–17)

As Riggs makes clear, the relationship between the experience of time and age, as one draws towards the end of life, becomes more pertinent.

As we saw with Scannell's comments above, time can be experienced in two important and different ways. Both find some articulation with and through television in general, and with the narrative form of mystery drama in particular. The first, linear time, is that time which moves forwards, and is non-reversible (Scannell 1996: 152). Clearly for those in the later years of life this becomes an ontological question, which is to say a question which concerns mortality and the finite nature of existence. Routine for these elderly audiences became especially important in this regard compensating for the 'ontological rupture' and the insecurity that this provokes. In this, the relentless unfolding of linear time and its threat to the self are ameliorated by the cyclical nature of daily time, time which is marked by repetition, security and ritual. Daily time in this sense is expected, safe and known in advance. It is time which gives life structure (Scannell 1996: 152). This woman is typical of the frustration felt when the US network, CBS, moved the long-standing slot for *Murder, She Wrote*:

> Elderly woman: I'm so mad they moved her. Every Sunday night for years, I have gone through the routine feeling the *60 Minutes* is over and now here comes Jessica! It just made my week.
>
> (cited in Riggs 1998: 29)

This, as Riggs suggests, 'provided them with such an intense and faithfully anticipated reward that they were willing to restructure their sense of the ordinary to ensure the experience' (Riggs 1998: 28).

The significance of the series was not however solely centred on the scheduling and the weekly ritual of watching and talking about the show. It was also about the closed nature of the narratives themselves, which became favoured over the open-ended nature of soap operas (Riggs 1998: 24). In this her respondents enjoyed the closure that *Murder, She Wrote* offered. This Riggs suggests reflects a number of the experiences of old age: the need for resolution, the need to be strong, and the need for reassurance.

The first of these, the need for resolution, is concerned with a sense of time as finite, 'with competing life's projects, rather than with starting everything over again each day'. Rather than starting new phases of life, taking on new challenges and responsibilities, this elderly audience were 'closing off life's corridors, shedding possession, and taking the final cruise'. As Riggs (1998) puts it, they needed a different sort of ritual than the multilinear form of soap opera offers, one which was cyclical and afforded closure at the end of each episode.

> So while they continued to need ritual in their lives, the ritual of soap opera does not resonate as strongly for them. They might instead crave rituals of reassurance and resolution, the latter of which have traditionally been linked with the male mind set.
>
> (Riggs 1998: 24)

In this sense the cyclical rather than linear nature of the narrative was reassuring, articulating both with the need for closure and resolution, that the plot 'worked out clean every time'. Indeed, significantly, this links to the ritualistic and weekly nature of the scheduling. Both of which were anticipated, giving structure to their lives (Riggs 1998: 51–3).

The second point relates more to the linear nature of time, with the onset of old age, and the weakening of the body and one's memory and sense of self. In the face of this Riggs's respondents felt the need to be strong, mindfully alert and active. They wanted to be independent, both in mind and in body. They worry about being labelled as senile and take pride and pleasure in engaging with the particular form of mystery narrative: to be 'alert'. Likewise, symbolically, they are faced with challenges in life; they need to stand up against those who would manipulate them now that they are older. They need to remain dignified in the face of indignity. This resonates with the characterization of the central protagonist, Jessica. Her small victories, her dignified persona and trimness meant a lot; it carried considerable 'symbolic weight for them' (Riggs 1998: 45–6).

In addition to this Riggs found that this linear sense of time found its expression in the traditional values, the stasis, represented in *Murder, She Wrote*. This is concerned with the need to 'feel the ground beneath one's feet', of finding the right balance between the familiar, the known, and the safe, and the adventurous the new, the exciting and the challenging. As Riggs puts it, this reflects the experience of time the women felt when they looking for familiarity:

> [*Murder, She Wrote*] amplified the mutual conviction that they were not looking for surprises in form and content, only surprises in the variations

within the predictable plot structures. Mystery dramas seemed to represent a particularly homologous fit for older people, who enjoy a comfortable routine and the confirmation of long-held beliefs.

(Riggs 1998: 29)

## Domestic time and interior space

In a quite different way we see this same concern with time and dailiness with housewives, other home-workers and unemployed people, all of whom may feel guilty about watching television during the day. Here for example is Janet from Gray's (1992) study, who has quite a strong sense of self tied up with her domestic responsibilities and the allocation of cyclical time in her life. Her daily episode of the soap *Falcon Crest* helped her to structure and find meaning in her time in quite a powerful ways. For example she used it to have a well anticipated break, as well as something to work towards. She also used it to set up a clear distinction between 'work' and 'leisure' in her life, a division which is harder to maintain for home-workers whose time and roles are less structured than those whose labours are based in the workplace. The distinction, as such, helped to give discursive weight to her self-identity and phenomenological experience as a housewife:

> Janet: If I was watching television throughout the day, I think I would feel guilty . . . I mean it isn't that my husband is coming home saying . . . I don't mean that, I'd just myself feel that I was cheating. I sort of look upon it as a job, you know, it's my work really . . . like you go out to work, but this is my job, that is, just in my own mind. If I had television on all day and didn't do anything, I'd feel guilty, it may be silly I don't know, because I don't have to answer to anybody, but . . . I look upon that hour [*Falcon Crest*] as a treat . . . I can be working, and I've got that hour to look forward to, that hour, to sit down and relax and that hour's mine.

(cited in Gray 1992: 63)

In focusing on the experiential aspect of television, the respondents seen here are not simply cognitive ones who think. They are also those who have experiences: who have emotions, pleasures, desires, interests and investments. They live through routines and habits; they experience time through unarticulated and bodily inscribed expectations, ways of being, acting and responding.

By recognizing this phenomenological aspect of viewing, Lembo (2000) argues that we need to think this through with the question of 'interiority'; of thinking not only about *how* and *when* audiences turn to television, but also where they want to be. The *where* is not only an 'external' space (the living room, the kitchen, the bedroom), but also an 'internal' space (being taken out of myself, engaged, stimulated, excited, calmed, numbed). As he puts it:

> Beyond this recognition that television use exists as one of many activities, analysts face the far more difficult task of documenting the *mindful* and *emotional* qualities exhibited by viewers at different stages of their turn both to television and to other activities; and, beyond that, they must also be able to assess where it is that people end up, mindfully speaking, after they have become involved in watching television or doing other things. Are people typically feeling tired, bored, anxious, alert, relaxed or some other way when they turn to television in any given situation?
>
> (Lembo 2000: 102, my emphasis)

We can see a sharp contrast between two different experiential states quite explicitly in the following example, taken from Gray's (1992) study. In this there is a clear distinction between Rene's desire to be taken 'out of herself' and her husband Bill's need to be 'alert' and 'tuned in' to the world when watching television. These are quite different 'mindful states' in Lembo's terms:

> Rene: But of course, he likes the factual side to it and he always watched *World at War*, and erm . . . he prefers the factual things actually to fiction does Bill . . . where as I like to be taken out of myself. I mean, I do agree with him that you should see these things to know what's gone on and to understand why they happened, but God, I was a kid growing up during that, I don't want . . . I feel as if . . . I don't want the Nazis invading my sitting-room again . . . you know. I really don't. I get so depressed and I don't want Scargill shouting every five minutes either, I know it's happening, but you see he will sit here and take that all day.
>
> (cited in Gray 1992: 90–1)

Likewise, typically tired after work, some of Lembo's respondents (shift-workers who would finish work early in the morning) habitually turned to television on their return home. This served as the primary focus of their activity until they decided to go to bed. The 'mindful orientation' to television for these workers – the state of mind they wanted to be in while watching – was focused. They wished to be engrossed in the world of the text; they wanted to be satisfied with it, so it took up all of their attention. They used television in order to claim some time back from their working lives, before they finally surrendered to sleep (Lembo 2000: 127). This might have been a way of getting away from the thoughts and feelings associated with work (or putting them out of your mind), a way of stimulating their imaginations in a playful state of mind, or of having thoughts provoked in a more reflexive mode.

What Lembo's audiences revealed was that these types of response were sought after, and anticipated. It is about changing the quality of phenomeno-logical mindfulness, the interiority that makes up our unfolding subjective experience. They were 'orienting themselves to television with such ideas in mind'. In doing so 'these men are representing to themselves something of where it is they have *come from*, mindfully and emotionally speaking, and where they would like to *move to*' (Lembo 2000: 132, emphasis in original).

Purnima Mankekar (1999) demonstrates this in her account of the ritual aspects of watching *Param Veer Chakra*, a hugely popular series broadcast on India's state-run television channel, Doordarshan. Briefly put *Param Veer Chakra* told the story of members of the Indian armed forces who had been awarded the eponymous medal for bravery. The address was both personal and national, taking the audiences through the life of each soldier, their youth, and family, their military career, and finally their acts of heroism for which they deserved the medal. As Mankekar (1999) explains, while the narrative was similar to soap opera insofar as they centred on psychological conflicts, in *Param Veer Chakra* the heroes were torn between their love of their family and their love of the nation. In all cases nationalist affect prevailed over the pull of family-based emotions. This structure, and the strong nationalist sentiments it provoked, were predictable, and indeed sought after. As Mankekar (1999) explains, 'despite its predictability and dependence on formula, many viewers I worked with claimed the *Param Veer Chakra* was their current favourite'. In this 'the pleasures in the series derived precisely from watching the story unfold through twists and turns that were familiar to them' (Mankekar 1999: 262). This mindful state (the melodramatic pleasure, pathos and nationalist senti-ments stirred up by the series) however were part and parcel of the ritualistic structuring of time and space in the homes she researched. Here is Mankekar's account, which is worth reproducing at length:

In the neighbourhoods where I did my research, television sets were turned on every Sunday morning, as soon as the family awoke. For the most part, people went around their morning routines with the soundtrack forming a background to their activities. But the title music of *Param Veer Chakra* functioned as a call to viewers to come and watch. Older members of the family, children, and men of all ages would stream in as soon as the opening notes of the song flowed through their home. Typically, many women would watch as they continued their household chores, but in their case as well, the signature tune would induce a heightened state of atten-tion towards the sounds and images they would try to snatch as they went about their work. As with many signature tunes, the title music of *Param Veer Chakra* functioned both to remind viewers that the episode was about to begin and to emotionally prepare them for the narratives. As far as I could tell, on hearing the title song at the beginning of the episode, viewers would relive the pathos of the closing scenes of the previous episode and slip into a mood of tragic expectancy as they sat down to watch that morning's show.

(Mankekar 1999: 265)

## Conclusion

In this, we see, in quite profound ways, the concrete and embedded nature of the public sphere and the ways in which semiosis is generated in everyday life. Notions of decoding, of negotiation and resistive readings simply cannot catch hold of these practices of meaning making. Meanings do not only function in the modalities of ideation, of emotion, of identity work, of memory and desire, of fantasy and reverie. They also function in several experiential dimensions: they articulate with our sense of time and space, with feeling secure in routines, of knowing that our favourite television programme will be available. There is a reassurance when we turn to the news, or that soap, this drama, or that reality show: that we won't have to do anything else; that we won't be alone, that our time will be filled. In this, however, meanings and identities are articulated: a husband asserts 'his right' to watch what he wants, undisturbed. Parents scrutinize their children's viewing, they set up rules and regulations, expectations and rewards. These may be negotiable, but in doing so children must reflect upon their responsibilities: have they done enough homework, or household chores, are they making wise choices, using their time well? In other ways television becomes a resource for teaching, something to push against: look at how it represents gender, one family will say, while another ponders the depths of evil, the supernatural, life and death.

In all of this, television becomes part of household life, its routines and rhythms. Not only are these activities of watching meaningful in themselves, but also they set the context for semiosis. It is in this knot of meanings that texts become meaningful, that life is worked through, and where meanings exchanged. We have used Lull's conceptual framework in this to clarify and extend our thinking about this. Television's uses, as we have seen, are organized through five core practices or uses (communication facilitation, affiliation and avoidance, social learning, environment, competence and domination). When we talk about the public sphere, we should also, it seems, attend to its concretization in both time and space, to the rhythms, dynamics and struggles of everyday life. It is to this that we turn in the final chapter: an examination of the intersection of global, community and domestic spaces, the public sphere, and of identity. In doing so it acts as a final test of this book's methodology: of doing things with audience research.

## Note

1 A 'highbrow' current affairs programme on BBC Radio 4, *Today* is broadcast between 6 and 9 a.m.

# 5 | TELEVISION, IDENTITY AND GLOBAL AUDIENCES

No doubt, as readers of this book will know, concepts such as 'globalization', the 'public sphere' and 'imagined communities' are a central part of the discourse of cultural and media studies. They are familiar terms with which we frame our debates and go about our business. However, despite this, as Colin Sparks (2004) notes, sometimes they are used rather less carefully than they should be. It is often assumed for example that the continued consolidation of the world's global media corporations results in a homogenized public sphere, a public sphere in which the same media content is available to all those who watch. It is assumed, in some way that, this constitutes a *global* space. Whether we approach this negatively or positively, Sparks argues that there is in fact very little evidence that it exists (Sparks 2004: 145). While there is of course a staggering concentration of ownership, it would be a mistake to assume that there is a resultant homogenization of content. Most media, and certainly television, continue to be based on national markets. Satellite systems for example are not global, and are exploited on a subscription basis territory by territory (Sparks 2004: 144). Programming, be it *Big Brother France* or localized versions of MTV, are targeted at ethno-specific markets (Sinclair et al. 1996). Indeed, CNN, perhaps the pre-eminent symbol of media globalization, has little more than 4 per cent market share in the United States, and less than 0.1 per cent in the UK. In most countries throughout the world it is viewed only by American executives in their hotel rooms (Hafez 2007: 61; Sparks 2004: 144).

While we certainly need to consider the impacts of ownership on television audiences, and the resultant attenuation of nationally based public spheres (McChesney 2008), this final chapter takes a somewhat different approach. In doing so it explores the relationships between television and globalization 'from below' by considering audiences' *experiences* of transnational television (Karim 2003). Drawing on the methods and concepts developed throughout the previous four chapters, this final chapter will consider broadly ethical questions about the television practices of migrant, diasporic and exiled audiences, who for one reason or another find themselves *between cultures*, making choices between watching the television of their country of origin, or that of the host country (Naficy 1993).

These are broadly ethical questions in two senses. First, they explore the provision of a public sphere, the circulation of discourses, representations and images with which audiences 'work through' questions of identity and their place in the world. The final case study for example will explore migrant audiences' use of news discourse following the 11 September attacks on New York. In these terms Stuart Cunningham (2001) argues that what we see here is less of a common public sphere, and more multiple public spheres. These overlap and interact as ethno-specific audiences move between different national spaces, community affiliations and ethnic identifications. Drawing on the idea of a shifting and mercurial form, he refers to these as public 'sphericules'. These at once undermine assumptions about television, which imagine a single and common public sphere (Scannell 1996). Instead it points to forms of citizenship which exist alongside a nationally based civil society. These are 'do-it-yourself' forms which are based on 'culture, identity, and voluntary belonging rather than based on rights derived from, and obligations to, a state' (Cunningham 2001: 134). To explore the public sphere, in these terms, is to look at those whose '*civitas* connects communities in dozens of countries while also embracing their situatedness in a given one' (Sinclair and Cunningham 2000: 28).

This at once raises the second ethical issue, for questions of identity become acutely foregrounded in this flux. In these terms the chapter also explores the ways in which audiences use the competing discourse and representations of different television systems to reflect upon who they are, and on what they should be. Such an ethical address is traversed by the vectors of generation, gender and ethnicity. These practices of 'working through' are always concrete however. They are organized through the practices of everyday life, whether it be subscribing to Turkish news channels and watching them in community based groups, or Indian families gathering together at home to watch *Neighbours* (Bird 2003). By investigating these practices this chapter explores the intersection of multiple spaces, most saliently of *domestic space* in which identity is played out in the negotiations between parents and their children. These are important for parents and their children will have very different investments in and experiences of the host country. These experiences are also deeply rooted in *community space*. In this, television acts as a mediator, and a common reference point for public discourse between those who share similar 'roots' (home) and 'routes' (journey and resettlement) (Georgiou 2006: 60). Finally this is embedded in *global space*, in the relationship between here and there, the past and the present, and also perhaps, of an imagined future. In these terms this chapter explores the intersection of television, identity, and the concrete spaces of the public sphere.

## Imagined communities: nostalgia and self-reflexivity

Asu Askoy and Kevin Robins' (2000) research offers a very useful way into these debates when they critique of the notion of an imagined community (Anderson 1983). It is particularly useful as they question the overly simplistic idea that migrant television audiences have a singular and untroubled relationship with their countries of origin (or indeed, that anybody could identify absolutely and unproblematically with a singular and uncontested imagined community). It is often assumed for example that transnational television simply reaffirms migrants' sense of belonging to the 'homeland' at the expense of their assimilation into the host country (Askoy and Robins 2000: 345). Such essentialism ignores the contingent and shifting nature of identity. It does so as it fails to account for the experiences and ambivalences which occur when television audiences 'think across spaces'. As they argue:

> What they are experiencing is never straightforwardly and unproblematic-ally the sense of being 'at home' or of 'keeping in touch with their roots'. And if we think carefully about what they are actually experiencing – how they are in fact using television – we believe it becomes difficult to sustain the rather simplistic notion that transnational television consumption could every simply, and unproblematically, be about extending an 'imagined community'.
>
> (Askoy and Robins 2000: 356)

These experiences are exemplified by the Turkish audiences that Askoy and Robins studied. Not only did the respondents enter into a complex negotiation with the European societies in which they now lived, but also they had to think through their relationship with the different versions of 'Turkishness' that are articulated in transnational television. On the one hand, the state broadcaster in Turkey, TRT, promotes a state sanctioned and official version of Turkishness. While rooted in a national past, it is more mythical than real, and remains aloof from the everyday cultures of its audience.

On the other hand, these audiences can watch the new commercial broadcasters, which were available following a period of technological expansion and liberalization in the 1990s. These channels presented alternative versions of

Turkey in which previously unacceptable taboos were suddenly represented. As Askoy and Robins explain, official 'untouchables' who had been censored and rendered invisible by the previous state monopoly of television, such as members of religious sects, ethnic groups such as the Kurds and Alevis, woman with headscarves, radical feminists, transvestites and homosexuals, were now highly visible on current affairs debates, talk shows and other forms of entertainment programming (Askoy and Robins 2000: 353).

In this expanded discursive environment, diasporic Turkish audiences have several choices to make. They no longer simply have to choose between watching the television of the new host country or transitional television. They also have to choose between watching commercial or state run Turkish television. This, they suggest, produces a process of reflexivity in which the choices, the investments and identifications that audiences make are brought under a self-scrutinizing gaze. In this ethicalization of existence (Rose 1999) painful and difficult questions of identity are worked through. As Askoy and Robins (2000) argue:

> Identities are no longer fixed – they are thought about, changed, abandoned and reclaimed. What is different and distinctive about the migrant experience of television culture – and what would be instructive for cultural critics in the host societies, if they could only grasp this other kind of cultural experience – is precisely the experience of *thinking across spaces*, with all the possibilities that this then opens up for thinking beyond the small world of imagined communities.
>
> (Askoy and Robins 2000: 358)

As we have seen in previous chapters, such an ethical project functions in various modalities of response. These are characterized by a movement between closeness and distance, between emotional identification, fantasy and nostalgia on one hand, and scrutiny, questioning and dialogue on the other. The former 'modality of fantasy' as Askoy and Robins (2000) put it, works when television viewers seek out idealized images of stability and coherence. These portray an eternal and essentialized version of Turkey.

An idealized version of another time is seen here as this respondent talks of his heartfelt desire to return to the Turkey of his youth, a fantasy which is 'longed for, desired and missed'. Old films on Turkish television, he suggests, 'take me back to Turkey':

> Turkish male: I sometimes ask myself 'what does a person outside his country miss the most?' We go out for picnics occasionally – if you can call it a picnic, since we can't find trees to sit under and we can't start our grill. It's at these moments that I start thinking about our meadows back home,

our pine trees, our water. I'm from the Black Sea region and I remember our cool waterfalls, our sea. I wish my children could see the plateaux, the summer feasts, and learn about our customs and traditions . . . I wish these were on Turkish television.

(cited in Askoy and Robins 2000: 359)

Another female respondent acknowledges not only this nostalgic yearning, but also the idealized fantasy that it produces, a 'rose tinted world' as she puts it, which bares little relationship to the Turkey she now sees on her television. It is possible, she says, 'to become lost in dreams and imaginings . . . it gives you a very sweet sense' (cited in Askoy and Robins 2000: 359). For the following viewer it was the sound of traditional Turkish folk music that was so appealing:

Cypriot respondent: When I listen to the regional tunes I am absorbed, lost in my old days. I wish the other channels would reflect our culture. Then everyone would be happy . . . I sit for hours watching, absorbed in my dreams.

(cited in Askoy and Robins 2000: 359)

In these three responses we see a nostalgic yearning. This has as much to do with *temporality*, of a return to a lost time, as a return to an imaginary *space*. In the following responses, however, we see a much more grounded relationship with present day Cyprus, a synchronization between the mediated space of the homeland and the 'banality of the here and now' (Askoy and Robins 2000: 352). This Cypriot for example explains that television brings the real, everyday reality of home closer. It 'gives you more freedom':

Cypriot respondent: You don't feel so far away, because it's only six foot away you don't feel so far away from it. Cyprus is like one switch of a button away, or Turkey even, mainland Turkey, you are there, aren't you?

(cited in Askoy and Robins 2003: 94–5)

Indeed television in this sense forms part of a complete semiotic space. It is used in James Lull's (1980) environmental function to create a Turkish environment at home, one which is replete with the signifiers of 'Turkishness' (Barthes 1972). For this respondent, 'it's almost as if we're living in Turkey, as if nothing has really changed for us'. For another, 'when you're at home, you feel as if you are in Turkey. Our homes are already decorated Turkish style, everything about me is Turkish, and when I'm watching television too' (cited in Askoy and Robins 2003: 94–5).

## Thinking across spaces: demythologization

There is certainly a sense in which these audiences are living in dual spaces, and using Turkish television to create a comfortable and familiar semiotic environment. However, Askoy and Robins (2003) see something else in this as well, a tension which disrupts a false polarizing logic of living in the 'here and now' or of becoming immersed in a 'nostalgic longing for home'. As they put it:

> What we regard as significant about transnational television is that, as a consequence of bringing the mundane, everyday reality of Turkey 'closer', is its undermining of this false logic. The 'here and now' reality of Turkish media culture disrupts the imagination of the 'there and then' Turkey. Turkey – thereby working against the romance of diaspora-as-exile, against the false identification of the 'homeland'. We might say, then, that transnational Turkish television is an agent of cultural demythologization.
>
> (Askoy and Robins 2003: 95)

This demythologization is explained with clarity by the following respondent. In it we see the tension between the nostalgia of a mythological and idealized Turkey of the past, one which is frozen in memory at the point of departure (Georgiou 2006: 86–9), and its disruption or demythologization by television's mediation of present cultural realities:

> Turkish respondent: In many ways you become frozen in your understanding of where your community is. The longer you are here the more you are likely to have views and attitudes which are more conservative and out of date. I've seen people my age and even younger, expecting things of their children that they have rebelled against . . . I wish that they would watch more Turkish television. Some of their attitudes are far behind what the messages are. You turn on Turkish television, and some of it is refreshingly modern. It's quite normal to watch people having affairs, or who are having relationships, who aren't married. You never would have had that twenty years ago. But some of the mindset is relating to that. The first time a girl is having a relationship is when they get married – you see that with second-generation people. They don't get that from satellite. They get that from their parents.
>
> (cited in Askoy and Robins 2003: 96)

This demythologization can be thought of as a distancing which causes audiences to reflect upon their own pleasures, investments and identities. While it may be provoked by drama and other non-factual forms, it is accentuated by other factual genres, such as news, documentary and current affairs programming. As these respondents from Myria Georgiou's (2006) research put it, 'there's too much violence on Turkish television, there's nothing good about the Turkish channels, only stress'. Another complains that 'as you sit down to eat your food with your family you are watching television, and you are seeing a young girl covered in blood. The news brings demoralizing stories'. Likewise, this Greek Cypriot complains about the change in values which challenges the ideological closure ensconced in her mythical and frozen version of Cyprus. She tells of her shame, and her impulse to cover her icon of the Virgin Mary, so she will not have to face the obscenities depicted on her television: 'What has Cyprus turned into?' she asks, 'and Greece as well . . . so much immorality, so much nudity, so much blasphemy' (cited in Georgiou 2006: 86–9).

Such a process of distantiation and identification is driven by strong feelings of ambivalence, discomfort and frustration. However, it is not driven by television alone. Quite paradoxically, those who had the most contact with the country of origin, whether through mediated or physical contact, were those who felt most estranged and dislocated from it. For this long-time resident of Australia, home is firmly rooted in his present geographical space, so much so that dreams and concrete plans of returning to the homeland have been abandoned:

> Turkish Australian respondent: Our place is here now. We wanted to go back and settle in Turkey for many years; we still talk about it with my husband but we don't fit there any more. The Turkey we left when we came here is long gone. I sometimes cry when we watch Turkish television. All those years I thought that once the time came we would buy a house and settle back in our village but we know now that it is not possible. Our Turkey was much more beautiful than the one we see on television today.
>
> (cited in Karanfil 2007: 65)

Rather than affirming their sense of belonging to the country of origin, watching television news brought home the realities of everyday life. Through this, cultural change was recognized along with truths about Turkey that had previously, when viewed from the inside, seemed impossible. Becoming synchronized with Turkish reality therefore did not result in a simple affirmation of identity. Rather it was an experience of dislocation. In this, respondents found themselves in an very unsettling position, 'to become removed, and even alienated, from the thing that they thought was theirs' (Askoy and Robins 2000: 361).

In this we see the ways in which identity is something that is lived, something that has an experiential dimension, something that is 'felt' as much as it is something that is constructed by discourses and symbols of nationhood:

> The crucial point is that individuals are endowed with the capacity for both emotions (feelings, moods) and thought (reflecting, comparing,

interpreting, judging, and so on). We should be concerned, then, with their minds and sensibilities, and not their cultures and identities – with how they think, rather than how they belong.

(Askoy and Robins 2003: 94)

## Dailiness and the public sphere

These experiences suggest some of the ways in which television's role as an organizer of a public sphere (or, indeed, of multiple public spheres) works less in an abstract space as it is quite often employed in academic arguments, and much more in the daily practices of ritual and experience. These are firmly rooted in domestic and community spaces. John Sinclair and his colleagues usefully point to the significance of transnational news in these terms. Its liveness, its fixed point in the schedules, and its temporality signifies 'what is going on, rather than what has been, what marks the particularity of this day' (Sinclair et al. 2001: 52–3). Their research in Australia found that Chinese diasporic viewers had a strong sense of investment in transnational news from China. They would receive the previous evening's news broadcasts the following morning. In this there was a complex negotiation of identity: a 'double imaginary of time, a sense of being in two temporalities: here and there, then and now'. One respondent found pleasure in her knowledge that what she viewed was being screened close to real time in Taiwan, and that this was the same bulletin that she used to watch with her father over lunch (Sinclair et al. 2001: 52–3). Indeed, Yu Shi (2005) suggests the ways in which Chinese audiences in Australia use television and other media as common reference points. Keeping up with Chinese news, with its near synchronized transmission, was an important resource in 'keeping alive old communal ties and uniting a dispersed population into an imagined transnational community' (Shi 2005: 66). This is one way in which they maintain close links with friends, colleagues and relatives back home.

Responses such as these suggest this effortless availability and meaningfulness of transnational television news, as well as a synchronization of lives and identifications across global space. However, Askoy and Robins make the important point that for some travelling audiences, who experience feelings of ambivalence, this address simply breaks down. As we saw in Chapter 4, in Paddy Scannell's (1996) terms, television works by orienting its viewers to the day to come, to current time, and of course, to a common space. This is both a national space and a 'shareable, accessible, available public world'. It creates a 'horizon of expectations, a mood of anticipation, a directness towards that which is to come, thereby giving substance and structure (a "texture of relevancies") to everyday life' (Scannell 1996: 55).

This care structure, television's communicative ethos, is precisely that which breaks down for some diasporic audiences. In this transnational television carries the risk of failure; it risks not 'working' properly, when its address (its care structures) are oriented not to those living overseas, but to the indigenous national audience for whom it was initially intended. In these terms it becomes disconnected from everyday life. Askoy and Robins (2003) argue that this has important consequences for how we theorize the relationship between television and global space:

Transnational broadcasting is not about magically transporting migrant viewers back to a distant homeland. It is about broadcasting services being diverted to them in a new location – in the case of the Turks we have been discussing it is London. What this means is that the world of broadcasting *is not seamlessly connected to the world of the street outside*, as it would be for those watching in Turkey. Migrant viewers cannot move routinely between media space and the 'outside' space of everyday Turkish reality. And since so much of what television is about has to do with connecting viewers to the life and rhythms of the real world of the nation, there are bound to be difficulties with the disconnected type of viewing that migrancy enforces (Askoy and Robins 2003: 102).

However, it is the embedded nature of this 'thinking between spaces' that we will now turn to, for it does serve to problematize Askoy and Robins' position. It does so, for not only is transnational television reception located in domestic space, but also it is firmly rooted in community space. The public sphere, in these terms, is deeply materialized in the spaces, practices and relationships of everyday life. This will allow us to further address the tensions and contradictions identified above. We will see the ways in which transnational television reception, when located in the larger community, re-establishes its links to common culture, common discourse, and audiences' orientation to their daily realities: when its care structures *do work*.

## Public sphericules and community spaces

What we see in the examples used in this chapter, as Cunningham (2001) argues, is perhaps not so much a singular public sphere, and certainly not a common global public sphere, but rather multiple public spheres, or 'sphericules', as he calls them. These are neither local nor global, but much rather dispersed across spaces, where affiliations are made between groups with common interests and identifications. As he explains, they 'provide a central site for public communication in globally dispersed communities, stage communal difference and discord productively and work to articulate insider ethno-specific identities'.

The media-centric spherical therefore becomes a space for the 'staging of difference and dissension in ways that the community itself can manage' (Cunningham 2001: 134–8).

Georgiou (2006) makes the important point in this regard that migrants tend to live in proximity to each other, and that these hybrid communities are important points of common identification. In these spaces the practices and signifiers of 'ethnicity' are circulated, exchanged, worked over and transformed. Television and other media are an important part in this. Migrant groups use television communally, in a community centre for example, or at a neighbour's house. In this they use television to negotiate the boundaries of community and to make television 'compatible with their everyday lives and their positioning in the local, the urban and the transnational space' (Georgiou 2006: 20–3).

In this, as we saw in Chapter 4, generational differences are especially pronounced. Parents and their children will have quite different relationships with the country of origin. Parents, Georgiou found, were not above enforcing the choice of Greek television on the main set (in the living room perhaps, or in a large kitchen) while younger generations would watch UK or US programming in the private spaces of their bedrooms. However, enforced communal viewing, as family time, was often observed for an hour or so in the evenings. Indeed, the children of some families would be regularly exposed to Greek television when they were cared for after school by grandparents (Georgiou 2006: 92–3). Throughout this there is a complex negotiation over the uses of space, identity, age and authority, which recalls Lull's (1980) functions of social learning, affiliation, avoidance and regulation:

> The coexistence and negotiation that takes place around viewing and around familial relationships creates some interesting dynamics. The children improve their Greek, which is the outcome of the close relationship with their grandparents and of their satellite television. The grandfather familiarizes himself with the British culture, even when he doesn't want to and doesn't understand it. His grandchildren interpret the language and the cultural codes when they watch together British soap operas. This space of cultural and intergenerational exchange reflects the hybridity of the diaspora. In the everyday interplay mediated by the relations of love, the members of this extended family develop their multiple connections to close and distant, diasporic and mainstream cultural hubs.
>
> (Georgiou 2006: 93)

Indeed, this generational negotiation works across multiple forms of identification and pleasure, for despite their professed dislike for Greek television, the younger audiences were respectful of its place in the community, and in the lives of their families. While younger audiences would often profess to shun Hellenic television, they would on occasion make playful investments in it, as one of Georgiou's respondents puts it:

> Greek teenager: People my age are forced to watch Greek TV, to listen to the radio [Greek radio stations]. But then, they end up liking them. For example, some funny programmes like *Kafenion*, we all get together on Friday night and watch it. We can relate to it. It's like having your parents on TV. It's the kind of stereotype of them, but it's funny!
>
> (cited in Georgiou 2006: 94)

While there is a clear reflexivity about identity in this, a negotiation between Greekness and hybrid identities and futures, in other community spaces the common identification with Greek ethnicity is more pronounced and less negotiable. Watching transnational television in a local community centre, for example, was a common social experience for the older generation of men (woman being excluded from this public sphere). This viewing took on a ritualistic quality, fitting into the wider use of time and space. When the Cypriot news was broadcast, for example, the chatting, joking and conversation which was characteristic of other viewing would stop, and there would be solemn attention to the bulletin. Once over, this, and the other material viewed, would become the focus of talk, discussion, debate and argument (Georgiou 2006: 110–11).

The relationship to Cyprus found in this viewing however is marked by the tensions and ambiguities that we explored above. On the one hand, communal watching renewed their traditional images of Cyprus, as well as their identifications with the community and the 'homeland'. On the other hand, it worked as a demythologizing process, as the men worked through their condemnation of contemporary values and morals in Cyprus (Georgiou 2006: 110–11). Nevertheless, the care structures here, and the relevance of Greek television, became pronounced. It was a shared resource, a common reference point, which through community and domestic affiliation, addressed their contemporary, if hybrid, reality.

Aswin Punathambekar (2005) makes a similar point, exploring the ways in which television screenings of Hindi film are used to imagine and work through contested values and identities. As she puts it, 'Hindi film narratives, viewing practices, and patterns of socialization in the American-Indian diaspora intersect to create a discursive realm of consensus regarding notions of "Indianness" ' (Punathambekar 2005: 152). Bollywood film in this regard is especially important as it is specifically addresses the diasporic audience, addressing them as part of the 'great family of India' as they move around the globe 'with India in their hearts' (Punathambekar 2005: 153).

As we examined above, however, it is insufficient to simply pose this as an abstract question of identity construction as if these identifications were not generated and sustained through domestic and community practices and relations. Punathambekar (2005), for example, explains how community screenings of Hindi films became popular during the 1960s, 1970s and 1980s, a time before the availability of videos, DVDs and satellite television. It was not uncommon for enterprising Indians living in the United States, Canada and the UK to rent 16mm or 35mm Hindi films to screen in community centres. This was a chance for the diasporic community to come together, to wear traditional clothes, speak in Hindi or other regional languages and generally participate in cultures and rituals of 'home'. As one such organizer put it:

> Preeti: We used to inform people by post. They used to come, buy tickets, get samosas and a cup of chai, coke for the kids and chitchat with their friends, exchange news, gossip, everyday things, you know that one starts missing when one is away from home. I remember, even when there were snowstorms, people would come and say, we wait the whole week to watch a Hindi film, don't cancel it.
>
> (cited in Punathambekar 2005: 154)

This activity, in which the films and customs 'resonated with their emotions, nostalgic longing and cultural values' was quite predictably privatized with the advent of videos in the 1980s, and then transnational satellite broadcasting throughout the 1990s. The former was sustained through a network of Asian grocery stores, which also served as points of contact where news of 'home' could be gathered. In a context of greater integration into the host society, as well as constraints of time and the ability to travel back to India, these televised films acted as a key point of emotional identification, and a chance to participate in the storytelling rituals so important in Indian culture. As Vinod and Mythili explain:

> Vinod: You've grown up watching the movies and you *continue*, that's all. You like the songs, you listen to them here also. You enjoy particular kind of drama . . . you see crowded streets, keeps you in touch with the way of life in India.
>
> Mythili: It doesn't matter what the story is like, I like to see the dresses, the Salwar designs, everyday life, even if it seems like a fantasy, you know.
>
> Vinod: And, you see, you want to keep that link with India even if you don't live there. Even though you've lived outside for many years, it's where you are from, isn't it?
>
> (cited in Punathambekar 2005: 155)

## Identity and the care of the self

It is significant that such identifications are rooted in the everyday spaces of home and the community. This, as Marie Gillespie's (2002) research has also indicated, is often a gendered practice, where women bear the burden of cultural transmission, of translating the films, and of interpreting them so that their children can understand 'all the Indian customs and traditions' (Punathambekar 2005: 159). Particularly pertinent to the socialization of girls is the question of sexuality and marriage, where western sexual practices were seen by many of Punathambekar's respondents as evidence of debauchery. These were contrasted with what was felt to be the 'traditional' and morally superior values of 'Indianness' found in Hindi films. In this, Bollywood films were viewed at home on television to produce a 'talking space' (Gillespie 2002: 184) in which sharply contrasting generational relationships with 'home' could be worked through:

Mythili:    You see the western community is very different from our culture. Like respect for parents and elders, how to behave, basic things, and when children go to school and make friends, you don't know the families that those children come from, what problems they may have. So your child will get influenced by all that.

Vinod:    With Hindi movies, there is no question of influence. But they portray nice moral values like . . . *Kabhi Khushi Kabhie Gham* we can get lessons for life from it.

Mythili:    We have to make sure our children do not get too much into this culture. Things like that happen here, and there are parents who are very orthodox and will not accept their children making their own choices, But we talk to our daughter and work out things.

Vinod:    But, you see, things have changed in India also. Like our niece in Bombay, she is very modern. So we have to change with the times, but we should hold on to some values. I think parents everywhere have such concerns and if they are not aware from the beginning, they pay the price in the end.

(cited in Punathambekar 2005: 159–60)

This is an ethical space (or a sphericule). Not only does it concern itself with cultural transmission and the rehearsal of values, but also it is a space of self-reflection. In this, audiences' reactions to the films and to 'India' can be turned inwards. As Punathambekar puts it, this rehearsal is 'accompanied by a gradual reworking of ideas and values concerning institutions such as marriage and, in the process, the questioning of India's status as the sole arbiter of "Indianness" ' (Punathambekar 2005: 161).

Such an ethical project is seen with clarity in Gillespie's (1999) research, which offers a very evocative account of the way in which television is used by the Punjabi community in London's Southall district. While the films themselves are important, she reports that the ritual act of coming together as a family for communal viewing took precedence over the meanings of the text themselves. The discussions prompted by these films, and the act of watching them in family settings contributed to the ongoing negotiation of cultural identity. It reflects, as she puts it, the characteristic cultural role of women as 'carriers of culture and tradition within the family' (Gillespie 1999: 79–80). Typically the older generations of the household would produce conservative readings of the films. These supported notions of tradition. Parents, grandparents, uncles and aunts would articulate such a discourse in discussion of the film, often against the resistance of younger generations, who would embrace discourses of change and modernity. This dialogue and discussion was one of the essential pleasures of the viewing, which was strongly marked along gender lines, boys feeling that viewing was more enforced, but at the same time valuing the act of communal viewing and of 'being together' (Gillespie 1999: 81).

It is also significant that there are multiple sphericules (Cunningham 2001) within the same household, and that these are transected by generational affiliations. In this, Gillespie (1999) found a marked distinction between the ways in which Asian films were viewed by families, and the ways in which western films and television tended to be watched by children without their parents. The parents and grandparents would often disapprove of depictions of sexuality and their moral values for example. In this we see 'an assertive circumvention of parental control and a rejection of their preferences' (Gillespie 1999: 95). These practices (of social learning, regulation, communication facilitation, affiliation and avoidance) are particularly marked in the ways in which mothers would watch western and 'sacred' soap operas with their children. Some mothers would condone their children's viewing of *Neighbours* and other soap operas as it served to regulate time and space (they knew what their children were doing and that they were safe and keeping out of trouble). For several mothers they also served as a welcome break from the domestic tasks. In this they would watch with children as a 'pretext for intimacy and conversation'. As Gillespie (1999) puts it:

Intimacy may be heightened by the act of sharing experiences regardless of what is shared. Given that some of the mothers understand and speak very little English, it may be the relaxed atmosphere of the viewing situation and the desire to be together, rather than the soap itself, which is appreciated.

(Gillespie 1999: 96)

However, such viewing could also serve the didactic purposes of social learning, competence and domination. This was one way in which the mothers showed that they cared for their children, insofar as they wanted to protect them by discussing the characters' morals, values and motivations. This was experienced differently by different participants. Some felt that *Neighbours* 'doesn't really relate to our lives 'cos it shows us things we are not allowed to do, like all the teenage romance'. Others found such discussion and moral teaching intrusive:

> Teenager: I don't really like watching *Neighbours* with my mum 'cos you might start off OK but as soon as she sees something she doesn't like she's off . . . she'll start on you – don't do this and do that and I'll start arguing with her . . . and we might not end up speaking for three days over something that is really quite trivial.
>
> (cited in Gillespie 1999: 96)

This question of identity, the interplay between television from 'here' and from the parental 'homeland' and the embedding of semiosis in domestic spaces and relationships are vividly depicted in all of its tensions in Meenakshi Gigi Durham's (2004) research. In this she argues that young people not only have to negotiate different cultures, but also have to navigate their journey through adolescence into adulthood. This means working through complicated changes in who one is, and how one is expected to behave. As Durham (2004) puts it:

> 'Adolescence' and 'diaspora' are terms that both invoke the metaphor of a journey: issues of border crossing, dislocations, time/space passages, and reorientation frame our understandings of both constructs. Adolescence struggles with identity can be compared with the identity questions experienced by transnational immigrants: in the liminal spaces between childhood and adulthood, or between one geopolitical state and another, the 'who am I?' question becomes imperative. The process of constructing a self that will bridge the gaps is the defining goal of these crucial life moments.
>
> (Durham 2004: 140)

Durham's research participants were all US citizens, born of first generation immigrants of South Asian Indian descent. They were all female, between the ages of 13 and 15 years old. In this, as Durham (2004) suggests, the girls were positioned between different cultures: the parental and US culture on the one hand, and the cultures of adulthood and childhood on the other. They all reported tensions over their degree of social freedom and sexual identity. All had been forbidden to attend the ritual 'rite of passage' of attending their school's senior prom, while they were not allowed to wear current teen fashions such as tank-tops and short skirts. For the girls it is clear that they thought that their parents' views had been formed less through first hand knowledge of their cultures, and more through the depiction of teen life in the media. These then, as we have seen previously, shaped their parents' interpretative repertoires:

Ria:    In every single teen flick . . . in every single one it's like there's a girl and a guy and they fall in love and they like do all this crazy stuff and most of the time it's stereotypical. . . . High school is nothing like in the movies! I don't really know, I think my parents might understand that now, but like . . . the way that people are portrayed in the movies there's always like the hot cheerleader and the hot football player and there's these segregated groups on there and school isn't really like that . . .

Malini:    My parents, I think they still have stereotypes about drugs and stuff like that.

Divya:    Like Malini said, they believe these dumb stereotypes about the drugs and the drinking and the sex and like all this stuff about 'just say no' or whatever and about having all these . . . I've never been asked so I've never had to say no!

(cited in Durham 2004: 15)

Whatever their parents think, the girls' use of television displays a much more complicated relationship between ethnicity and sexual identity. While they regularly watched the sitcom *Friends*, for example, and participated in the fan culture which surrounded the series at school, they were nonetheless very critical viewers, moving between closeness and enjoyment, and a more distancing scrutiny:

Ria:    On *Friends* they're always sleeping with different guys and hopefully I'll never ever do that. I don't want to use it as an example of what a relationship should be.

Divya:    We own DVDs of *Friends* . . . my parents are worried about it. They think, if they see me watching *Friends*, oh my God, she's watching this and she'll think these are role models and she's going to do all these things . . . but it's like no.

(cited in Durham 2004: 152)

While they enjoyed such television series, much of this was in terms of the gossip and friendships that it sustained in school with their non-Indian peers. Indeed, this was rather a matter of communication facilitation (Lull 1980) as their peers had little common ground with the girls' preferred media of Hindi films (Durham 2004: 152). As Durham suggests, the girls oriented to these films in culturally specific ways, seeing them as 'fantastic' rather than realistic portrayals of Indian culture, one which nevertheless made them feel like members of the Indian community:

| | |
|---|---|
| Researcher: | Do you watch the movies, too, that the songs are from? |
| Girls: | Yeah. |
| Lekha: | All of our . . . like mom's friends with all these Indian people . . . like they'll all get Indian movies and we share them. |
| Researcher: | Do you get together and watch them? |
| Girls: | Yeah, we do. |
| Divya: | I love Indian movies. |
| Ria: | The movies give you something to talk about with other Indian people, I guess. They can make us feel more like part of an Indian community, the way *Bal Vihar* does too. |
| Rita: | If there's a film like playing in town, I'll go and see it before I go and see anything else. It's like they're about us. |
| Malini: | Those kinds of movies aren't more real than the others . . . I mean, I know they're exaggerations, too, but they are familiar situations. |
| Ria: | They're sort of inside jokes. We get them. |

(cited in Durham 2004: 154)

In many ways, as they did so, they were transported across global space, albeit one which was rooted in their local networks. As children of Indian parents, born in the United States, they identified themselves neither as American, nor as Indian in any straightforward way. In this their sense of 'Indianness' was somewhat different from their parents'. Questions of sexuality most clearly demarcated the lines between themselves and their parents. In this regard Durham (2004) argues that television was a key resource in their articulation of this difference:

> The girls in this study saw both Indian and American popular culture as marking the boundaries of those two worlds, neither of which they claimed to be their milieu. Rather than attempting to find a place in both cultural sphere, they recognized the need to assert a new identity position that, in a sense rejected the options offered by both Indian as well as American media texts. As consumers, therefore, their textual readings involved a radical questioning of the sexual mores instantiated by the television shows, films and popular music they consumed.
>
> (Durham 2004: 155)

Rita and Malini for example talked about their relationship to films such as *Bend It Like Beckham* and *Mississippi Masala*. These resonated with the tensions they had in their own relationships with their parents, such as their own expectations of having a 'western marriage', or of their growing desire for freedom and independence. Indeed, as Durham (2004) argues, this diasporic media (whether the films were watched on television through DVD and satellite, or in cinemas) opened up a space of negotiation with their parents as they worked through their themes of inter-ethnic love, romance and cultural difference. Such themes of hybridity are precisely those which the girls face in their everyday lives, an 'interlacing of the global and the local' as she puts it. Television opens up a discursive space from which they can interrogate the 'fusions, material and symbolic collisions' of this new global space: 'a cultural form', as Durham puts it, in which 'the seemingly irreconcilable differences between cultures are articulated and worked out' (Durham 2004: 156).

## News, semiosis and global space

In this last section we will continue to explore these questions of identity and look at the relationship between news discourse and everyday life, the latter which is played out in the intersection of global, community and domestic spaces. We will do so to explore the ways in which the discourses of television news are drawn into semiosis within particularly complex identifications, experiences and perspectives. Our case study in this regard will be to consider diasporic television audiences' relationships with the news reporting of the 11 September attacks. As I have emphasized throughout this chapter, for migrant or diasporic audiences, television news is encountered in complexly embedded contexts: at the meeting points not only of different global news discourses, but also of the imaginative spaces of identity, homeland, memory, nostalgia and desire, and their articulation in the interpersonal and material spaces of the home and the wider community. In this, then, we see a movement, as Dina Matar (2006) puts it, between 'complex social, familial and political activity' in which texts are drawn into semiosis. This operates through several different modalities of response:

> People's talk of news shifts from the discussion of any news story, to representations of that story, to the realities of their own lives. Thus it plays a significant role in processes of collective identity formation as well as providing a context and resource for people's experimentation with private and group definitions.

> (Matar 2006: 1038)

As we saw above, audiences for transnational news make meaning through a complex discursive framework. This includes a range of national and transnational media, from the BBC in the UK, CNN from the United States and

Al-Jazeera and Al-Manar from the Arab world, to email, websites, Arabic-language newspapers and radio. Indeed, as Matar points out, these audiences have a heightened awareness of different perspectives which allow them to think and challenge the dominant discourses of the western news media (Matar 2006: 1031). She reports for example that her Palestinian respondents often refer to themselves as 'news junkies'. A common conversational opening is 'Have you heard the latest?' News discourse is both a common reference point in the wider community, and part of the semiotic environment at home. As these two respondents put it:

Palestinian woman, early 30s:    If I don't listen to the news or feel what is going on in the world, I feel there is something missing, particularly what is happening in our homeland.

Palestinian woman, late 60s:    The television is on all the time. If there is something important on the news, then I turn the volume up. Otherwise I turn it down while doing the housework. If I am out of the house, or if I have visitors, I record the news on Al-Jazeera. I record everything. Even though things have happened, I still watch the news when I get back home. I do not go out of the house often. Do you believe this? I have to watch the news. I have a friend who is like me. She always follows the news and calls me when something happens. Also, she would turn on Al-Jazeera if I am watching another channel and then we compare the news.

(cited in Matar 2006: 1036)

For these respondents, television news is not simply a form of cultural synchronization in which they keep up with events in Palestine, it is also practice through which identity is maintained across the private spaces of family life and the collective spaces of community. Here for example is a 60-year-old woman, of Muslim faith. Forced to live in exile, she fled Palestine for London more than 20 years ago:

Palestinian female: I watch the news and live with the story. I live with it. I imagine myself there and feel as if they [the Israelis] have hit me, killed me. Those children are like my children. I am always there [in Palestine]. I start to cry. This little girl was martyred at Mohammed al-Durra. . . . We live with them, with him. They [the Arab satellite channels] always show this picture, dying in her father's arms. Also the songs of the revolution and the *intifada*. But these children, their images, I cannot forget. I dream of them all the time. You see, I imagine myself. I am a mother. God forbid I have a son or daughter and this happened to them, but I imagine myself there, with them.

(cited in Matar 2006: 1037)

This woman displays a particularly rich modality of response, one that connects her experience of being an exiled mother with politicized acts of memory, imagination and fantasy.

In other cases Askoy found that the turn to transnational television news was born of the frustration viewers experience with news of any one channel or country. Many respondents were critical of the news for its lack of adequate explanation, contextualization and analysis. Some Turkish men for example complained about the insufficient analysis in the Turkish coverage, suggesting that 'on the whole they showed pictures of the atrocities . . . but they didn't do very much in the way of interpretation' (cited in Askoy 2006: 936). Another complains that the coverage was 'opportunistic' and 'hypocritical' rather than objective. It sought to inflect the coverage to Turkish political gain: 'creating the impression "Look we were right, we too have been suffering from terrorism, this is what terrorism is like" '. Others in contrast switched to Turkish channels as they found the BBC television coverage too emotive: 'they were talking about the last phone calls from the planes, and as you listened your eyes filled with tears' (cited in Askoy 2006: 936). Worse still however is the way in which the attacks were set up as a 'clash of civilizations'. As this man complains:

Turkish male: British television started putting the blame on Muslims, interpreting the events as a war between Muslims and Christians. There was no logic to this, only an aggressive attitude, a sensationalist attitude.

(cited in Askoy 2006: 936)

Likewise Mr B and Mr E, who both complain about the stereotypical representations that dominate news coverage of the Muslim world as barbaric, backwards and uncivilized:

Mr B: The media portrays Afghanistan as a country with no culture, with ragged people wearing tatty traditional clothes and hanging turbans, carrying a Kalashnikov. The people were portrayed as understanding only fighting and killing. You would think from the media coverage that the people of Afghanistan had never known civilization.

(cited in Mousavi 2006: 1055)

Mr E: The BBC would talk about the 'uncivilized world'. It referred to [11 September] as an 'attack on the civilized world', implying that the Muslims were barbaric and uncivilized. The picture of Islam given is of a religion of repression, prejudice and war-mongering, devoid of democratic values, and Islamic regimes as authoritarian and brutal. Furthermore, all Muslims [are portrayed] as backwards, barbaric, and ignorant of justice. In other words, the opposite of civilized.

(cited in Mousavi 2006: 1059–60)

This channel flicking was therefore born out of a desire to get a balanced and contextualized view of events. This respondent from Askoy's (2006) study puts it with clarity:

Respondent: When there's a news item about a world event, we always look at British television as well. We compare them both [British and Turkish]. . . . To see who says what; a bit of curiosity, a desire to catch a bit more detail about something. We think they all report in a biased way. Maybe we're mistaken, maybe what they are reporting is correct, but we're not satisfied. . . . That's why we change channels, move across different channels, to have more knowledge, to be reassured, to be better informed. . . . As long as I'm not satisfied, I look at other channels, to see what this one is saying, what that one is saying . . . it's a kind of small-scale research on our part.

(cited in Askoy 2006: 937)

Despite these very reasoned accounts, other respondents displayed a range of different responses to the coverage. These were characterized in particular by what we might call a 'conspiracy repertoire'. In these the attacks were seen as an 'inside job'. Some of Askoy's Kurdish respondents, for example, suggested that 'I think it was the CIA, the CIA's own men, not Bin Laden. Anyway, Bin Laden was working for the CIA'. Another suggests that 'I think that this is an internal US matter, an act by the deep state, that America hit herself' (cited in Askoy 2006: 939). As Askoy suggests, in the context of the focus group discussion, these respondents formed a consensus that the United States initiated the attack as a pretext to invade Afghanistan. While this interpretative repertoire is clearly a part of more general conspiracy theories that circulated following the attacks, Askoy also points to a more situated reason for such dogmatic thinking. He suggests that the veil of secrecy, paranoia and suspicion that followed the attack was compounded by the stark polarization 'war on terror' discourse, which framed the events as a clash of civilizations. Responding to their own marginalization in the media, Askoy argues that these respondents foreclosed what could have been a creative opportunity for thinking between spaces (as neither 'western' nor 'Islamic', neither 'us' nor 'them') (Askoy 2006: 943). Rather they fell back on their own experiences of persecution and exile, 'resorting in a rigid template which subordinates all realities to a defensive scheme' (Askoy 2006: 939).

In some cases, however, this conspiracy repertoire was replaced by one in which there is a confrontation between two modalities of response. One which privileges emotional reactions and identification with the victims of the attack, and another which stands back from a dispassionate position to privilege 'invested collective experiences and commitments'. As Askoy suggests, 'in the first, what is being valued is the honesty of the emotional response to the events, while in the second, the premium is out upon emotional detachment and lucidity'. This latter response is regarded as more reliable by many, 'the only way to get at the truth of the events' (Askoy 2006: 940). The following response therefore must be considered in relation to these Kurds' own exile on one hand, and their experience of death, persecution and exploitation at the hands of powerful states on the other:

> Ayse: Personally I don't have any anti-American feelings. But when I came home that day, when I looked at my parents – and there were lots of neighbours in our house, my parents were saying: 'it's not right that people should die [in the World Trade Center], but something like this was necessary for them [the United States], they needed to experience this pain . . .' But this was very different from what I felt. How could you think anything like this? My mother's reaction was . . . she said 'Thousands of Kurdish people have died in the Middle East, and this was a result of America's politics, or British politics'. OK, there are these politics, people being massacred. But quite honestly it seemed very wrong to me to be glad about people massacred in the United States.
>
> (cited in Askoy 2006: 940)

Ayse's response caused much discussion and some dissent in Askoy's focus group. Some respondents criticized her, claiming that it was not suitably analytical and political. One suggested that she herself was not 'affected by it emotionally'. This was based on her personal experiences, as well as on the group's collective experience of suffering: 'What you are saying is, lots of children are dying. We're more used to these things. We've heard it from our relatives or from people who have been tortured' (cited in Askoy 2006: 940).

Certainly, as Askoy suggests, there are shortcomings in each of these modalities of response. The complexity of the situation was poorly served by both the British media and Turkish transnational television, which did little to salve their anti-Americanism. The former was viewed with suspicion as 'propagators of the crusader mentality' while little from the latter 'would resist these viewers' anti-American drift' (Askoy 2006: 942). Nevertheless, Askoy sees hope in this public sphere, where the dogmatic position of the conspiracy repertoire, the empathy displayed by Ayse, and the collective identifications of the rest of the group existed in a dialogic relationship to each other: 'rather than defending their corner to the exclusion of the other position, they were prepared to allow themselves to move in and out of these different modes of thinking' (Askoy 2006: 943).

In many ways, however, responses such as Ayse's above demonstrate the importance of emotional responses to news discourse. Indeed, as we saw in Chapter 1, audiences often want hard-hitting stories, which have the power to shock people and move them to respond. These, as Elizabeth Bird has found, are the ones that audiences engage with, the ones that they remember, and the ones which may stop them falling back on simplified opinions and stock responses (Bird 2003: 25–31). Sayed Askar Mousavi's (2006) respondents for example move between various different modalities of response, all of which involve the interplay of memory and experience, and the articulation of critical and ethical discourses. In these powerful comparisons are made between different accounts of the events of 11 September 2001 and the subsequent war in Afghanistan. The first of these, Mr A, clearly and movingly demonstrates the emotional aspects of television news, its ability to transport the audience imaginatively into different spaces, to recall past experiences, and to identify with those involved:

Mr A: A woman was screaming and someone else was throwing himself out of the building. I am a very emotional person, I felt my tears rolling. There were tears both of sadness and anger. When we saw the towers crumbling I tried to put myself in the place of jumping from the buildings and the ones burning in the planes. At the same time, I was remembering the [frightening] situations I had been in the fighting in Afghanistan. When the rockets were fired [in Afghanistan] my son [who is sitting here] was very young; he would squeeze himself in my lap and say 'I'm not frightened, I'm just cold'. I remember those wars, when I was in Kabul. Once I was at a clinic with my daughter when particularly heavy fighting broke out. In half an hour the whole clinic was filled with the dead and injured. I went to the toilet and saw somebody's arm was on the floor. After I left the clinic I went to a friend's house. As we were going in, someone from the household was leaving; two minutes later his body was brought back. Those scenes went through my head as my eyes were fixed on the screen. My wife and I both cried as we watched the reports on the TV; as did my daughter and my son. I didn't sleep that night.

(cited in Mousavi 2006: 1051)

The following three responses, however, demonstrate much less by way of empathy with those killed in New York. Rather they are characterized by a harsh ethical judgement born of the coverage which dominates western television, and the resultant absence of their own suffering in the public sphere. It is worth quoting these in full, such are the ways in which they demonstrate the deeply embedded and contextualized nature of semiosis, and the ways in which responses move between ethical, emotional, ideational and interpretative modalities of response. Each of these is deeply invested with memory, with identity, and with a sense of injustice born of the crisis in representation in the news media:

> Mr C: The events in New York reminded both of us of the many 11 Septembers [similar tragedies] suffered by people in Afghanistan every moment of every day. We remember the massacres and campaigns of ethnic cleansing carried out by different political and ethical groups against one another.
>
> (cited in Mousavi 2006: 1051)

> Daughter E2: I was doing my homework in my room when I heard the commotion. My grandmother, who was staying with us, shouted my name. When I saw the planes hit the building I said 'so what?' I wasn't interested. Because my own country is at war and nobody cares about that. Thousands of people have been killed and when I cry [about that] my classmates tell to go to parties and discos and have fun with them.
>
> (cited in Mousavi 2006: 1052)

> Mr B: I thought of Muslims the world over, and Afghanis and Afghanistan, and wondered what would happen to them. I really thought World War Three was going to break out and was terrified. But the scenes of the towers crumbling or of the suffering of so many Americans did not really upset me that much. Because nobody has bothered by what the people in Afghanistan has been enduring over the past 20 years. Was an American's life more valuable than anyone else's? The images of [the destruction of] New York were so exaggerated – justifiably or not – that you would think that the whole of the population had been involved in a catastrophe. As if the whole world is now a different place.
>
> (cited in Mousavi 2006: 1054)

## Conclusion

It is noteworthy then, as we conclude this chapter, that these accounts point to some significant aspects of semiosis, both of those who identify across global spaces, and those for whom globalization figures less strongly. What we see in particular are the ways in which audiences are engaged in much more than the simple 'decoding' of television, and the ways in which their meaning making far exceeds the hypothetical positions of the 'preferred', 'negotiated' and 'oppos-itional' decodings suggested in much thinking about news audiences. While of course audiences display very different responses to the discourses of television news, these seem to be based on the interpretative communities of response, and on individual and shared *emotions* and *experience*, as much on *cognition* and *thinking*.

Semiosis in such an account is always situated: situated in relation to ques-tions of identity (to whom one is, to where one has been, to where you are now, and what the future might hold) as much as it is to the formal and informal knowledge, discourses and interpretative repertoires that are at one's disposal. Indeed, to place emphasis on 'cognition' and 'thinking' alone quite misguided, as we see in accounts of the classic Habermasian public sphere. Rather, semiosis is always tinged by emotion and feeling: this drives audiences' *investments* and *attachments* to ideas in the first place and provides a framework for reaction and response. These are always contextualized; they arise out of, and occur in, the multiply embedded spaces of home, of community, of nation, and of globalization.

It is in the intersection of these spaces that complex questions of identity are worked through. In this television acts as a key resource. At once it serves as a common point of identification: it may synchronize the everyday cultural real-ties of audiences in one country with those of another, while also serve to demarcate the boundaries of communities at home. It is rarely straightforward in this, however: the acts of nostalgia and yearning that some respondents demonstrated, the 'imagining of communities' they engaged in, were undercut by the realization that things had not frozen in time, that the homes that they left in fact no longer existed. In this, there is a profound ethicalization of existence: questions of gender and sexuality, or morality and familial responsi-bility are foregrounded, struggled over as they watch at home, with parents, siblings, grandparents and peers. In each moment the discourses are reinflected: by who is present, by the uses that television is put to, by wider experiences, biographies, dreams and aspirations. There is little consistency in this: it is contingent, embedded, but not unpredictable. It is this, rather than notions of 'decoding', 'negotiation', 'preferred readings' and 'resistance' which should inform our textual analysis. This is but one of the things 'to do with audience research'.

# CONCLUSION: TELEVISION AND ETHICS

This book started with the intention of reviewing the available audience research in order to bring it together, revisit and summarize it. The intention was not only to describe and document what it is that we do when we are watching television, but also to think about how we can use audience research more usefully and consistently. If nothing else I hope that I have demonstrated that we need to think about the television audience with a greater degree of sensitivity and clarity. In particular I have been concerned about theorizations of decoding, that the idea of 'negotiation' fails to account for the profoundly dialogic nature of semiosis, the embedded nature of audience practices, and the ubiquitous place of television in everyday life. While it is a useful starting point, an essential rejection of textual determinism, it obscures many modalities of semiosis, and the sheer complexity of the meanings that we make with television.

## Ethics

In reviewing the literature I have sought to revisit some of the 'established' research, to look at it anew in the light of current developments. These encompass not only what it is that we call television, but also developments in research, in theory and in method. I hope that I have shown not only how the established research literature continues to be relevant for television today, but also for what it will become. The issue of *media ethics* in particular has emerged as a key theme, not only in reality programming, or with reference to talk shows, but also in the ways in which audiences talk about soap operas or respond to transnational television from afar. All these genres share in common a concern, in John Ellis's (1999) term, to *work through* questions of morality, of right and wrong, of who we are, who we should be, how we feel, and what it would be to live, and let others live, a good life (Couldry 2006).

The question of ethics, likewise, is central to television news. In approaching this issue, the public sphere has been employed as both a normative concept, as something that television and its audience should aspire to, and also as an empirical concept, as something which is found to exist, in one form or another, out there in everyday life. In many ways this book has found the audience for television news to be lacking, not only influenced by what they watch, but also ethically defunct, disengaged and apathetic. They forget what it is they have watched just a few minutes before, they misunderstand essential points of fact and analysis, they form interpretative repertoires which are little more than stripped down versions of its discourses. Worse still, news was seen to have clear and demonstrable effects. These repertoires remain dormant, on hold, ready to be reactivated at some later date, taken up as the self evident truths of the matter which need no further explanation.

While we have good reason to be deeply pessimistic, there is also, however, a glimmer of hope. This ethical failing, this crisis in the public sphere, is not solely the fault of audiences. Given just a modicum of context, given the opportunity for historical insight, for alternative accounts and background, audiences come alive: they get angry, engaged, they blush at their former gullibility. They demand more. In this the audience for television news is dialogic: viewers argue, they mull over and work through, they lay down their own words, and anticipate those of others. They get angry, they are moved. Most of all they demand respect.

In this we see a clear use of audience research. We feed these insights, and these concepts, back into our thinking about institutions, texts and politics; we can also use them to make a case for a more adequate form of broadcasting. As I write this, the BBC has refused, in the name of impartiality, to broadcast a humanitarian appeal for the occupants of Gaza. Worried that this would appear to be 'taking sides', that it would be *criticizing* a disproportionate use of force by a heavily militarized state against an impoverished people, the BBC has refused to engage ethically and has sat, impotent, on the fence. Responding on the BBC's blog, one dissenting viewer deplored the lack of ethical resolve: 'do they think we cannot tell the difference between a humanitarian appeal and a political commentary,' he asked, 'do they think that we are stupid?' In this we see that news, like all genres, is drawn into semiosis in numerous ways. Not only do people argue and debate, not only do they form interpretative repertoires, but also they emote. They respond emotionally, with passion and distress, anger and despair.

Sometimes they respond, as we have seen, with a steely ethical resolve. In this the injustices which have been dealt against them are balanced with the injustices that others face: those who appear are judged; often they are found lacking.

Ethics as we have seen are also central to the formats of reality television. We have seen that the scandalous, the scurrilous, the prurient and the carnivalesque can also be the vehicles of ethical thought and judgement. This however is far removed from the pristine space of Habermas's public sphere. At once audiences get involved and identify with those on the screen. They see themselves in the experiences, the feelings, and the dilemmas that they face. They form character relationships and closely felt affiliations; they become loyal and they excitedly anticipate the next instalment of their favourite shows. In these audiences reflect upon their own behaviour. We have referred to this as an ethicalization of existence, a reflexive space in which standards of conduct are interrogated, worked through: from how to bring up one's children, to what to eat, to how to treat others, and thyself. Television shapes who we are, not behind our backs as theories of ideology and socialization might imply, but rather as audiences come to terms with who they are, who they should be, and what is expected of them. This works as much through fantasy and desire as it does through sober thought and reflection.

While this ethical judgement may well be turned inwards, towards the self, it is just as likely to be projected onto others. Here we have seen how the genres of reality television invite speculation and gossip. At once audiences delight in moral transgressions, but reinforce these same boundaries in doing so: game show participants are judged, mocked, jeered and scorned. The differences between the private self and the public self, between the front and backstage behaviours are scrutinized for the slightest forms of hypocrisy, of inconsistency, ineptitude, indiscretion, for character flaws and moral failing. The audience for daytime talk shows share much in this. On the one hand, difference is likely to be stigmatized, held up as a spectacle, to be laughed at. We have seen how this works as a discursive recuperation where the transgressive is judged and normative values applied. On the other hand, the lives and dilemmas of those that appear become a problem, something to be worked through, understood, reflected upon. For better or worse, these are modern rituals through which society reflects upon itself: in which the central values and meanings that it shares, the points of tension, conflict and ambiguity are displayed and worked through. There is no certainty in this ethics, only heteroglossia and a constant struggle over meaning.

While ethics may be a question of judgement, of engagement, and of working through the gaps between everyday experiences and media discourses, we have also seen some of its playful modalities. Play, as we have seen, can be thought of as a liminal space, a space of ambiguity, protected somewhat from immediate consequences but also from the risks inherent in the struggle to find meaning. For some, this is a dangerous space, a space of ethical challenge. In this we see some of the power of soap opera. These are the ludic pleasures and powers of speculation, gossip, remembrance, laughter and expertise. The pleasures of talk, of affiliation, and of common knowledge are central to this play. In these small moments scandal, laughter and gossip become transgressive: they resist that which will constrain and limit, and suggest the possibility of new, if slight, freedoms. These are shared pleasures, knowing pleasures that are snatched from other demands and responsibilities.

While soap opera's ethics may be about solidarity and a knowing laughter, some of this play is about closeness, with following the lives of characters over many, many years: of knowing them, often more intimately than we do others in our lives. This is the pleasure of narrative, of story, of decentring, of traversing the text. In this soap opera speaks to viewers, sometimes profoundly; they know who we are and how we feel. They convey a tragic structure of feeling, of what life feels like in its lived, affective and experiential dimension. They express, work through and give form to the ineffable experiences of everyday life, the ordinary pain of living, the injustices of domesticity, the impositions of the social order. In this play we see the pleasures of emotional realism, and the ethical problematization that it might provoke.

## Semiosis and everyday life

The picture of the audience that emerges from this is far from simple; it cannot be essentialized; it is neither ideologically progressive nor conservative. Rather, I think, that such a notion of ethics has emerged as a more flexible, more nuanced term for understanding what it is that audiences do with television. In this we see that meaning making is always embedded in everyday life, that we are always more than this thing that we call 'an audience'. We turn to television as parents, lovers, sons and daughters, as busy housewives, tired flatmates or distracted commuters heading out the door.

In this we have seen how semiosis outruns, by far, conceptions of 'decoding'. These have informed much thinking about audiences. Their usefulness has been exhausted; much too much of the complexities of meaning, of the modalities of response that we have seen, are hidden by this term. They restrict the constant flow of meaning to single textual encounters. Despite its claims, the model is monologic rather dialogic, it describes a linear circuit rather than an ebb and flow of meaning making. Semiosis has been seen to involve multiple practices, many modalities of response; it is embedded in everyday life. We are always *more than an audience*; we are always attending to other business, other uses, distractions, investments and pleasures.

We see in this that to study television is not just to talk about its texts, its histories and institutions. Television's texts mean and are *drawn into semiosis*, only through the practices of everyday life. We have seen for example how television serves to maintain a semiotic environment (to stop one being lonely, as background noise and familiarity: its presence can be deeply comforting). It facilitates communication; it not only brings people together, but also keeps them apart. At once it is a shared and deeply pleasurable means of companionship, a shared resource. The simple act of watching together, of feeling together, of perhaps a knowing glance, or a companionable silence, communicates more than words can sometimes say. Television in these ways can also act as a pedagogic device: it can be drawn into semiosis as a tool for learning. At once, television acts as an instrument of regulation, and also of resistance. Identities are asserted, values articulated, struggled over, worked through: from gender, to sexuality or generation to ethnicity. These practices are played out at different levels, in different times and spaces: from the imagining of 'home' on a global scale (with nostalgic identifications of a mythical past) to the establishment of home on a daily basis, in domestic space, and community space, in the here and now. Television's care structures, *its ethics*, in all of this, come to speak to *somebody*: to everyone as someone. It is unlikely, whatever the future holds, that television will change in this.

## Media ethics: where do we go from here?

While the review of the empirical research is as thorough and as extensive as space allows, it is obviously not complete. The selection of work to be reviewed has been based on several factors, including quality and applicability, the academic tradition in which it is situated, as well as issues of quantity. Where a significant body of research into a particular genre does not (at least to the best of my knowledge) exist, these areas have been ignored. So sports coverage, situation comedies, religious programming and drama for example are not covered, nor are documentaries and current affairs programming. Clearly this suggests the need for more sustained empirical research in these areas, and I hope a book such as this may prompt it. As I have argued elsewhere, this is not to abandon a concern with texts, their address and their meanings (Briggs 2007b). Rather it is to approach meaning making as an encounter between the text and the audience, an encounter which is always overdetermined by the complexity of everyday life. In this audience research is a fundamentally semiotic endeavour: this book's key term, *semiosis*, attests this.

Television is certainly a medium in transition. For media professionals and academics alike, what was once a relatively stable medium is now shifting under our feet. In this it is clear that television can no longer be seen as a discrete medium, not the least as it converges on the Internet, mobile phones and DVDs and PVRs (Ross 2008). Audiences are increasingly likely to engage with texts across a variety of platforms; indeed they are encouraged to do so by those that produce and distribute them (Spigel and Olsson 2004). These issues have been most rigorously addressed by studies of television fandom and new media audiences, such as the work of Henry Jenkins (2006) and Kurt Lancaster (2001). While this book has touched on these issues in passing, it has not reviewed studies of audience fandom in any sustained way: these are *exceptional audiences*, typically 'high investors' and 'early adopters' of new technologies who have unusual relationships with their media.

This study, in comparison, has focused on 'ordinary television' (Bonner 2003) at the expense of the 'exceptional'. It has done so for despite the ways in which television is changing I believe that it will continue to be ordinary and unexceptional, an assumed right, and a habitual part of everyday life. In this manner it is hoped that the concepts that have been presented, the debates and issues that have been raised, will spur research into what television is becoming, *in all its ordinariness*. In this as Raymond Williams (1975) demonstrated in his pioneering study of television, we will benefit by keeping our eyes fixed as firmly on the past as on the future, to look for *continuity* as well as *change*. It may be this question of ethics which proves to be important as television continues to proliferate and fragment; that it is an ethical agenda that forms this bridge between what television is now, in all its ubiquity, and what television will become, in all its uncertainty. It is this ethical question which asks what it is that television *does*, what it is that its audiences *do*, and what it is that it should *become*. It is a question that we should now pursue.

# GLOSSARY

**Affiliation:** One of James Lull's (1980) media uses, affiliation refers to the manner in which audiences use television texts to sustain relationships, through the focus of joint attention and common activities. Affiliation may also serve to ease the need for constant conversation and attentiveness and foster comfortable silences.

**Audience:** The position adopted in this book is that audience is a problematic term, as audiences are usually something else as well (a child doing homework, a worker trying to relax after work, a mother trying to get half an hour's peace and quiet or non-confrontational contact with her children). Audiences are therefore always embedded in multiple practices as well as identities and experiences. These shape the nature of the meanings which are generated (modalities of response) as texts are drawn into semiosis.

**Avoidance:** One of Lull's (1980) media uses, avoidance refers to the way in which television can be used to insulate television viewers from those around them, to be 'unavailable' for social interaction.

**Backstage:** Erving Goffman's (1969) term refers to the behaviours which are normally hidden from public view; backstage behaviours are in contrast to frontstage activities. The distinction is valuable as it points to the performative nature of identity in which we present different aspects of 'the self' depending on the expectations, participation roles and social location of the interaction. Identity is therefore a relational and social category rather than a fixed property as we perform culturally agreed upon and acceptable roles. Reality television programmes in particular allow us to see backstage behaviours, such as poor parenting or the intimate details of the participants' sexual lives. Audiences are invited to take an ethical stance and judge those behaviours; this allows for introspection and an ethicalization of existence.

**Care structure:** Paddy Scannell's (1996) phenomenological term for the fact that television seems to speak to individual people rather than to mass audiences (to 'everyone-as-someone') and seems to care for us, care structure is closely related to dailiness, as it links audiences together and refers to common events and common cultural experiences, knowledges, discourses and values ('a structure of relevancies').

**Carnivalesque:** Carnival for M.M. Bakhtin (1965) was an open space of inversion and laughter, where existing hierarchies were overturned through excess, parody and nonsense. For some, such licence can be subversive and serves to foster alliances between oppressed groups. Carnivalesque practices often highlight the arbitrary nature of the constraints which are placed upon us in everyday life and allow participants to speak freely and frankly and circumvent the face-saving constraints of politeness and status. In this carnivalesque behaviours and practices are closely related to ideas about play and ritual.

**Centrifugal forces:** According to Bakhtin (1986) any concrete utterance, whether text in the making (e.g. audience gossip) or materialized text (e.g. a television talk show), is dialogic and involved in the struggle over meaning which occurs in language. To a greater or lesser extent the utterance is characterized by centripetal forces, which either guide semiosis to the centre, towards consensual languages, meanings, values and discourses, or by centrifugal forces, which open up the realm of meaning and discourse, towards multiple points of view. The latter is marked more strongly by heteroglossia, and the former by 'monologia'.

**Centripetal forces:** See **Centrifugal forces**.

**Character relationship:** This term is used by Annette Hill (1997) to account for the strong feelings and opinions that audiences develop for or against characters. Soap operas, series drama and reality programming encourage particularly strong character relationships as they involve the extended hermeneutic processes of retension, protension and lateral reference. As a character's history and relationships are stressed, audiences often have a deep understanding of their motivations and feelings, more so than with many of those who they interact with in everyday life. This encourages the process of personalization and focuses on the relationship between backstage and frontage behaviours.

**Competence and domination:** These terms refer to Lull's (1980) media uses, in which social roles are maintained, enacted, resisted or enforced. Examples of competence and domination include who controls the remote control or watches on the main set, and parental restrictions that are placed on children's viewing.

**Dailiness:** Scannell's (1996) phenomenological term dailiness refers to the relationship between the institutional and textual address of television, which is always there, and considered as an entitlement (the news is on every night, without fail, usually at the same time, referring to this day, and no other), and the organization of our routines and habits. Scannell argues that we come to rely on this entitlement as it makes up a key resource in our expectations and experiences of 'normality' (what others have termed our 'ontological security').

**Decoding:** Taken from Stuart Hall's (1973) encoding/decoding model, decoding refers to the ways in which audiences interpret the preferred meanings that a television text communicates. Three commonly used hypothetical reading positions are 'dominant decodings', which accord with the preferred meanings encoded into the text, 'negotiated decodings', which recognize the preferred meanings but enter into a dialogue with them, and 'resistant decodings', which recognize the preferred meanings, but argue against them.

**Dialogic:** A term from Bakhtin's thought, dialogic refers to the *processes* through which meanings are made. The emphasis is on language and meaning as unfolding through dialogue (as diachronic) rather than meaning as a fixed property of the language system (as synchronic). Any discourse, or any instance of its use (the utterance), replies to previous meanings and anticipates possible responses. It is therefore a view of language and communication which emphasizes the relational and contextual features of semiosis.

**Discourse:** From the work of Michel Foucault, discourse refers to the ways in which language is used to construct knowledge about the world, rather than to reflect it. Discourses are therefore involved in acts of power as they govern the ways that a subject can be meaningfully talked and reasoned about. Discourses are plural, however, in the sense that sexuality, for instance, can be talked about through medical, moral, educations, legal, feminist or psychiatric discourses. Each will generate different 'truths', although they might support each other. Many discourses emerge from particular institutions and professions (the church, the judiciary, schools, clinics and social sciences for example) but go on to find expression in the mass media. As discourses define normative and acceptable ways of being they can be said to create subjects of particular kinds.

**Domination:** See **Competence and domination.**

**Embedded audience:** Initially coined by Abercrombie and Longhurst (1998), the term embedded audience refers to the way in which audiences make meanings in the context of their everyday lives. These contexts are multiple and overlap, and can be defined along the lines of concrete social spaces (such as the home), in terms of our biographies (accumulated cultural experience), our identities (beliefs, memories, fantasies and desires), roles (mother, son, Muslim, bus driver, 'Brit' etc.) and relationships (colleagues, siblings, spouse, friends, partners etc.).

**Emotional public sphere:** A term employed by Lunt and Stenner (2005) to describe a media forum in which emotional expression, the disclosure of secrets or the revelation of intense personal conflict is placed at centre stage and made the focal point of the action. It exists either alongside, or as part of the critical public sphere in the way that it encourages, manages and reflects upon emotional conflict in a public context. It tends therefore to be concerned with backstage behaviours, as well as the ethicalization of existence. Others have stressed its carnivalesque properties as a disruptive space.

**Emotional realism**: Emotional realism places emphasis on what life feels like, rather than how it exists in an objective or realistic sense (see **empirical realism**). Ien Ang (1985) describes it in terms of the authenticity of a character's emotional life, a portrayal which resonates with those of the audience, regardless of any melodramatic excess. Emotional realism is associated with the perspective of phenomenology which places emphasis on the experiential aspects of identity and semiosis; it therefore constitutes a broadly construed modality of response.

**Empirical realism**: Ang's (1985) term empirical realism refers to audience expectations of objectively realistic representations in which there is a strong resemblance between the diegetic world and their everyday lives. Judgements may be made on the basis of what is readily *recognizable* in terms of setting, for example, or in what is *probable*, in terms of character motivation and the *story*. See also **emotional realism**.

**Encoding**: Derived from Hall's (1973) model, encoding refers to the institutional, discursive, economic, technical and professional processes of production. This nexus determines how the text is produced, what is produced and how the world is represented. As you might expect, there are persistent logics that are readily identifiable in the encoding process. Hall (1973) argued that the encoding process tends to produce 'preferred meanings' in the media, and that these legitimize existing social relationships. The term has close associations with 'discourse' and 'power'. See also **decoding**.

**Environmental functions**: One of Lull's (1980) media uses in which television is used to create a comfortable and familiar environment, environmental functions might be to stop one feeling alone in an empty house, for example, or to import the signifiers of ethnicity into domestic or community space.

**Ethicalization of existence**: If Foucault's model of discourse and the subject places emphasis on the functioning of power, Nikolas Rose's (1999) concept ethicalization of existence allows us to think about the ways in which audiences use discourses to reflect upon their own identities and their conduct. In this, questions of identity are based on ethical questions such as 'Who am I?', 'What should I be?', 'How should I act?'. Rose suggests that people use discourses to 'cast a grid of visibility' over their existence to shape and gauge their own conduct in the terms it provides. This may act not only through conscious self-reflection and introspection, but also through the activation of fears, fantasies and aspirations. Those that appear on television may be judged for their behaviour, although pleasure may be found in their transgressions of ethical standards. These represent different modalities of response.

**Evaluative accent**: Valentin Vološinov's (1973) term evaluative accent refers to the 'struggle over meaning' that is always found in language. Because language is highly receptive to context, the inflections of meaning will change in relation to that context. The same discourse or representation can therefore be subject to different ideological 'accents'. This is a property of media texts as well as audience responses.

**Experiential:** Experiential, or relating to subjective experience, the audience's phenomenological engagement with the world not only can be on a moment-to-moment basis but also concerns interior states and processes, such as suddenly remembering something, feeling repulsed by or attracted to a character, or having a thought of getting angry. Ron Lembo (2000) refers to these as 'mindful states'.

**Frontstage:** Goffman's (1969) term refers to the 'presentation of self' in everyday life, in contrast to backstage activities. The term frontstage problematizes assumptions of a true or fixed identity and places emphasis on what audiences are trying to achieve when they talk in focus groups, or gossip and argue over television in everyday life. People might speak carefully using a political discourse as they want to appear as 'concerned citizens' or as 'intelligent', for example. It accords with Bakhtin's view of language which sees meaning as unfolding between people in real concrete situations. Although Goffman refuses the distinction, we can also think about this in psychological terms as a relation between what we say to others and what we think and feel in different contexts, which might be discrepant.

**Gossip:** Gossip may refer to a lot of the talk that surrounds television, both as it is watched, serving the functions of affiliation, and later as it works in the function of communication facilitation. Writers such as Elizabeth Bird (2003) stress the ways in which gossip at once celebrates the transgression of ethical standards of conduct, and also secures these by judging those who transgress in conservative ways. Other writers, notably Mary Ellen Brown (1994), sees in this more space for transgression and for small resistances. She argues that women in particular use gossip to scorn those who judge and control, as well as pointing to contradictions between expected cultural standards and actual conduct. Gossip is therefore closely related to the idea of working through and is subject to centrifugal and centripetal forces. It may also usefully question assumptions about the 'rationality' of the public sphere.

**Heteroglossia:** Closely associated with Bakhtin's ideas about dialogic nature of language, heteroglossia refers to the availability of numerous types of speech, discourse and communication, as well as to the knowledges that they produce. Any instance of language use, be it in everyday conversation, debate, opinion and thought, or in a media text, will call upon, adopt, quote and assimilate these ways of speaking.

**Identification:** A concept which has been widely discredited in cultural and media studies as it suggests an effects model of behavioural influence, identification nevertheless retains some heuristic value because audiences use it to account for their own experiences. It is more usefully described along the lines of personalization and the building of character relationships.

**Identity:** Cultural and media studies generally presents a theorization of identity as a process rather than a fixed quality, although we strive for a centred and stable sense of self through our daily rituals and relationships, as well as through narrative and other symbolic forms. Goffman stresses the performative nature of identity, making a distinction between frontstage and backstage behaviours while post-structuralism stresses the ways in which our identities or subjectivities are an effect of discourse; see **subject**. Rose's (1999) notion of an ethicalization of existence bridges these two approaches.

**Imagined community:** A phrase coined by Benedict Anderson (1983), imagined community refers to the ways in which nations and nationalism are created through representational forms such as maps, flags, museums, statues of national heroes, national events (such as annual sporting fixtures) and wider symbols, such as those found on television (the BBC as a national institution, or regular newscasters for example). These articulate values which are held to express the national character, and serve as common points of identification for those who would otherwise never meet. It is therefore a semiotic and mythological process.

**Interpretative repertoire:** This term from discursive psychology (Potter and Wetherell 1987) refers to the way in which thought and dialogue draw upon the available discourses that construct knowledge about a specific area of cultural life. Interpretative repertoires are 'stripped down' versions of these discourses, often employing stock phrases and images. They aid memory and function as shared resources in an audience's conversations and debates. The concept helps us to understand the ways in which beliefs and opinions are discursively formed, contingent and open to change. Audiences will use various interpretative repertoires differently in different contexts depending upon what they want to achieve and how they wish to present themselves. This will also depend upon their saliency and other factors which may make them more readily available.

**Lateral reference:** Wolfgang Iser's (1978) term lateral reference refers to the hermeneutic activity of making comparisons between different storylines in a single narrative, of speculating on or working out or anticipating the implications of one set of actions for other characters and storylines.

**Liminal:** Derived from the anthropological writings of Victor Turner (1980), liminal spaces are 'in-between' spaces which blur cultural boundaries and classifications. In doing so they place emphasis on ambiguity, openness and indeterminacy. Liminal states are normally associated with rituals and rites of passage. In these the normal limits to thought, self-understanding and behaviour are relaxed; this can be disruptive and illuminating.

**Modality of response:** A term introduced by Barker and Brooks (1998), modality of response refers to the varying types of meaning that are produced as audiences respond to texts. Closely related to ideas about semiosis, this view of language stresses the differences between thinking and imagining, or judging and emoting for example. Modalities of response are 'cued' by textual and generic modes of address as well as the practical activities, anticipated outcomes and expectations which shape television viewing. The concept is used to extend or 'get behind' the concept of decoding, which tends to obscure important differences in semiosis.

**Monologia:** A term derived from the writing of Bakhtin, monologia is a centripetal force that tries to unify discourse and limit difference between languages and representations. Monologia is essentially opposed to the centripetal forces of dialogue and heteroglossia, which seek to open up rather than close down the accepted universe of discourse.

**Personalization:** Closely associated with emotional realism and working through, personalization refers to the way in which audiences bring their own feelings and experiences to bear on their interpretation of characters' actions, motivations, feelings and experiences, and feed these back into their own lives. This often allows them to broach difficult subjects, to share them, and reflect upon them in new ways. This may have implications for identity formation and the ethicalization of existence.

**Phenomenology:** Phenomenology is the examination of subjective experience or of 'Being-in-the-World', and derives in and particularly from the work of Martin Heidegger and Maurice Merleau-Ponty.

**Play:** Play is a pervasive activity across culture, and is not confined to childhood. It is theorized as a liminal space between 'reality' and 'fantasy' which is insulated from normal constraints and responsibilities. Closely associated with the carnivalesque, play sets up a subjunctive or 'as if' space in which audiences can look at the world, their experiences and identities in new ways. Play is usually pleasurable because it allows for a degree of freedom and release through emotional recognition, companionship and excess. Media texts and the practices that surround them can therefore be viewed as 'games' which are played; their mode of address and the positions they imply are analogous to 'rules'.

**Power:** According to Foucault (1977a) power is usually productive rather than repressive; it is closely linked to the production of discourses which have the power to define the ways in which any aspect of the world can be thought about and acted upon. Discourse functions in the service of power to produce 'knowledge' and 'truth'. However, because discourses are plural, knowledge and power are always struggled over, as competing discourses vie for acceptance.

**Protension:** Iser's (1978) term for the hermeneutic activity of guessing ahead, protension concerns asking questions, solving puzzles, and generally being involved and invested in a story's future.

**Public sphere:** Arguably one of the most important concepts in cultural and media studies, the public sphere refers to a space for the exchange of ideas, for debate and opinion formation. This is vital for democracy, where citizens are called upon to make informed choices, as well as to hold those with power responsible for their actions. Classical accounts stress the insistence on rational debate, while later accounts allow for the possibility of a greater range of communicative activities, as well as emotional responses. The role of television and other media in the public sphere is contested and subject to much debate and analysis.

**Regulation:** One of Lull's (1980) media uses in which domestic time and space become organized around programmes, choices or schedules, regulation might enforce bedtime routines, mark mealtimes, or bring the household together for a period of shared attention and social contact.

**Retension:** Iser's (1978) term for the hermeneutic activity of remembering a story's past, retension works through intra-diegetic references not only to events, actions and motivations in recent or distant episodes (sometimes dating back many years, sometimes to a previous episode), but also to inferred extra-diegetic knowledge which have not been shown, but are implied based on our knowledge of characters.

**Ritual:** The term ritual suggests the ways in which television fosters joint cultural participation in large scale media events such as the reality programme *Big Brother*. These are viewed as symbolic practices in and through which a culture reflects upon itself by working through its central values and meanings. This is closely associated with the concept of play.

**Semiosis:** A diachronic view of language stresses the unfolding nature of meaning making. Semiosis is ongoing rather than static, a constant conversation between texts, discourses and audiences. Semiosis therefore stresses heteroglossia and the dialogic nature of communication. Semiosis occurs through various modalities of response, the variety and complexity of which are usually obscured by the concept of decoding.

**Social learning:** One of Lull's (1980) media uses, social learning refers to the numerous ways in which television can be used to 'teach' values and aspirations. At the most general level this relates to ideas about discourse and representation, but more specifically Lull points to the active ways in which parents, for example, may comment upon particular representations to discuss the issues they raise with their children. The concept is closely related to the public sphere and working through.

**Sphericule:** The term sphericule extends assumptions of a singular and nationally based public sphere, which is in principle open to all, and considers the possibility of multiple and perhaps overlapping public spheres, based on ethnic affiliation, for example, or on specific interests.

**Subject:** Post-structuralism stresses the ways in which institutional discourses produce regimes of intelligibility through which we come to be identified as subjects of a particular kind. Particularly associated with the writings of Foucault, this approach stresses the ways in which those who have the means to generate knowledge exercise power over individuals as they create the truths about homosexuality, motherhood and criminality for example. Foucault stressed the institutional nature of these discourses and the practices through which their effects were generated (in the clinic, the nursery school and the prison).

**Text:** Any communicative form involves the production of text. In this sense there is little difference between texts which have a fixed material form, such as an episode of a soap opera, or ephemeral texts which unfold as audiences speculate and gossip as they watch or converse more generally. More radically we can treat our thoughts as texts insofar as they are semiotic in nature: responding to particular representations, discourses, memories, associations and experiences. While fixed material texts have boundaries and offer meanings, and must be analysed as such, this view of text stresses intertextuality and the fluid nature of semiosis.

**Transnational television:** Television which is either produced for a diasporic audience and initially distributed on satellite and cable systems in specific territories, or television which is produced for a national audience, but subsequently distributed in other counties, are examples of transnational television.

**Working through:** The concept of working through refers to the constant and open-ended process through which television defines, narrates, makes intelligible, worries over, sensationalizes and speculates about culture and society, the events and experiences which define it, as well as its values, discourses and ethical codes of conduct, all of which are in tension and flux. The concept helps to specify what happens within the public sphere.

# FURTHER READING

## Chapter 1: Television, news and the public sphere

Corner, J., Richardson, K. and Fenton, N. (1990) *Nuclear Reactions: Form and Response in Public Issue Television*. Luton: University of Luton Press.

Gamson, W. (1992) *Talking Politics*. Cambridge: Cambridge University Press.

Madianou, M. (2005) *Mediating the Nation: News, Audiences and the Politics of Identity*. London: UCL Press.

Morley, D. (1980) *The Nationwide Audience: Structure and Decoding*. London: British Film Institute.

Volkmer, I. (2006) *News in Public Memory*. New York: Peter Lang.

## Chapter 2: Reality television, audiences and ethics

Bell, D. and Hollows, J. (eds) (2005) *Ordinary Lifestyles: Popular Media, Consumption and Taste*. Buckingham: Open University Press.

Couldry, N., Livingstone, S. and Markham, T. (2007) *Media Consumption and Public Engagement: Beyond the Presumption of Attention*. Basingstoke: Palgrave Macmillan.

Ellis, J. (1999) 'Television as working through', in J. Gripsrud (ed.) *Television and Common Knowledge*. London: Routledge.

Rose, N. (1999) *Governing the Soul: The Public Shaping of the Private Self*, 2nd edn. London: Free Association Books.

Silverstone, R. (2007) *The Media and Morality: On the Rise of the Mediapolis*. Cambridge: Polity.

## Chapter 3: Soap opera and play

Bailey, S. (2005) *Media Audiences and Identity: Self-Construction in the Fan Experience*. Basingstoke: Palgrave Macmillan.

Harrington, L. and Bielby, D. (1995) *Soap Fans: Pursuing Pleasure and Making Meaning in Everyday Life*. Philadelphia, PA: Temple University Press.

Machado-Borges, T. (2003) *Only for You: Brazilians and the Telenovela Flow*. Stockholm Studies in Social Anthropology 52. Stockholm: Almqvist and Wiksell.

Spence, L. (2005) *Watching Daytime Soap Operas: The Power of Pleasure*. Middletown, CT: Wesleyan University Press.

Tufte, T. (2001) *Living with the Rubbish Queen: Telenovelas, Culture and Modernity in Brazil*. Luton: University of Luton Press.

## Chapter 4: Television and domestic space

Briggs, M. (2006) 'Beyond the audience: *Teletubbies*, play and parenthood', *European Journal of Cultural Studies* 9(4): 441–60.

Gillespie, M. (1999) *Television, Ethnicity and Cultural Change*. London: Routledge.

Mankekar, P. (1999) *Screening Culture, Viewing Politics: An Ethnography of Television, Womanhood and Nation in Postcolonial India*. Durham, NC: Duke University Press.

Morley, D. (2000) *Home Territories: Media, Mobility and Identity*. London: Routledge.

Silverstone, R. (1994) *Television and Everyday Life*. London: Routledge.

Silverstone, R. and Morley, D. (1990) 'Families and their technologies: Two ethnographic portraits', in T. Putnam and C. Newton (eds) *Household Choices*. London: Futures.

## Chapter 5: Television, identity and global audiences

Browne, D. (2004) *Ethnic Minorities, Electronic Media and the Public Sphere*. New York: Hampton Press.

Cunningham, S. and Sinclair, J. (eds) *Floating Lives: The Media and Asian Diasporas*. St Lucia, Qld: University of Queensland Press.

de Block, L. and Buckingham, D. (2007) *Global Children, Global Media: Migration, Media and Childhood*. Basingstoke: Palgrave Macmillan.

King, R. and Wood, N. (eds) (2001) *Media and Migration: Constructions of Mobility and Difference*. London: Routledge.

Lull, J. (1988) *World Families Watch Television*. Newbury Park, CA: Sage.

Naficy, H. (1993) *The Making of Exile Cultures: Iranian Television in Los Angeles*. Minneapolis, MN: University of Minnesota Press.

# REFERENCES

Abercrombie, N. and Longhurst, B. (1998) *Audiences: A Sociological Theory of Performance and Imagination*. London: Sage.

Allan, S. (1999) *News Culture*. Buckingham: Open University Press.

Anderson, B. (1983) *Imagined Communities*. London: Verso.

Ang, I. (1985) *Watching Dallas: Soap Opera and the Melodramatic Imagination*. London: Methuen.

Askoy, A. (2006) 'Transnational virtues and cool loyalties: Responses of Turkish-speaking migrants in London to September 11', *Journal of Ethnic and Migration Studies* 32(6): 923–46.

Askoy, A. and Robins, K. (2000) 'Thinking across spaces: Transnational television from Turkey', *European Journal of Cultural Studies* 3(3): 343–65.

Askoy, A. and Robins, K. (2003) 'Banal transnationalism: The difference that television makes', in K.H. Karim (ed.) *The Media of Diaspora*. London: Routledge.

Bakhtin, M.M. (1965) *Rabelais and his World*. Cambridge, MA: MIT Press.

Bakhtin, M.M. (1981) 'Discourse in the novel', in M. Holquist (ed.) *The Dialogic Imagination: Four Essays*. Austin, TX: University of Texas Press.

Bakhtin, M.M. (1986) *Speech Genres and Other Late Essays*. Austin, TX: University of Texas Press.

Barker, M. and Brooks, K. (1998) *Knowing Audiences: Judge Dredd, its Friends, Fans and Foes*. Luton: University of Luton Press.

Barthes, R. (1972) *Mythologies*. London: Jonathan Cape.

Bausinger, H. (1984) 'Media, technology and everyday life', *Media, Culture and Society* 65(4): 343–52.

Baym, N. (2000) *Tune In, Log on: Soaps, Fandom and On-line Community*. Thousand Oaks, CA: Sage.

Beattie, L., Miller, D., Miller, E. and Philo, G. (1999) 'The media and Africa: Images of disaster and rebellion', in G. Philo (ed.) *Message Received*. London: Longman.

Bignell, J. (2004) *An Introduction to Television Studies*. London: Routledge.

Billig, M. (1991) *Ideology and Opinions: Studies in Rhetorical Psychology*. London: Sage.

Billig, M. (1997) 'From codes to utterances: Cultural studies, discourse and psychology', in M. Ferguson and P. Golding (eds) *Cultural Studies in Question*. London: Sage.

Billig, M. and Shotter, J. (1998) 'A Bakhtinian psychology: From out of the heads of individuals and into the dialogues between them', in M. Bell and M. Gardiner (eds) *Bakhtin and the Human Sciences*. London: Sage.

Billig, M., Condor, S., Edwards, D., Gane, M., Middleton, D. and Radley, A. (1988) *Ideological Dilemmas: A Social Psychology of Everyday Thinking*. London: Sage.

Bird, E. (2003) *The Audience in Everyday Life: Living in a Media World*. New York: Routledge.

Bonner, F. (2003) *Ordinary Television: Analyzing Popular TV*. London: Sage.

Briggs, M. (2006) 'Beyond the audience: *Teletubbies*, play and parenthood', *European Journal of Cultural Studies* 9(4): 441–60.

Briggs, M. (2007a) 'Meaning, play and experience: Audience activity and the "ontological bias" in children's media research', *Participations: Journal of Audience and Reception Studies* 4(2).

Briggs, M. (2007b) 'Teddy bears, television and play: Rethinking semiosis in children's media culture', *Social Semiotics* 17(4): 503–24.

Briggs, M. (2009) 'BBC children's television, parentcraft and pedagogy: Towards the "ethicalization of existence" ', *Media, Culture and Society* 31(1): 23–39.

Brown, M.E. (1994) *Soap Opera and Women's Talk: The Pleasure of Resistance*. New York: Sage.

Buckingham, D. (1987) *Public Secrets: EastEnders and its Audience*. London: British Film Institute.

Buckingham, D. (1993a) *Children Talking Television: The Making of Television Literacy*. London: Falmer Press.

Buckingham, D. (1993b) 'Boy's talk: Television and the policing of masculinity', in D. Buckingham (ed.) *Reading Audiences: Young People and the Media*. Manchester: Manchester University Press.

Buckingham, D. (2000) *The Making of Citizens: Young People, News and Politics*. London: Routledge.

Buckingham, D. and Sefton-Green, J. (2003) 'Gotta catch 'em all: Structure, agency and pedagogy in children's media culture', *Media, Culture and Society* 25(3): 379–99.

Corner, J. (1999) *Critical Ideas in Television Studies*. Oxford: Clarendon Press.

Corner, J., Richardson, K. and Fenton, N. (1990) *Nuclear Reactions: Form and Response in Public Issue Television*. Luton: University of Luton Press.

Couldry, N. (2002) 'Playing for celebrity big brother as ritual event', *Television and New Media* 3(3): 283–93.

Couldry, N. (2006) *Listening Beyond the Echoes: Media, Ethics, and Agency in an Uncertain World*. London: Paradigm.

Couldry, N. and McCarthy, A. (2004) *Media Space: Place, Scale and Culture in a Media Age*. London: Routledge.

Couldry, N., Livingstone, S. and Markham, T. (2007) *Media Consumption and*

*Public Engagement: Beyond the Presumption of Attention.* Basingstoke: Palgrave Macmillan.

Cunningham, S. (2001) 'Popular media as public "sphericules" for diasporic communities', *International Journal of Cultural Studies* 4(2): 131–47.

Curran, J. (1997) 'Rethinking the media as public sphere', in P. Dahlgren and C. Sparks (eds) *Communication and Citizenship.* London: Routledge.

Dahlgren, P. (1995) *Television and the Public Sphere: Citizenship, Democracy and the Media.* London: Sage.

Dahlgren, P. (2005) 'Television, public spheres and civic cultures', in J. Wasko (ed.) *A Companion to Television.* London: Blackwell.

Dayan, D. (2001) 'The peculiar public of television', *Media, Culture and Society* 23(6): 743–65.

de Certeau, M. (1984) *The Practice of Everyday Life.* Berkeley, CA: University of California Press.

Douglas, M. (1991) *Purity and Danger: An Analysis of the Concepts of Pollution and Taboo.* London: Routledge.

Durham, M.G. (2004) 'Constructing the "new ethnicities": Media, sexuality, and diaspora identity in the lives of South Asian immigrant girls', *Critical Studies in Media Communication* 21(2): 140–61.

Ellis, J. (1999) 'Television as working through', in J. Gripsrud (ed.) *Television and Common Knowledge.* London: Routledge.

Ellis, J. (2000) *Working Through: Television in the Age of Uncertainty.* London: I.B. Tauris.

Elsaesser, T. (2003) *European Cinema: Face to Face with Hollywood.* Amsterdam: Amsterdam University Press.

Fiske, J. (1987) *Television Culture.* London: Routledge.

Foucault, M. (1977a) *The History of Sexuality, Volume 1: An Introduction.* New York: Vintage.

Foucault, M. (1977b) *The History of Sexuality, Volume 3: The Care of the Self.* New York: Vintage.

Fraser, N. (1992) 'Rethinking the public sphere: A contribution to the critique of actually existing democracy', in C. Calhoun (ed.) *Habermas and the Public Sphere.* Cambridge, MA: MIT Press.

Gamson, J. (1998) *Freaks Talk Back: Tabloid Talk Shows and Sexual Nonconformity.* Chicago, IL: University of Chicago Press.

Gauntlett, D. and Hill, A. (1999) *TV Living: Television and the Culture of Everyday Life.* London: British Film Institute.

Georgiou, M. (2006) *Diaspora, Identity and the Media: Diasporic Transnationalism and Mediated Spatialities.* Creskill, NJ: Hampton Press.

Giddens, A. (1990) *The Consequences of Modernity.* Cambridge: Polity.

Gillespie, M. (1999) *Television, Ethnicity and Cultural Change.* London: Routledge.

Gillespie, M. (2002) 'Dynamics of diasporas: South Asian media and transnational cultural politics', in G. Stald and T. Tufte (eds) *Global Encounters: Media and Cultural Transformation.* Luton: University of Luton Press.

Gitlin, T. (1998) 'Public spheres of public sphericules?', in T. Liebes and J. Curran (eds) *Media, Ritual and Identity: Essays in Honor of Elihu Katz*. London: Routledge.

Goffman, E. (1969) *The Presentation of Self in Everyday Life*. London: Allen Lane.

Goffman, E. (1981) *Forms of Talk*. Philadelphia, PA: University Press of Pennsylvania.

Goode, L. (2005) *Jürgen Habermas: Democracy and the Public Sphere*. London: Pluto.

Gray, A. (1992) *Video Playtime*. London: Routledge.

Gripsrud, J. (1999) *Television and Common Knowledge*. London: Routledge.

Habermas, J. (1989) *The Structural Transformation of the Public Sphere*. Cambridge, MA: MIT Press.

Hafez, K. (2007) *The Myth of Media Globalization*. Cambridge: Polity.

Hall, S. (1973) *Encoding and Decoding in the Television Discourse*. Occasional Papers No. 7. Birmingham: Centre for Contemporary Cultural Studies.

Hall, S. (1982) 'The rediscovery of ideology: The return of the repressed in media studies', in T. Bennett, J. Curran, M. Gurevitch and J. Wollacott (eds) *Culture, Society and the Media*. London: Routledge.

Harrington, L. and Bielby, D. (1995) *Soap Fans: Pursuing Pleasure and Making Meaning in Everyday Life*. Philadelphia, PA: Temple University Press.

Harrison, J. (2006) *News*. London: Routledge.

Hawkins, G. (2001) 'The ethics of television', *International Journal of Cultural Studies* 4(4): 412–26.

Hepburn, A. (1997) 'Teachers and secondary school bullying: A postmodern discourse analysis', *Discourse and Society*. 8(1): 27–48.

Hill, A. (1997) *Shocking Entertainment: Viewer Response to Violent Movies*. Luton: John Libby.

Hill, A. (2000) 'Fearful and safe: Audience response to British reality programming', *Television and New Media* 1(2): 193–213.

Hill, A. (2005) *Reality TV: Audiences and Popular Factual Television*. London: Routledge.

Hill, A. (2007) *Restyling Factual TV: Audiences and News, Documentary and Reality Genres*. London: Routledge.

Hobson, D. (1982) *Crossroads: The Drama of a Soap Opera*. London: Methuen.

Hobson, D. (2002) *Soap Opera*. Cambridge: Polity.

Hollows, J. (2008) *Domestic Cultures*. Buckingham: Open University Press.

Holmes, S. (2004) ' "But this time you choose!": Approaching the "interactive" audience in reality TV', *International Journal of Cultural Studies* 7(2): 213–31.

Hoover, S.M., Schofield Clark, L. and Alters, D.F. (2004) *Media, Home and Family*. New York: Routledge.

Iser, W. (1978) *The Act of Reading: A Theory of Aesthetic Response*. London: Routledge and Kegan Paul.

Jaworski, A. and Coupland, N. (eds) (2006) *The Discourse Reader*. London: Routledge.

Jenkins, H. (1992) *Textual Poachers: Television Fans and Participatory Culture*. New York: Routledge.

Jenkins, H. (2006) *Convergence Culture: Where Old and New Media Collide*. New York: New York University Press.

Jones, D. (1980) 'Gossip: Notes on women's oral culture', *Woman's Studies International Quarterly* 3: 193–8.

Jones, J. (2003) 'Show your real face: A fan study of the UK Big Brother transmissions (2000, 2001, 2002). Investigating the boundaries between notions of consumers and producers of factual television'. *New Media and Society* 5(3): 400–21.

Karanfil, G. (2007) 'Satellite television and its discontents: Reflections on the experiences of Turkish-Australian lives', *Continuum* 21(1): 59–69.

Karim, K.H. (2003) 'Mapping diasporic mediascapes', in K.H. Karim (ed.) *The Media of Diaspora*. London: Routledge.

Kelly-Byrne, D. (1989) *A Child's Play Life: An Ethnographic Study*. New York: Teachers College Press.

Kitzinger, J. (2000) 'Media templates: Patterns of association and the (re)construction of meaning over time', *Media, Culture and Society* 22(1): 61–84.

Kitzinger, J. (2004) *Framing Abuse*. London: Pluto.

Kress, G. (1997) *Before Writing: Rethinking the Paths to Literacy*. London: Routledge.

Kress, G. (2000) 'Text as the punctuation of semiosis: Pulling at some threads', in U. Meinhof and J. Smith (eds) *Intertextuality and the Media: From Genre to Everyday Life*. Manchester: Manchester University Press.

Lancaster, K. (2001) *Interacting with Babylon 5: Fan Performances in a Media Universe*. Houston, TX: University of Texas Press.

Lee, M. and Cho, C.H. (1990) 'Women watching together: An ethnographic study of Korean soap opera fans in the US', *Cultural Studies* 4(1): 30–44.

Lembo, R. (2000) *Thinking through Television*. Cambridge: Cambridge University Press.

Liebes, T. and Katz, E. (1993) *The Export of Meaning*. Cambridge: Polity.

Livingstone, S. (1998) 'Relationships between media and audiences: Prospects for future audience reception studies', in T. Liebes and J. Curran (eds) *Media, Ritual and Identity: Essays in Honor of Elihu Katz*. London: Routledge.

Livingstone, S. and Bovill, M. (1999) *Young People, New Media*. London: London School of Economics.

Livingstone, S. and Lunt, P. (1994) *Talk on Television: Audience Participation and Public Debate*. London: Routledge.

Lull, J. (1980) 'The social uses of television', *Human Communication Research* 6(3): 197–209.

Lunt, P. and Stenner, P. (2005) 'The Jerry Springer Show as an emotional public sphere', *Media, Culture and Society* 27(1): 59–81.

McChesney, R.W. (2008) *The Political Economy of the Media: Enduring Issues, Emerging Dilemmas*. New York: Monthly Review Press.

Mackay, H. and Ivey, D. (2004) *Modern Media in the Home: An Ethnographic Study*. Luton: University of Luton Press.

Madill, A. and Goldmeier, R. (2003) 'EastEnders: Texts of female desire and of community', *International Journal of Cultural Studies* 6(4): 471–94.

Manga, J. (2003) *Talking Trash: The Cultural Politics of Daytime TV Talk Shows*. New York: New York University Press.

Mankekar, P. (1999) *Screening Culture, Viewing Politics: An Ethnography of Television, Womanhood and Nation in Postcolonial India*. Durham, NC: Duke University Press.

Masciarotte, G.J. (1991) ' "C'mon girl": Oprah Winfrey and the discourse of feminine talk', *Genders* 11: 81–110.

Matar, D. (2006) 'Diverse diasporas, one meta-narrative: Palestinians in the UK talking about 11 September 2001', *Journal of Ethnic and Migration Studies* 32(6): 1027–40.

Meyrowitz, J. (1987) *No Sense of Place: The Impact of the Electronic Media on Social Behavior*. New York: Oxford University Press.

Miller, T. (ed.) (2002) *Television Studies*. London: British Film Institute.

Moores, S. (1996) *Satellite Television in Everyday Life*. Luton: University of Luton Press.

Moores, S. (2000) *Media and Everyday Life in Modern Society*. Edinburgh: Edinburgh University Press.

Morley, D. (1980) *The Nationwide Audience: Structure and Decoding*. London: British Film Institute.

Morley, D. (1986) *Family Television: Cultural Power and Domestic Leisure*. London: Comedia.

Morley, D. (1992) *Television, Audiences and Cultural Studies*. London: Routledge.

Morley, D. (2000) *Home Territories: Media, Mobility and Identity*. London: Routledge.

Morley, D. and Silverstone, R. (1990) 'Domestic communication: Technologies and meanings', *Media, Culture and Society* 12(1): 31–55.

Mousavi, S.A. (2006) 'Transnational Afghani audiences after September 11', *Journal of Ethnic and Migration Studies* 32(6): 1041–61.

Naficy, H. (1993) *The Making of Exile Cultures: Iranian Television in Los Angeles*. Minneapolis, MN: University of Minnesota Press.

Philo, G. (1990) *Seeing and Believing: The Influence of Television*. London: Routledge.

Philo, G. (ed.) (1995) *Industry, Economy, War and Politics: Glasgow University Media Reader: Volume 2*. London: Routledge.

Philo, G. (ed.) (1999) *Message Received*. London: Longman.

Philo, G. (2002) 'Television news and audience understanding of war, conflict and disaster', *Journalism Studies* 3(2): 173–86.

Philo, G. (2008) 'Active audiences and the construction of public knowledge', *Journalism Studies* 9(4): 535–44.

Philo, G. and Berry, M. (2004) *Bad News from Israel*. London: Pluto.

Potter, J. and Wetherell, M. (1987) *Discourse and Social Psychology*. London: Sage.

Price, M.E. (1995) *Television, the Public Sphere, and National Identity*. New York: Oxford University Press.

Punathambekar, A. (2005) 'Bollywood in the Indian-American diaspora: Mediating a transitive logic of cultural citizenship', *International Journal of Cultural Studies* 8(2): 151–73.

Riggs, K.E. (1998) *Mature Audiences: Television and the Elderly*. New Brunswick, NJ: Rutgers University Press.

Rose, N. (1999) *Governing the Soul: The Public Shaping of the Private Self*, 2nd edn. London: Free Association Books.

Ross, K. and Nightingale, V. (2003) *Media Audiences: New Perspectives*. Buckingham: Open University Press.

Ross, S.M. (2008) *Beyond the Box: Television and the Internet*. New York: John Wiley.

Scannell, P. (1989) 'Public service broadcasting and modern public life', *Media, Culture and Society* 11(2): 135–66.

Scannell, P. (1996) *Radio, Television and Modern Life*. Oxford: Blackwell.

Scannell, P. (2002) 'Big Brother as a television event', *Television and New Media* 3(3): 271–82.

Shattuc, J. (1997) *The Talking Cure: Women and Daytime Talk Shows*. New York: Routledge.

Shi, Yu (2005) 'Identity construction of the Chinese diaspora, ethnic media use, community formation, and the possibility of social activism', *Continuum* 19(1): 55–72.

Shotter, J. and Billig, M. (1998) 'A Bakhtinian psychology: From out of the heads of individuals and into the dialogues between them', in M.M. Bell and M. Gardiner (eds) *Bakhtin and the Human Sciences*. London: Sage.

Silverstone, R. (1994) *Television and Everyday Life*. London: Routledge.

Silverstone, R. (1999) *Why Study the Media?* London: Sage.

Silverstone, R. (2007) *The Media and Morality: On the Rise of the Mediapolis*. Cambridge: Polity.

Silverstone, R. and Morley, D. (1990) 'Families and their technologies: Two ethnographic portraits', in T. Putnam and C. Newton (eds) *Household Choices*. London: Futures.

Sinclair, J. and Cunningham, S. (2000) 'Go with the flow: Diasporas and the media', *Television New Media* 1(9): 11–31.

Sinclair, J., Jacka, E. and Cunningham, S. (1996) *New Patterns in Global Television*. Oxford: Oxford University Press.

Sinclair, J., Yue, A., Hawkins, G., Pookong, K. and Fox, J. (2001) 'Chinese cosmopolitanism and media use', in S. Cunningham and J. Sinclair (eds) *Floating Lives: The Media and Asian Diasporas*. St Lucia, Qld: University of Queensland Press.

Sparks, C. (2004) 'The global, the local and the public sphere', in R.C. Allen and A. Hill (eds) *The Television Studies Reader*. London: Routledge.

Spence, L. (2005) *Watching Daytime Soap Operas: The Power of Pleasure*. Middletown, CT: Wesleyan University Press.

Spigel, L. and Olsson, J. (eds) (2004) *Television After TV: Essays on a Medium in Transition*. Durham, NC: Duke University Press.

Stallybrass, J. and White, A. (1986) *The Politics and Poetics of Transgression*. Ithaca, NY: Cornell University Press.

Thompson, J.P. (1990) *Ideology and Modern Culture*. Cambridge: Polity.

Turner, V. (1980) *The Anthropology of Performance*. New York: PAJ.

Volkmer, I (ed.) (2006) *News in Public Memory: An International Study of Media Memories across Generations*. New York: Peter Lang.

Vološinov, V. (1973) *Marxism and the Philosophy of Language*. Cambridge, MA: Harvard University Press.

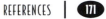

Walkerdine, V. (1997) *Daddy's Girl: Young Girls and Popular Culture*. Cambridge, MA: Harvard University Press.

Williams, R. (1975) *Television, Technology and Cultural Form*. London: Schocken.

# INDEX